MW01288541

The UFO Phenomenon and the Birth of the Jewish, Christian, and Muslim Religions

ROBERT ITURRALDE

authorHOUSE®

AuthorHouse™
1663 Liberty Drive
Bloomington, IN 47403
www.authorhouse.com
Phone: 1-800-839-8640

First published by AuthorHouse 4/14/2009

ISBN: 978-1-4389-7570-2 (sc)

Printed in the United States of America
Bloomington, Indiana

This book is printed on acid-free paper.

Dedicated to my wife
and in memory of my father and sister

CONTENTS

Introduction

I started researching this book in 1987. The UFO phenomenon has been a major news story in the world in the past 55 years. UFOs have been seen on every continent and country of this planet. There have been witnesses from every race, culture and religion, and all social, economic and intellectual levels. The most reliable witnesses—like police officers, the military, and the government—are on record with the most amazing sightings.

I first became interested in the UFO phenomenon when I bought an old book about UFOs at a flea market and read about incident reports by U.S. Air Force pilots. The most amazing case was that of Capt. Thomas Mantell, who died on January 7, 1948, chasing a UFO. I decided to check the *New York Times* for an article about the incident. To my surprise, I found one article with details about the event. However, the Air Force denied it had taken place, saying that Capt. Mantell died while chasing the planet Venus. This incident is elaborated on in Chapter 2.

I discovered that many people, including UFO researchers, don't know that the UFO phenomenon is the source of religion, folklore, myth, and the supernatural. In this book, I explain this relationship. My job seems easier than that of philosopher George Berkeley (1685-1753), who tried to prove that the world ceased to exist after one walks away. I may be wrong in my conclusions, but the subject needs to be examined.

Robert Iturralde

CHAPTER 1

UNEXPLAINED ARCHEOLOGICAL FINDINGS AND ANCIENT MONUMENTS

"We find ourselves faced by powers that are far stronger than we had hitherto assumed, and whose base of operations is at present unknown to us."

— Dr. Wernher Von Braun, 1959, on the deflection from orbit of a U.S. satellite.

The possibility that the earth has been visited by an advanced extra-terrestrial civilization was seriously considered by the late astronomer Dr. Carl Sagan. Throughout the archeological and anthropological history of our planet, scientists have found items that only fit the description of "out of this world."

DISCS IN ARCHEOLOGICAL HISTORY

In 1967, a Russian magazine named *Sputnik* published an article about a Chinese archeologist claiming spaceships had visited the earth 12,000 years ago. The revelations were so shocking, said the article, that the Peking Academy of Prehistory had banned its publication. The work, entitled "Groove writing relative to spaceships, which as recorded on the discs, existed 12,000 years ago," explores 716 odd-looking stove discs that were found in caves in the Bayan Jara Ula Mountains on the border of China and Tibet. The "Grooves" are puzzling to scholars because they look like UFOs, which we think of only as a modern phenomenon.

England is very rich in Bronze Age artifacts that look like discs, cigars, and cloud-like designs very similar to UFOs. In various parts of Norway, Sweden and Denmark, archeologists have found Bronze Age engravings of discs with legs.

In a museum in Salzburg, Austria, is a perfect little cube of meteoric nickel-iron which is actually a form of stell that is about two inches square, though the opposing sides are somewhat convex or domed. It weighs about 28 ounces and has a specific gravity of 7.75. A precisely turned, deep groove or incision completely encircles it. The object has been examined endlessly by technicians and their conclusions are astonishing: they declare that because the components are nickel and iron, the object definitely was constructed by machine manufacture and came from a block of meteorite. However, the most amazing thing is that it was found in a block of coal taken from a Mioceno stratum 65 million years ago.

Most surprising are the disc and cigar-shaped designs of what today we call UFOs that have been found next to those of bison, bear and deer in prehistoric caves in Altamira, Niaux, La Pasiega, Les Trois Freres and Ussat. A cave in Altamira in Santander Province in Spain has the most remarkable collection of disc paintings. These designs are positioned across the sky on the ceiling with herds of bison cowering below. The drawings are disc-shaped with a flat bottom and a dome on top. Archeologists have found identical forms at Fort De Gaume 500 kilometers away in France's Dordogne Province. The cave La Pasiega in Spain also has saucer-like designs similar to the UFOs seen by thousands.

The most convincing drawing is in the cave at Niaux in France. There are two discs, one with dotted lines that looks like a picture of an aircraft in flight. At the cave in Ussat is a painted object remarkably similar to the lunar module complete with ladder and antennas that stands on four crane legs. Beneath is an erect human figure.

Of course skeptics will say that there is nothing in this design, but if we accept the designs of bison, deer and antelope as real, why not the spaceship-like designs? The reason is simple: it is too much for modern man to accept the idea that we have been visited by extraterrestrials since prehistoric times. We must remember that the great philosophers, like Hume, Locke, and Descartes, have maintained that there is nothing in our ideas that are not also in our senses or perceptions. All of our ideas are a reflection of the material world. So where did prehistoric man get the ideas for designing saucer-shaped objects?

The Pyramids

Moreover, the most enigmatic stone configurations that defy explanation about technique, labor and forms of construction exist around the world. There are monuments of vast proportions that are a challenge to our modern engineers and technology, such as the pyramids in Egypt. The Great Pyramid is believed to have been built in 2,500 BC during the reign of Pharaoh of Cheops. The dimensions are breathtaking. It was built with approximately 2,300,000 stone building blocks weighing from three to seventy tons. The base covers 13 acres, which is the equivalent of eight square blocks in New York City.

Napoleon's engineers believed the Pyramid of Cheops consisted of enough stone to build a wall around France. The Pyramid is big enough to contain all of the cathedrals of Rome, Milan, and Florence and still have room for the Empire State Building in New York and Westminster Abbey, St. Paul's Cathedral and the English House of Parliament in London. It is calculated that there is more stone in the Pyramid than all the masonry used to build every church in England since the time of Christ.

The Cheops Pyramid was originally 485 feet tall. All the locomotives in the world could not pull the Pyramid because it weighs six and a half million tons. Some of the individual stones weigh up to one hundred tons. The stones are fitted so closely together that it is impossible to detect the line where they are joined. How these stones were raised has perplexed many scientists.

The Egyptians didn't leave any record of the technology used to build the pyramids. The most popular theory is that workers slid the massive blocks up ramps onto the pyramid, but little evidence exists. The only written record came from the Greek historian Herodotus, who said it took 20 years and 100,000 men to build the Great Pyramids. The only problem is that he wrote this 2,000 years after they were built.

There are many considerations to take into account: How were the thousands of workers taken care of and fed? Where did they sleep? How were they transported? An army so vast requires supervisors, foremen and police.

We know that Egypt was not a big slaveholding society. How did they get enough people to hack out

2,600,000 giant blocks from the quarries? What kind of quarries were they? What kind of tools did they use? There was no dynamite or other explosives at that time.

After the rocks were quarried, how were they dressed? Dressing many of these stones would require a minimum pressure of two tons. How did primitive man get the necessary equipment to apply that kind of pressure? How did they get the stones to the building site?

Some historians believe that the Egyptians used ropes to pull those blocks of stone. Where did they get the ropes? Where did the Pharaoh find an architect who could design a building with such precise measurement? Historians say that three to one hundred tons were pushed over land on wooden rollers. Trees were chopped down, dressed out to logs and used as rollers under the blocks. It is a good theory except that there are no forests in Egypt. The Great Pyramid would have required 26 million wooden rollers. To import them would have required the largest fleet in history. Where did they get the wood to build such a fleet?

STONEHENGE IN ENGLAND

Another architectural mystery is the famous stone monument of Stonehenge, which is located about 75 miles south-southwest of London and eight miles north of Salisbury. It is a popular tourist attraction with nearly 200,000 visitors per year. Stonehenge was built with so-called bluestone, a separated kind of rock with a bluish color. Most bluestones are dolerite.

The site of the quarry is 240 miles away. Keep in mind that each stone weighs up to five tons. Stonehenge was built between 1900 and 1600 BC, a thousand or so years after the pyramids in Egypt. It was a few hundred years before the fall of Troy, and the Minoan civilization was flourishing.

Nobody knows the purpose of these stones or who built Stonehenge. Some think they were built for astronomical or religious purposes. The Druids came after they were built, and the prehistoric people left no evidence of their work.

Like the challenge to logic presented by the pyramids, many questions remain: How were these stones weighing up to five tons transported in a very irregular and hilly terrain? Where was the forest to provide the building wooden rollers? What kinds of tools were used to quarry the stone? How were the thousand of workers taken care of?

Some believe an enlightened man from Greece had them built. But who was he? Why don't we know the name of the man who accomplished such a feat?

Where did prehistoric people get the ideas to build such monuments?

THE STONE PLATFORM OF BAALBEK IN LEBANON

Another puzzle is the stone Platform of Baalbek in Beirut, Lebanon, a gigantic terrace composed of stone blocks, most of them with sides more than 60 feet long and weighing up to 2,000 tons. It is located on a section of the Beirut-Homs railway line and road at a height of 3,760 feet.

The Platform is incredibly old and has no historical date. It is first mentioned in Assyrian writing under the name of Ba'li as early as 804 BC. The Greeks and Romans both made use of it. It is inconceivable that these stones were transported with wooden rollers or sledges. There is no technical aid in ancient time, or even a crane today, that can lift 2,000 tons.

THE RUINS OF SACSAYHUAMAN IN PERU

Another archeological site that defies rational explanation is the Ruins of Sacsayhuaman in Peru—or more exactly in Cuzco—in South America. The local archaeologists don't think the Incas built this fortress of stone, situated at a height of 11,480 to 12,415 feet. The monolithic block weighs more than 100 tons; the ramparts are 18 feet high. The terrace wall is more than 1,500 feet long and 55 feet high. The rarified atmosphere makes it difficult to breathe. The rocks are well-polished stones that look as though they were cut out by a cheese knife.

Again, there are questions of who created these massive stones. To have built such immense structures in a terrain so elevated and irregular would have been a fantastic feat that the poor peasants who populated the area did not have the technology to accomplish.

In my opinion, most of the ancient civilizations of 5,000 to 6,000 years ago did not have the technology or the enlightenment to have created such massive structures. Who built them? I believe the answer is that we have been guided culturally, religiously, and historically to evolve from the lowest form by an ancient extraterrestrial civilization that is still around us but in different forms that are hard to understand by the vast majority of people.

CHAPTER 2

A SHORT HISTORY OF UFOS

"We are sending them out. Why shouldn't someone be sending here? Just think, when Pioneer 10 finally leaves our solar system, it becomes our first UFO to all the other star systems."

— Dr. Margaret Mead, Anthropologist

The best introduction to the subject of UFOs is by H.G. Wells in the beginning of the first chapter of *The War of the Worlds*, which he wrote in 1898. Later, in 1938, Wells adapted the book into the famous radio program that caused panic among listeners because they thought that Martians really had landed. The book begins:

"No one would have believed in the last years of the 19th century that this world was being watched keenly and closely by intelligences greater than man's and yet as mortal as his own; that as men busied themselves about their various concerns they were scrutinised and studied, perhaps almost as narrowly as a man with a microscope might scrutinise the transient creatures that swarm and multiply in a drop of water. With infinite complacency men went to and fro over this globe about their little affairs, serene in their assurance of their empire over matter. It is possible that the infusoria under the microscope do the same. No one gave a thought to the older worlds of space as sources of human danger, or thought of them only to dismiss the idea of life upon them as impossible or improbable. It is curious to recall some of the mental habits of those departed days. At most, terrestrial men fancied there might be other men upon Mars, perhaps inferior to themselves and ready to welcome a missionary enterprise. Yet across the gulf of space, minds that are to our minds as ours are to those of the beasts that perish, intellects vast and cool and unsympathetic, regarded this earth with envious eyes, and slowly and surely drew their plans against us. And early in the 20th century came the great disillusionment."

This introduction is excellent for the UFO sightings in modern times, but since the beginning of history, there has been evidence of sightings of what we now call UFOs or flying saucers.

UFOs in Ancient Times

One very well known document from the times of the Egyptian King Thothmes III, who died about 1450 BC, is the *Tulli Papirus*. The report is compelling: "In the year 22, third month of winter. The scribes of the house of life found it was a circle of fire that was coming in the sky. They went to the king to report it. Now after some days had passed, LO! They were more numerous than anything, and they were shining in the sky. The army of the king looked on, then, upon the circles went up higher and to the south. It was a marvel never occurred since in this land."

We see in this report that the witness is trying to explain something beyond the limits of his milieu, industrial and technological development. The famous Roman historian, Livy, reported "phantom ships" in the sky in 213 BC in Hadri, and an altar was also in the sky. In 216 BC, at Praenest, "burning lamps" fell from the sky. In 170 BC, at Lanupium on the Apian Way 16 miles from Rome, a remarkable fleet of ships was seen in the air. In 104 BC, "A rumbling sound was heard in the sky over Italy. A pillar was seen to fall to earth. In day-time over Rome, a burning torch was seen in the air." In 234 BC at Rimini, three moons were seen while the Gauls invaded Italy.

"In 223 BC portents occurred which threw the people of Rome into great fear. A river in Picenum had the color of blood. In Etruria, a good part of the heavens seemed to be on fire. In Ariminium, a light like the day blazed out at night. In many cities of Italy three moons became visible in the night time and in the Forum, a vulture perched for several days."

In 218 BC, Livy, reported in *Book XXI-XXII*, "phantom ships had been seen gleaming in the district of Amitemym; in many places apparitions of men in shining clothing had appeared in the distance, but had not drawn near to anyone."

Lycosthenes also reported, "The apparitions of ships were seen in the sky…dreadful earthquakes shook the ground." In that year Hannibal invaded Etruria and the Romans lost the battle at Trasimene.

Livy mentions in *Book XXIV-X* that amazing things were seen in the sky. "Prodigies in large numbers were reported in that year. At Hadria an altar was seen in the sky and about it the forms of men in white garments. At Alba they said two suns were seen and at Fregellae that light had appeared in the night. In 163 BC at Capua, the sun was seen by night. At Forini, two suns were seen. The sky was on fire. In Cephoalonia, a trumpet seemed to sound from the sky. There was a rain of earth. A windstorm demolished houses and laid crops flat in fields. By night an apparent sun shone at Pisaurum. In 152 BC, in many places in Rome, apparitions in toga were seen; on approaching, they vanished from view."

Pliny writes, "It is also reported that several suns were seen at midday at the Bosphorus and this lasted from dawn to sunrise. At Praeneste, a torch was seen in the sky. In 113 BC, a light from the sky by night, the phenomenon usually called 'night suns,' was seen in the consulship of Gaius Caecilius and Gnaeus Papirius and often on other occasions, causing apparent daylight in the night." (Pliny, *Book II)*

"In 106 BC, an uproar in the sky was heard and javelins seemed to fall from heaven. In 100 BC, In the consulship of Lucius Valerius and Gaius Marios a burning shield scattering sparks ran across the sky at sunset from west to east." (Pliny, *Book II*, xxxlv)

"In 93 BC, at Volsinii, flame seemed to flash from the sky at dawn. After it had gathered together, the flame displayed a dark grey opening and the sky appeared to divide. In the gaps, tongues of flame appeared." (Obsequens)

"In 91 BC, at sunset a glove of fire in the northern region rushed across the sky emitting tremendous sound. In Spoletium, a gold-coloured fireball rolled down to the ground and, growing larger, rose from the earth towards the east becoming large enough to blot out the sun." (Obsequens, confirmed by Orosius)

As we can see, the names of what we call UFOs varies with the culture and stage of development of a particular society. In ancient times there were no flying machines and the only way to describe what was seen was with familiar words like flammable torches, shining shields, sun or moon apparitions, shining altars, and flying swords or ships. Ancient people believed that these were good or bad omens from the gods with hidden messages just as some people in modern times still believe that when there is an eclipse of the sun or moon, something bad is going to happen. Superstition and ignorance go hand-in-hand and haven't changed for many people in the 21st century.

UFOs in the Year of Our Lord

Dio Cassius wrote in *Book LVI* in AD 9, "The temple of Mars in the field of the same name was struck by lightening and many locusts flew into the city and were devoured by swallows, the peaks of the Alps seemed to collapse upon one another and to send up three columns of fire, the sky in many places seemed ablaze and numerous comets appeared at one and the same time, spears seemed to dart from the north and fall in the direction of Roman Camp. In AD 14, thus the sun suffered a total eclipse and most of the sky seemed to be on fire, glowing embers appeared to be falling from it, and blood-red comets were seen."

We see that the descriptions are close to what we call UFOs. Since ancients used words that were familiar to them, they could transcend their milieu or stage of development. Admiral Pliny, the great nature historian who died while trying to study the eruption of the Vesubios that buried Pompey and Herculano wrote in AD 79 in *Historia Naturales, Book XL-XXLV,* "There are also meteoric lights that are only seen when falling, for instance one that ran across the sky in midday in full view of the public when Germanicus was giving a gladiatorial show. Of these are two kinds. One sort are called 'lampades' which means 'torches'; the other 'bolides', 'missiles', that is the sort that appeared at the time of the disaster at Modena (when Decimus Brutus was besieged there by Anthony in 445 BC)."

Ovid, who died in AD 18, wrote: "In the middle of the night I saw the sun truly a glittering white."

We can't say that these people were dreaming. These events were recorded by witnesses of great integrity like Plutarco, Pliny and Livy, and they described what they saw.

In AD 51, "Three suns were seen during the consulship of the future Emperor Claudius when Cornelius Ofitus was his colleage." (Pliny)

In AD 60, "Indeed we have been able to contemplate for six month that comet which appeared in the happy reign of Nero." (Seneca)

In AD 65, the Jews were oppressed by the Romans and there were portents and signs in the sky which prophets interpreted as omens of happiness instead of misfortune. Josephus wrote in *War of the Jews, Book VI, Chapter V-3*, "Thus there was a star resembling a sword, which stood over the city, and a comet that continued a whole year, thus also before the Jew's rebellion and before those commotions which preceded the war, when people were come in great crowds to the feast of unleavened bread, on the eighth day of the month Xanthicus and at the ninth hour of the night, so great a light shone round the altar and the holy house, that it appeared to be bright day-time, which light lasted for half-an-hour."

In AD 71, Lycosthenes wrote: "Moreover, in the East and West two suns were seen at the same time, of which one was faint and pallid, the other powerful and clear."

In AD 98, he wrote, "At Tarquinia, an old town in Campania, Italy, a burning torch was seen all about the sky. It suddenly fell down. At sunset a burning shield passed over the sky at Rome. It came sparkling from the west and passed to the east."

In AD 192, during the rein of Commodius, a particularly bright object crossed the sky. The historian, Elio Lampridio, hints at it. He is one of the *scriptores historiae augutae* and it is in his *Life of Commodius*. Herodian, too, in his *History of the Empire after Marcus Aurelius* supports this with, "There were many marvels in those days. Stars were seen in mid-air and in broad daylight." (*Book 1*)

"In AD 193, three men attempted to secure control of affairs: Severus, Niger and Albinus. These were the three men portended by the three stars that suddenly came to view surrounding the sun when Julianus in our presence was offering the Sacrifices of Entrance in front of the Senate House. These stars were so very distinct that the soldiers kept continually looking at them and pointing them out to one another declaring that some dreadful fate would befall the Emperor." (*Dio Cassius, Book LXXXLV*).

In AD 393, "Strange lights were seen in the sky in the days of the Emperor Theodosius. A sudden, bright globe appeared at midnight. It shone brilliantly near the daystar (planet Venus), about the circle of the Zodiac. This globe shone a little less brilliantly than the planet, and little by little, a great number of other glowing orbs drew near the first globe. The spectacle was like a swarm of bees flying round the beekeeper, and the light of these orbs was as if they were dashing violently against each other. Soon they blended together into one awful flame, and bodied forth to the eye as a horrible two-edged sword. The strange globe which was first seen, now appeared like the pommel to a handle, and all the little orbs, fused with the first, shone as brilliantly as the first globe. This sword burned for 40 days and nights, and then vanished."*(Dio Cassius)*

In AD 384 a terrible sign appeared in the sky, shaped like a pillar. It was in the time of the Roman Emperor, Theodosius.

UFOs in the Middle Ages (AD 400-1400)

As we see from these reports, people have seen things in the sky that in modern times we call UFOs. The Middle Ages had its share of sightings that defy our common sense:

In 457, over Brittany, France, a blazing like a globe was seen in the sky. Its size was immense, and on its beams hung a ball of fire-like a dragon out of whose mouth proceeded two beams, one of which stretched beyond France, and the other reached towards Ireland, and ended in fire-like rays. In 577, a thing like a lance passed across the sky, from north to west, over France. In 596, armies were in rout, and a great noise like thunder and flashes of lightening were seen in the skies over Surrey, England. Many drops the color of blood fell from the sky.

In 746 and 748, dragons were seen in the sky and ships in which men were seen in the air. In 773, a red cross appeared after sunset in the sky over England. In 796, small globes were seen circling round the sun. In 919, a thing like a burning torch was seen in the sky, and glistening balls like stars moved to and fro in the air over Hungary.

In 1011, a burning torch like a tower was seen to flame in sky with a great noise. This was in the year of the Emperor Henry II, and happened in Lorraine, at the Hill Castrilocum. In 1097, on 3 Kalends of October, a comet appeared for 15 days. Several said this wonderful sign burnt almost like a cross in the sky. In 1104, burning torches, fiery darts, flying fire were often seen in the air. Near the stars were what looked like swarms of butterflies and strange little fiery worms. They flew in the air and took away the light of the sun as if they had been clouds.

In 1269, on December 6, at twilight, a strange brightness shaped like a cross gave light from high in the air and shone down on the city of Cracow, Poland, and on all the country.

Scholars have found very interesting sightings recorded in Chinese history of what we now call UFOs. Shen Kua was a famous scientist and scholar more than 900 years ago. He wrote about "a big pearl that rose from marshes near the town, and hovered over a nearby lake. It had a round double shelf and several people had seen it open. Inside was a bright silvery light the size of a fist, which dazzled anyone who looked at it. All the trees around had their shadows cast to the ground. The shelf would leave suddenly, as though flying through the waves. It seemed to be surrounded by flames."

In 1387, in November and December, a fire in the sky, like a burning and rcvolving wheel or round barrel of flame emitting fire from above, and others in the shape of a long fiery beam, were seen through a great deal of the winter in the county of Leicester, England. In 1472, diverse kinds of crosses and fiery bowls fell to the ground from the sky in Switzerland, leaving tokens behind.

THE 16TH – 18TH CENTURIES

In 1554, two red crosses were seen in the sky at Nebra, Saxony, and the same day at Griessesie, a town in Thuringia, amidst the sun, then shining very brightly, appeared a red cross which covered the whole disc of the Sun, and on both sides a huge beam with diverse circles, appeared in the elements.

On September 20, 1676, a strange spectacle was seen in Northamptonshire and other parts of England. It passed very near the earth. It appeared in the dusk, with a sudden light like that of noonday, so that the smallest pin or straw could be seen on the ground. Above in the air was seen, at not great apparent distance, a long arm with a great knob at the end. As it vanished, it seemed to break into small fires or sparks, like rockets.

In 1686, strange reports came from Gottfried Kirch, Germany. An astronomer reported this event: "On 9 July, 1686, at 1:30 a.m., a burning globe, furnished with a tail, appeared approximately eight and one-half degrees from Aquarius and remained immovable for one-eighth of an hour. Its diameter was about half that of the moon. It emitted so much light that at first one could read without a candle. Afterwards it vanished in its place, but very gradually. This phenomenon was also seen by others at the same time."

In May 1677, the famous astronomer, Edmond Halley, Savilian professor of geometry at Oxford University, reported observing a "great light in the sky all over southern England, many miles high." Later, on July 31, 1708, from 9:00 to 10:00 p.m., a similar apparition, thought to be 50 miles high, passed over Sheerness, and London. It moved with incredible speed and was very bright. It seemed to vanish and left a pale white light behind it. There were no hissing sounds and no explosion.

Astronomer Edmond Halley on March 6, 1716, about 7:00 p.m. again witnessed a phenomenon: "A man could easily read print in the light thrown out by these spears from the same body. It did not change for two hours, and then it seemed as if new fuel had been cast on a fire."

On March 17, 1735, about 8:15 p.m. Halley was observing Mars from the top of his house in Buckingham Street in London and saw a phenomenon. "It was quite unlike the Aurora Borealis, being steady and not tremulous in motion. The stars could be seen through it. It was not a comet, for I could see no nucleus through my 17-foot optical glass. It grew dim in the middle in half an hour, and then seemed *to split into two very luminous parts* which grew dimmer till about 9:00 p.m."

Thomas Short, M.D., of Sheffield, said that on December 5, 1937 at 5:00 p.m., he had been startled "by the appearance of a deep red cloud under which a luminous body sent out streamers of very bright light by which I could easily read in a large church Bible. It differed entirely from the Aurora Borealis, for the streamers of light moved slowly for some time and stood still."

On December 11, 1741, Lord Beauchamp reported that in Old London at 9:45 a.m., "The sky was serene, the sun shown brightly. I was on the mount in Kensington Gardens, London, when in the south I saw a ball of fire, as it seemed 8 inches in diameter, but oval in shape. It grew to the size of a yard and a half in diameter, and seemed to drop over Westminster. In its course, it assumed a tail 80 yards long, and before dispensing, it *divided* into *two heads*. It left a trail of smoke all the way, and where it dropped or seemed to drop, smoke ascended for 20 minutes and at length formed into a cloud which assumed different colours."

On December 31, 1758, a football-shaped fire of immense size came down from the sky over Colchester, Essex in England. A conical object with a tail passed over London, twice changed course, and seemed to burn, with no tail. Three objects came out and vanished.

THE 19TH CENTURY

It seems clear that every century has a share of UFO sightings that defy common sense and everything we know about nature and the technology of the times. Although I am sure there were sightings all over the world in the 19th century, most of the available research data is from Europe and the United States. Many were probably misinterpretations of natural and man-made objects, but there was a concentration of sightings in the United States that defy rational explanation. Although 1896 was the beginning of a wave of airships in the United States, there were sightings well before that date of unknown objects in the sky.

In 1883 in Segeberg, Germany, "All the children and teachers in the public elementary school saw in the sky two fiery balls, the size of full moons, traveling side by side, not very swiftly from north to south, on a clear and sunny day."

John Staveley of Hatton Garden, London, was so astonished by what he saw during a thunderstorm on August 10, 1809, that he wrote to the *Journal of Natural History and Philosophy and Chemistry:*

"I saw many meteors moving around the edge of a black cloud from which lightening flashed. They were like dazzling specks of light, dancing and traipsing thro' the clouds. One increased in size till it became of the brilliance and magnitude of Venus on a clear evening; but I could see no body in the light. It moved with great rapidity, and coasted the edge of the cloud. Then it became stationary, dimmed its splendour, and vanished. I saw these strange lights for minutes, not seconds. For at least an hour, these lights, so strange, and in innumerable points, played in and out of this black cloud. No lightning came from the clouds where these lights played. As the meteors increased in size, they seemed to descend."

In March 1890, F. W. Banner, the captain of the British ship, *Lady of the Lake*, saw a remarkable object in the North Atlantic. He wrote in his log:

"March 22, 1870, in Lat. 5.47, Long. 27.52, my crew reported a strange object in the sky. I saw it. It was a cloud of circular form, with an included semi-circle divided into four parts, and a central shaft running from the center of the circle and extending far outward and curving backward. The thing was traveling against the wind. It came from the south and settled right into the wind's eye. It was visible for half an hour, much lower than other clouds, and was lost to sight in the sky as dusk came on. I drew it. It looked like a half-moon with a long shaft radiating from the center."

The term "flying saucer" was heard for the first time on January 24, 1878, when John Martin, a Texas farmer, saw a dark object in the shape of a disc cruising high in the sky "at a wonderful speed" and used the word "saucer" to describe it. Sixty-nine years later another man, Kenneth Arnold, would use the term "flying saucer" and get worldwide attention.

On August 29, 1871, the astronomer Trouvelot of the observatory of Meudon observed "a number of very complex objects and a UFO that seemed about to fall, then descended like a dead leaf or like a disc falling through water."

On June 11, 1881, at 4:00 a.m. between Melbourne and Sydney, the two sons of the Prince of Wales, one of them the future King of England, saw a strange celestial object similar to a fully illuminated ship.

On November 1, 1885, at 9:30 p.m. at Adrinanople, an elongated object giving off a strong luminosity seemed to float in the air and its apparent disc was four or five times larger than the full moon. It traveled slowly and cast light on the whole camp behind the station with a brightness about ten times greater than a large electric bulb.

On April 2, 1897 at 2:00 a.m. in Chicago, amazed citizens clambered to the top of a skyscraper to observe an enormous flying object that seemed to have fins at each end and a beacon. On the 15th, an object in the shape of a cigar was seen in Benton, Texas, and several other places. It cruised toward the southeast and was described as "a magnificent sight."

On November 15, 1899, an enormous star, white, then red and blue, was seen moving like a kite in the sky near the moon at 7:00 p.m. in observation over Dourite, in Dordogne, France. In 1885, a singular triangular object was seen in the sky over Bermuda, and trailing things, like grapnels, hung under it. It descended, then ascended and passed out toward the ocean. In 1882, travelers on the British steamer *Salisbury*, 800 miles off Ascension Island in the south Atlantic, saw a huge object showing two lights in the sea. As the steamer approached, the mysterious object was seen to be 800 feet long. It slowly sank. There were sounds in it of working machinery. Often the UFO phenomenon keeps ahead of the technology of the times and that is part of the cosmic game.

In 1880 in eastern Venezuela, a 14-year-old boy saw a luminous ball descending from the sky and hovering near him. He reportedly felt somehow "drawn" to it, but succeeded in backing away in spite of his terror. That same year on March 26, in Lamy, New Mexico, four men walking near Galisteo Junction were surprised to hear voices coming from a "strange balloon" which flew over them. It was shaped like a fish and seemed to be guided by a large fan-like device. There were eight to ten figures aboard. Their language was not understood. The object flew over Galisteo Junction and rose rapidly toward the east.

On April 14, 1897, in Cleveland, Ohio, Joseph Singler, captain of the *Sea Wing*, was fishing with S.H. Davies of Detroit, when they saw on the lake what they thought was a ship about 13 meters long with a canopy. A man about 25 years old, wearing a hunting jacket and a cap, was fishing from the deck of the object. Near him were a woman and 10-year old child. When the *Sea Wing* came close to the craft, a large colored balloon rose from the object, flew up with it to an altitude of about 150 meters and circled "like a hawk before flying away." This event is very interesting, because it shows the versatility of a phenomenon able to change to human form.

THE 20TH CENTURY

The 20th century began slowly. Nobody paid any attention to the phenomenon until the World War II and the big UFO wave after the Kenneth Arnold sighting. However, in March 1909, a narrow, oblong object with powerful lights was seen in the sky over Peterborough, England. From the sound of the motor, some thought it was an airplane in a pioneer stage. The same object also was seen in skies from Essex and Midlands to Wales. The object must have had a speed of 210 miles an hour to cover that distance in one night. A Welshman said it was tube-shaped, and he saw "creatures like monkeys emerge from it." This is another event where the aliens seem to be a little ahead of the technology of our times. In January of 1912 at Porto Principal, Peru, a "ship in the sky" appeared over the town at treetop level. It was shaped like a large square globe, but matched no known type of terrestrial airplane.

In Georgian Bay, Canada, Willian J. Kiehl and seven other people saw a spherical craft on the surface of the water. On its deck were two small men wearing green-purple clothes. They seemed to be busy with a hose, plunging it into the water. On the opposite side were three men dressed in light brown, wearing square masks down to their shoulders. Seeing the witnesses, they reentered the craft except for one dwarf, wearing shoes with a curved, pointed tip, who remained outside while the craft rose three meters above the water and shot upward, leaving a short trail.

On June 12, 1929, in Fermeneuve, Canada, Levis Brosseau, 20, was returning home when he saw a dark object with a yellow light and his horse became very nervous. Within six meters of the object, four or five dwarfish figures were running back and forth. He heard their pointed, child-like voices, then saw the dark object take off with a machine-like sound and a rush of air. Estimated size of object was 15 meters in diameter and five meters in height.

In September 1943, in Oncadvo, Argentina, Navarro Ocampo was driving between Rosario and Cordoba, when he saw a large, saucer-shaped object on the ground 500 meters to the left of the road. It glowed with a bluish-green light, made a whistling sound, rose to 100 meters altitude, then left at fantastic speed. A strange metal block was said to have been found at the spot.

The best way to introduce the modern age of UFOs is with the most prominent scholar of our time and a famous disciple of Dr. Sigmund Freud. In 1946, Dr. Carl Jung started collecting newspaper clippings, reports, statements from the scientific, military and go environmental establishments and he read every book on the subject. In 1951, he wrote to an American friend, "I am puzzled to death about these phenomenon, because I haven't been able yet to make out with sufficient certainty whether the whole thing is a rumour with concomitant singular and mass hallucination, or a downright fact. Either case would be highly interesting. If it's a rumour, then the apparition of discs must be a symbol produced by the unconscious. We know what such a thing would mean seen from the psychological standpoint. If on the other hand it is a concrete fact, we are surely confronted with something out of the way."

In the preface to the first English edition of his book, *Flying Saucers: A Modern Myth of Things Seen in the Skies*, Jung wrote, "The worldwide rumour about flying saucers presents a problem that challenges the psychologist for a number of reasons. The primary question, and apparently this is the most important point, is, are they mere fantasy products. This question is by no means settled yet. If they are real, exactly what are they? If they are fantasy, why does such a rumour exist?"

And in the introduction Jung wrote, "So, I am fully aware of the risk I am taking in proposing to communicate my views concerning certain contemporary events, which seem to me important, to those who are patient enough to hear me. I refer to those reports reaching us from all corners of the earth, rumours of round objects that flash through the troposphere and stratosphere and go by the name of flying saucers, soucoupes, discs and UFOs. These rumours *or the possible existence of such objects seem to me so significant that I feel myself compelled, as once before, when events of fateful consequence were brewing in Europe, to sound a note of warning."*

The modem age of UFOs began with a sighting by Kenneth Arnold on June 24, 1947. Mr. Arnold left at 2:00 p.m., taking off in his private plane from Chehalis Airport in Washington on a flight to Yakima. He was an hour late searching for a U.S. Marine Transport plane which was missing on the southwest side of Mount Rainier. At a height of 9,200 feet, Arnold was startled by a bright flash of light reflected from his plane. The weather was beautiful. Suddenly, to the left of Mount Rainier he saw nine odd-looking aircraft that were flying in formation like geese. Mr. Arnold estimated their speed at about 1,000 mph and the chain of UFOs to be five miles long, which means that each machine in the chain was half a mile long.

The sighting by Mr. Arnold received world-wide publicity. The next day people all over the planet were seeing UFOs. Two weeks later, Mr. Arnold was approached by U.S. Army or Federal Bureau of Investigation (FBI) authorities and all news about UFOs was censored from the newspapers. On one occasion, he made a statement to the staff of the *Saturday Evening Post*, but it was not published. He said, "At my home, I have been visited by unseen entities whom I believed to be pilots of these weird discs. They were invisible to me and made no attempt to communicate. But I was aware of their presence because I could see my rugs and furniture sink down under their weight as they walked about the room or sat on various objects in the room."

I believe Mr. Arnold is telling the truth with this statement because there is evidence that UFOs, including the occupants, can make themselves invisible. Before the sighting by Kenneth Arnold in 1947, there were sightings of strange aircraft during and after World War II. The Foo Fighters were balls of fire that followed the British, American, German and Japanese planes. A British pilot said, "We saw a strange flare come from them, and it twinkled in and out." The Allied pilots thought it to be a German or Japanese secret weapon, while the German and Japanese thought it was a secret weapon of the Allies.

On December 24, 1944, two pilots witnessed a very shocking event: "A glowing red ball shot straight up to us. It suddenly changed into an airplane, which did a wing over! Then it dived and disappeared." This is an amazing event because besides making themselves invisible, it seems that they can change their molecular make up and adopt any material form that they want or they can make us believe that they have changed form. The Allied, Germans and Japanese governments never explained this phenomenon. It was swept under the rug.

The wave of UFOs in 1947 was after the nuclear explosions. After World War II, during the height of the Cold War, Scandinavians were seeing weird aircraft, like the German V weapon. The United States sent military experts to Sweden to investigate, but never found any explanation about these sightings.

The decade of the 1950s was a busy time for UFOs researchers. In the summer of 1952, more precisely in July, 29 UFOs turned the nation's capitol into the center of world attention. The first report came on July 22. UFOs were picked up on radar and scopes at Washington National

Airport, Andrews Air Force Base and Bollin Air Force Base. Newspapers were quoting Air Force officials about sightings picked up on radar, some flying in formation while others looped across the sky. The UFOs were tracked at speeds from 100 to 8,000 miles per hour.

The UFOs were also seen by airline employees. Capt. Casey Pierman and his crew on Capital Airlines Flight 807 traveling between Washington and Martinsburg, West Virginia, saw seven objects flash across the sky. The pilot said, "They were like falling stars without the tails."

In another event, an Air Force radar installation was tracking eight UFOs as they flew over Washington, D.C. The Air Force sent its interceptor F-94 jets to chase the UFOs. The speed of the jets was 600 mph, no match for the UFOs. The Air Force finally admitted on July 29 that it had detected UFOs. The UFOs returned to Washington, and this time the radar picked up 12. After this sighting, the Air Force held the largest press conference since the Second World War.

The Washington event is very important for UFO researchers as evidence of the reality of the phenomenon. Skeptics can deny the reality of this event, but to deny it happened is to deny human senses and the existence of the cognitive process when confronted with the UFO phenomenon.

In August 1951, the Lubbock Lights event was on front page of every newspaper in the United States. It took its name from the town of Lubbock, Texas, even though the first sighting happened in Albuquerque, New Mexico, where there were dozens of witnesses and the lights were tracked by radar. The Air Force couldn't find an explanation for the sightings. One witness took a good picture of the phenomenon.

During the UFO wave of 1954, there were sightings in every country in the world. On October 9, 1955, the *New York Times* quoted General Douglas MacArthur's warning that "the nations of earth soon will make a common front against attack by people from other planets. The next war will be interplanetary one." Addressing the graduating class of West Point in 1962, he said, "We deal now not with things of this world alone. We deal with the ultimate conflict between a united human race and the sinister forces of some other planetary galaxy."

The 1960s was another decade of sightings and abductions, but not everything was mentioned by the media. One event that became well known involved a policeman. On April 24, 1964, in Socorro, New Mexico, Patrolman Lonnie Zamora was chasing a speeder. The patrolman heard a roar and saw a flash of light. The patrolman went to investigate, thinking it was a dynamite explosion. Instead he saw a white bright object. He walked toward it and saw some aliens scramble back to the UFOs. This case had worldwide attention and is a classic in the UFO literature.

In 1966, the citizens of Michigan were so alarmed by UFOs that they put pressure on U.S. Representative Gerald Ford to call for an open congressional hearing on the subject, saying, "The American public deserves a better explanation than thus far given. We owe it to these people to establish credibility regarding UFOs." United Nations Secretary-General U Thant once said that UFOs are "the most important problem facing the world next to the war in Vietnam."

In 1965, the government of Argentina issued the first official communiqué documenting the sighting of a UFO. According to the report, Argentinean, Chilean, and British sailors stationed at Deception Island Naval Base in Antarctica spotted a green, red and yellow flying object that made no sound. It zigzagged across the sky and hovered at 15,000 feet for 20 minutes. The document said that "the occurrence was witnessed by scientists of the three navel bases and the facts agree completely."

The 1970s was another very busy decade for UFO researchers. Former U.S. President Jimmy Carter, then Governor of Georgia, was sitting out on his veranda in 1973 with 20 other people after an official dinner at Tomastown. In Carter's words, they witnessed a UFO "which looked as big as the moon and changed colors several times from red to green."

Sir Eric Gairey, Prime Minister of the Caribbean Island of Grenada, tried unsuccessfully in 1978 to have the United Kingdom investigate UFOs. The Minister saw "a brilliant golden light traveling at tremendous speed." The famous boxer Mohammed Ali, while training in Central Park in 1972, encountered a UFO. "I was out jogging just before sunrise when this bright light hovered over me. It just seemed to be watching me. It was like a huge electric light bulb."

Former Ohio Governor John Gilligan reported seeing a UFO near Ann Arbor, Michigan in 1973. He described it as a "vertical shaft of light that glowed amber." In 1978, famous actress Elke Sommer was in the garden of her Los Angeles home when "a shiny orange ball, 20 feet in diameter, appeared out of the blue. It was glowing and floating about like a big moon." She said, "It came toward me and I fled into the house. When I reappeared, it had vanished."

U.S. Senator Barry Goldwater confirmed in 1979 that the United States government withheld UFO data from the American public. The famous 1973 case of the abduction of two men in Pascagoula, Mississippi, got the attention of the country. They were fishing when they saw a strange object land and several robot-like creatures with wrinkled skin and pointed ears come out of the UFO and abduct them. The two men claimed that they were floated to the UFO and examined. The two witnesses, Charles Hickson and Calvin Parker, were submitted to lie detectors tests and interrogated by law enforcement and all agreed that the two men really had gone through this experience. The case is very important for UFO researches because it shows that many times the UFO entities are monsters, and it corroborates the sightings of such monsters seen in many parts of the world.

One case that is still a mystery is that of Capt. Thomas Mantell. On January 7, 1948, at approximately 2:00 p.m., Kentucky State Police reported to Fort Knox Military Police that they had sighted an unusual aircraft or object flying through the air, circular in appearance, approximately 250-300 feet in diameter, moving westward. This in turn was reported to the commanding officer at Godman Field in Fort Knox, who called Godman Tower and asked them to have Flight Service check to see if they had any experimental aircraft in that area. The captain of the flight-training unit replied, "We have no experimental aircraft in that area." So the commanding officer of Godman Field requested Capt. Thomas Mantell, who was the leader of four P-51s that were already in the air, to investigate the object overhead. Two pilots returned because they didn't have oxygen equipment and another went back because he didn't see the object.

At about 3:45, Capt. Mantell crashed five miles southwest of Franklin, Kentucky. The police went to check the site of the accident. Officer Walker stated that when he arrived, the body of the pilot had been removed from the aircraft. The police learned that the plane had exploded in the air, but did not burn upon contact with the ground. The wreckage was scattered over an area of about one mile, and at the time, the tail section, propeller, and one wing had not been located. The last words of Capt. Mantell were, "The object is traveling at half my speed, and 12 o'clock high. I'm going to close in right now for a good look. It's directly ahead of me. The thing looks metallic and of tremendous size. It's going up now and forward as fast as I am. That's 360 miles an hour. I'm going up to 20,000 feet, and if I'm no closer, I'll abandon chase."

This is said to have been the last radio contact with the base. The official report from the Air Force said, "Capt. Mantell was chasing planet Venus." The captain's wife didn't get a complete report of the incident. On the day of the crash a report came from Columbus, Ohio, that a glowing disc was seen hurtling across the sky at an estimated speed of 550 mph. It was white and orange and emitted an exhaust five times its own length. At the Clinton county Army Air Base at Wilmington, Ohio, one witness reported "a flaming red cone trailing a gaseous green mist tore through the sky." One witness said, "It seemed to hang suspended in the air at intervals. Then it came down. It then ascended at what looked like a terrific speed. The intense brightness from this phenomenon in the sky pierced through a heavy cloud layer which intermittently passed over the region." Thousands of people saw this phenomenon in places as far apart as 180-190 miles and at immense height. It was calculated by radar and theodilite measurements that the machine struck Capt. Mantell at 15,000 feet. The captain had a first class record in the Second World War and he would know the difference between an aircraft and planet Venus.

On July 4,1975, in Parsippany, New Jersey a college student and his date were returning from the movies when they spotted a cigar-shaped object about 60 to 80 feet long, moving slowly parallel to the ground and only 75 feet in the air. They heard no sound, but observed a bright light coming from the vehicle illuminating the surrounding area but with no glare. The witness also noticed a white light coming from the front bottom that appeared to sweep the ground. The object then moved and hovered for a few minutes before whizzing off into the sky in a flash.

In January 1975, in North Bergen, New Jersey, a liquor store owner was driving through North Hudson Park about 3:00 a.m. when he began to notice some interference on his car radio. Soon the signal faded and the witness heard a droning hum to his left. Then a bright object flew past, stopped, and hovered a few feet over a park lawn. The object was a circular vehicle about 30 feet across and flat on the bottom with vertical sides. The witness reported that a ladder descended from the craft. A door opened and eight to eleven creatures three and a half feet tall came out. They were dressed in helmets and jump suits and appeared to scoop up samples from the soil and put them in bags. The witness came back the next morning and found in the soil holes four to five inches wide and six inches deep. UFO sightings were reported in the area on the same night.

In 1956, a night watchman at a Trenton construction firm became the first person to receive a worker's compensation claim for having been assaulted by a UFO. On the evening of October 2, the witness spotted a red light hurdling toward him. He was overcome by vile odor and collapsed with strong stomach pains. A New Jersey Workman's Compensation referee ruled that this extraordinary claim was legitimate and true.

On October 12, 1966, a UFO visited the Waneque Reservoir. Residents and policemen said they saw a brilliant unidentified object flying above the Reservoir. Witnesses described the object as saucer-shaped about the size of a car and glowing with a white brilliance. The reservoir is part of the Newark water supply system and is about 25 miles northwest of Newark. Sgt. Ben Thomson said he saw the object as he drove a patrol car along the reservoir. "I saw the object coming at me. It went straight over my head, stopped in mid-air and backed right up. It then started zigzagging from left to right. It was so bright, I couldn't make out any of its features." He turned on the flashing red dome light on his car. "The instant it started to flash, the object sped away over the reservoir and without passing over the horizon, disappeared," he said.

Chinese airmen and scientists have sighted UFOs. On July 1977, astronomer Zhan Zhousheng and several other scientists at the Yunnan Observatory watched a glowing object pass overhead from north to west. "It was yellow at the core with a giant spiral extension. It was very bright in the moonlight and its color was greenish blue."

The air force pilot Zhou Quington and other pilots were watching films outside their barracks when a huge glowing object crossed the sky. "It passed over our heads at 21,000 feet and disappeared behind some houses. It seemed to have two large searching lights at the front and a bright taillight. The lengths of the columns of light kept changing, creating a misty haze around the object," said the pilot.

In the decade of the 1980s there were many sightings. One of the most important came from a former President of the United States Ronald Reagan. In 1988 it was revealed that in 1974 while he was governor of California, he had witnessed a UFO. "We were flying near Bakersfield when we saw a big light flying behind my plane. It appeared several hundred yards away," Reagan's pilot reported. "It began to accelerate, then it appeared to elongate, then the UFO went from a normal cruise speed to a fantastic speed instantly. Reagan himself described the incident to the Washington Bureau chief. Reagan said, "When I got off the plane I told Nancy all about it and we read up on the long history of UFOs."

In China in 1987 in Wuxi City, three aviation engineers reported that at 7:57 p.m. an unidentified object flew across the sky. "It was flying across the sky on a spiral course, leaving a trail."

On March 24, 1983, there were many sightings of UFOs in all of central and northern Westchester County, in Putnam County, and in Danbury, Connecticut. On December 31, 1982, there were sightings of UFOs in Kent, Carmel and Putnam County. In 1983 there were many sightings in the Hudson Valley that went on for three years. UFOs were constantly seen by thousands of people—housewives, engineers, and children—with more than 5,000 sightings in the five years following the first one. That's three sightings per day.

In the 1980s, the most spectacular sightings happened in England over a period of a week between Christmas and New Years. These took place in the Rendlesham forest very close to Woodbridge Base, where U.S. and NATO forces are stationed. "Early in the morning of December 27, 1980, two USAF security patrolmen saw unusual lights outside the back gate of RAF Woodbridge Base. They thought that an aircraft might have crashed or been forced down. ...The on-duty flight chief responded and allowed three patrolmen to proceed. The individuals reported seeing a strange glowing object in the forest. They described it as being metallic in appearance and triangular in shape, approximately two to three meters across the base and approximately two meters high. It illuminated the entire forest in a white light. The object itself had a pulsing red light on top and a bank of blue lights underneath. It was hovering on legs. As the patrolmen approached the object, it maneuvered through the trees and disappeared." (Excerpted from a memo entitled "Unexplained Lights," released under the Freedom of Information Act.)

The sighting of this UFO was such a spectacular event that it was recreated by the *Unsolved Mysteries* television show, and the witnesses of the event were interviewed by Robert Stack.

On August 25, 1988, there was another sighting in Russia by a housewife who reported, "We had returned from the cinema with the girls at 11:00 p.m. and were in our room when we saw a hemisphere of dull white rise from behind the house opposite. It was foggy, like a cloud and close to the Great Bear. It began to grow. Then from the hemisphere came a ray of the same color, long, narrow and steady."

Mikhail Gorbachev later remarked, "The phenomenon of UFOs does exist, and it must be treated seriously."

In the 1990s there were many sightings, and although very few got publicity, UFO researchers found out about them. On July 1, 1991, a father and his 12-year-old daughter observed a large bright, silvery object, 15-20 degrees above the horizon. The object was pencil- or cigar-shaped and approximately a half to one mile away from their home.

On January 24, 1992, in Tetbury, Gloucestershire, UK, a woman reported a sighting early in the morning of a large, gold, five-pointed star, which moved slowly at 500 feet over her home between Tetbury and Malmesbury. The object appeared to rotate slowly and made a humming sound, then took off at a terrific speed. On November 22, 1990, in the outskirts of Moscow a young woman was lying in bed when an intense light penetrated the room. She got out of bed and saw a glowing object in front of her house that took off after approximately five minutes.

THE 21ST CENTURY

In May 8, 2000, in Juniper, British Columbia, in Canada, a large triangular object was observed hovering above Blue Juniper Mountain. Suddenly, the craft split into four triangular small objects with flashing lights. They give an aura of changing colors and a powerful strobe light that lit up the mountain. Finally one of the small objects merged into the craft before it shoot into the sky.

In May 2004, a group of UFOs were sighted in Mexico and the Mexican government released a video, but at the moment it is not available. The 1990s had been a big decade for UFO sightings in Mexico, especially in Mexico City, and there are many good videos of these events.

On January 12, 2000, in Northeastern, Missouri, at 8:45 p.m., a family had the incredible experience of watching close to 30 UFOs within two hours, having spotted a lone light they chased in the car. The UFO came closer enough to hover over them, following them home as they proceeded to speed in panic.

Since 1947, UFO researchers have reported a cycle of sightings every 64 months: 1947, 1953, 1958, 1964, 1968, 1973, 1978. In the '80s and '90s and in 2000 and 2004, there were sightings, but nothing like years past.

At least 62 American astronomy professors have revealed that they have sighted and recorded UFOs. According to a Gallup poll, more than five million Americans claim they have seen UFOs. People around the world have seen at least 31 different types of UFOs.

These events raise many questions. If UFO sightings have been registered for centuries, it means that they probably coexisted with the human race from when culture began to evolve and probably are responsible for much of our cultural evolution. An extraterrestrial race that has been so involved in our religion and culture might well have also influenced our biological evolution as well, but I haven't researched that topic.

CHAPTER 3

A SHORT HISTORY OF HUMAN AVIATION

"In the firm belief that the American public deserves a better explanation than thus far given by the Air Force, I strongly recommend that there be a committee investigation of the UFO phenomenon."
— Former U.S. President Gerald Ford, 1966

I would like to review briefly the history of human flight and compare it with the UFO phenomenon as seen from the beginning of human history. As I have shown, the UFO phenomenon presents unique characteristics: they appear as glowing lights; they can become invisible; they do turns impossible for the human body to withstand; they have been tracked at speeds of 20,000 miles per hour. The difference between human aviation and UFOs is obvious.

On December 17, 1903, an American inventor, Orville Wright (1871-1948) made the first flight in history at Kitty Hawk, North Carolina in an airplane he had built with his brother, Wilbur (1867-1912). It flew only 850 feet, barely skimming the ground and was in the air less than a minute.

Although it was the first human flight, the Wright brothers weren't the first to think of flying or to try to fly. The American astronomer Samuel Pierpont Langley (1834-1906) began experimenting with airplanes in 1896, and before the Wright brothers' flight, he had made three attempts to fly planes. The third time, he nearly made it. His third plane, fitted with a bigger engine, was successfully flown, but after Langley had died.

Some 2,000 years ago, the ancient Greeks created fanciful tales of constructing feathered wings that enable men to fly and from those tales came the legend of Icarus.

The Italian engineer and artist Leonardo da Vinci (1452-1519) made drawings of flying machines. Although Orville Wright was the first to fly a vehicle that was heavier than air in 1903, three years earlier on July 2, 1900, the German inventor Ferdinand von Zeppelin successfully launched the first flight of a gondola capable of carrying people suspended beneath a hydrogen-filled, cigar-shaped bag that could float in the air. The device was called a dirigible balloon or zeppelin. Many dirigibles were built and used for commercial flights. In the 1920s and 1930s, it seemed the way of future human flight, but in the end the dirigibles lost the race. The Hindenburg, the largest dirigible ever built, suddenly burst into flames as it was docking at Lakehurst, New Jersey, on May 6, 1937.

In 1852, 48 years before Zeppelin, the French engineer Henri Giffard (1825-1882) had placed a steam engine in a gondola under a saucer-shaped balloon. It could move at six miles per hour.

English engineer George Cayley (1773-1857) was the first to study scientifically the conditions under which air might keep an artificial device aloft. He built the first glider capable of carrying a man through the air in 1853. However, before his unpowered airplane, there were unpowered balloons. The first were built in 1783 by two brothers, Joseph Michel Montgolfier (1740-1810) and Jacques Etienne Montgolfier (1745-1799). The first balloon filled with hot air flew on June 5, 1783, and on November 20 that year a large balloon capable of carrying a human being was built. In fact, it carried two people. Jean Francois Pilatre de Rozier (1756-1785) and Marquis d'Arlande were the first human beings to fly through the air in a man-made device 120 years before the Wright Brother's flight. On January 7, 1785, Pilatre de Rozier was carried with two others across the English Channel. On the return trip the balloon ignited and he died.

However, many Brazilians claim a flight by Santos Dumont should be considered the first airplane flight in history because the Wright brothers' test was private and their claims therefore questionable. Dumont was born in Brazil in 1873 and lived much of his life in Paris, where he invented many flying machines. In 1906 he publicly demonstrated, to cheering crowds in Paris his 14-Bis, which he made from box kites and a car motor. In his first demonstration of a flying machine, also in 1906, he had circled the Eiffel Tower in a No. 6 dirigible. He became known around the world.

Since the beginning of the 20th century, the technology has improved and planes fly faster. In 1903 the Wright brothers flyer flew 30 mph; in 1909 the Bieriot X1 flew 36 mph, in 1911 the Curtiss Hydro-Aeroplane flew 55 mph; in 1913 the Deperdussin Monocoque flew 127 mph; in 1922 the Curtiss HS D-12 flew 233 mph; in 1928 the Macchi M 52 Bis flew 318 mph; in 1931 the Supermarine S6-b flew 407 mph; in 1939 the Messerschmitt Bf209 flew 606 mph; in 1945 the Gloster Meteor flew at 606 mph; in 1947 the Bell X-1 flew 700 mph.

Chuck Yeagar became the first pilot to break the sound barrier in 1951 in a Douglas D-588-2 Skyrocket at 1,238 mph. In 1953 the Bell X-1A flew 1,650 mph; in 1956 the Bell X-2 flew 2,115 mph; in 1961 the North American X-15 flew 3,300 mph; in 1961 the same plane flew 4,104 mph; in 1967 it flew 4,104 mph; in 1976 the Concorde, a commercial plane, flew 1,450 mph.

In 1989 came the Stealth bomber, which depends on radar-absorbing sheathing to evade air defense instead of speed. The F-16 Falcon flew at 1,500 mph.

CHAPTER 4

THE UFO PHENOMENON AND NATURAL DISASTERS

"It is imperative that we learn where UFOs come from and what their purpose is."

—Vice Admiral R.H. Hillenkoetter,

former CIA Director

Since the beginning of history it has been noted that many natural disasters like earthquakes and big storms have been preceded by aerial phenomenon—what we now call UFOs.

In 63 BC, an earthquake shook the region of Spoletium, Italy, only a few minutes after a blazing beam swept across the sky. Many people believed one of the most devastating plagues in history, the bubonic plagues of Justinian, which engulfed the east Roman Empire from 540 to 590, was a punishment from God because of the unusual aerial phenomena that took place both before and after the plague. Gregory of Tours reported that before the plague invaded the Auvergne region of France in 567, three or four bright lights appeared around the sun and the heavens appeared to be on fire. Other celestial phenomena were seen before the outbreak, including what looked like an immense dragon.

Much more recently, on August 7, 1970, a red glowing ball swept through the village of Saladane in Ethopia. It destroyed houses, uprooted trees, melted asphalt on the road, burned grass, and broke the stone wall of a bridge into pieces. The object made an ear-splitting sound, then became stationary. About 50 buildings were damaged, eight people were injured and one little girl died.

On September 11, 1967, at about 9:30 in the evening during a storm in Rosario, Argentina, an entire family watched a huge, glowing orange object that remained stationary in a field about 230 yards from their house.

Witnesses have also reported that after a UFO has left a site, there is an abnormal fast growth of grass and weeds.

Just before an earthquake struck Caracas, Venezuela, on July 31, 1967, many people saw a huge, glowing red ball sweep across the sky. A UFO researcher matched a map given to him by the government that showed earthquake epicenters matched UFO sightings. In the 1960s, UFO researchers found a relationship between magnetic anomalies and UFOs. Researchers also know that UFOs give special attention to earth faults. In a study in 1954, French researchers discovered that 31 percent of UFO sightings appear near or in faults. A later study showed a 40 percent correlation between UFOs and seismic natural disasters.

The idea of a super-race able to determine natural disasters or cause them is not impossible. Researchers know that after the flood at the end of the last Ice Age, a great diversity of religious belief sprung up around the world. Every religion, folklore and culture has legends of space-gods. A great coincidence is that many of those who allege to have been abducted by UFOs claim that the message of the entities has been about future natural disasters, like earthquakes, pole axis change and, of course, World War III.

Since ancient times, things that look like what men in the 20th and 21st centuries called UFOs have been associated with natural disasters. One night in Rome in 41 BC, a light shone as strong as the sun. It was so strong that people arose from their sleep thinking it was time to work. In 106 BC something like a bird flew in the skies and set houses on fire in some parts of Rome. In 1067 people saw a fire that burned fiercely in the sky. It suddenly came down to the ground and lit up the surroundings for sometime, then revolved and ascended high after burning woods and trees.

On September 15, 1749, a glowing object roared and whirled in the countryside in England, frightening cattle. A witness saw the object sucking water from a pond before roaring away, splitting and smashing trees, and seeming to dart arrows of light into the ground. On January 1, 1751, a glowing object again smashed trees, killing a woman on the ground and unroofing houses for a radius of 15 miles.

So what can we make of all this? What we see in the 20th and 21st centuries that we call UFOs have been seen during all of our history. The UFO phenomenon has been with us, probably since before humankind arrived on this planet.

CHAPTER 5

CROP CIRCLES AND THE UFO CONNECTION

"Any sufficiently advance technology would appear indistinguishable from magic."

— Arthur C. Clark

Researchers have found a drawing that appears to be a crop circle from the 1600s, which at the time would have been perceived as a devil but today looks like an alien being. Some farmers claim to have seen crop circles in the 1930s and 1940s. However, researchers know for sure that the crop circles began to appear in the mid to late 1970s. Coincidentally, cattle mutilation appeared at the same time.

Between the years 1980 and 1988, nearly 100 circles were reported. They varied in size between six and twelve feet in diameter, and occurred between late May and early September. The flattened corn was laid out in perfect geometric precision. Many of the circles were discovered to be hoaxes, but others were too perfect to have been made that way. Some were attributed to "descending atmospheric vortices" or "stationary whirlwinds," but common sense tells us that whirlwinds or vortices usually cause destruction.

Another peculiar pattern in this phenomenon is that the circles appeared overnight and no one seems to know when or how. On one occasion, a witness driving with his wife on a clear and beautiful night in August at about

11:00 p.m. reported, "We saw a huge red ball, fiery and glowing, which rolled slowly over a clump of trees and above a hill on the right. It hung suspended for a time in the air. The rolling motion ceased." The witness stopped his car for a better view and "gradually the large ball commenced to turn on its axis, revolving and changing color as though cooling down from immense heat. It was now a florescent egg flattened somewhat, a brilliant orange in the sky. A deep crimson band spread along or through the center of the egg, jutting out slightly from either end. We looked on in amazement as four small red balls of light shot out of the main scarlet beam and protruded into the air."

The witness estimated the balls to be 20 feet or so, and "at no time were these smaller spheres disconnected from the main object. They seemed to be linked to it by a slender thread of paler red light that swayed like the tentacles of an octopus. They remained in that position, dancing vaguely from side to side, for about two or three minutes; then they quickly shot back into the larger shape and disappeared from sight."

This episode took place in 1966 in the middle of a great UFO wave. The interesting thing is that most of the corn circles are found in Warminster and adjacent areas in England, not too far from the great ruins of Stonehenge . A similar object was sighted in August of 1985 on the night before a great circle was found. A witness was driving with his wife and son when they saw a very bright, white light hovering over the field. After a couple of minutes the object vanished. The witness found the sighting disturbing, "It was weird, but we know what we saw," he said.

The great majority of crop circles in England in the 1980s were mostly in the area of Wiltshire and Hampshire. They have also appeared in Silbury Hill, where a witness saw a bright object in the sky a day before a crop circle was found. Another witness was driving home when she saw an intense golden white glow in the clouds. Then she saw a long, narrow beam of white light directed to the ground where the circles form.

The energy that produced the circles is invisible and researchers have found various effects like electrical cracking noises, humming and beating noises, bright flashes and UFOs. Wherever this super-intelligence came from, it is clear that everything they do is with the idea of making us believe and wonder about the truth and real facts of life. Some examples are the cattle mutilations, the hairy monsters, and the sightings of humanoids without a clear message for the human race. One thing is sure: every major mystery in this world has something to do with UFOs. I am talking about the strange disappearances of large groups of people, miracles, and the paranormal in general.

CHAPTER 6

THE UFO PHENOMENON AND THE ELECTROMAGNETIC EFFECT IN CARS AND ELECTRICAL APPLIANCES

"After he told the citizens it was only stars and had talked to me, he decided to look for himself. He noticed an object in the sky similar to a star, but bigger and brighter. He decided to scramble an F-4 from Shahrokin Air Force to investigate."

—U.S. State Department, report if an attempted interception of a UFO in Iran, September 19, 1976

One of the phenomena very well known throughout the history of UFOs is their effect on cars. Since the 1940s, a pattern has been seen where car engines stop completely when a UFO is present. Researchers have also reported that sometimes electrical appliances stop and television screens go blank. However, it is not well known that UFOs are probably responsible for blackouts. Not all blackouts, certainly, but when UFOs are present, we can assume a blackout is more than a coincidence because a machine as sophisticated as a UFO is capable of feats inconceivable to us humans. Here are a few incidents that seem like more than a coincidence.

In April 1952, there was a sudden blackout of a power system in northeastern Ohio and two days later an unexplainable blackout at a power station in Evanston,

Indiana, which lasted for two hours. Experts and police were puzzled that at the same time strange objects were seen in the sky. In another incident in Ohio, the power suddenly went on and off. The authorities checked every instrument, test, and recorded charts, but no clues were found. The power company issued the statement, "The only logical assumption is that some object or foreign substance came across the line and grounded it out, but we don't have a clue at what it was."

In July 1952, a brand new power station in a midwestern state suddenly blew up with violence. Nobody knew the reason, but UFOs were seen in the sky.

The record year for electrical failures and blackouts was 1965, which was also the record year for UFO sightings. During the Big Blackout of November 9, 1965, a city aviation commissioner of Syracuse, New York, was flying a plane in the company of other individuals when the lights went out at 5:22 p.m. He managed to land safely but reported a "ball of fire south of us, toward Thompson Road and Carrier Traffic Circle. It appeared to be about 100 feet in the air and 50 feet in diameter. All I could think of was a mushroom effect."

The blackout put 80,000 square miles and 30 million people in seven states and parts of Canada in the dark. There were many eyewitnesses to UFOs just before the lights went out. A witness near Syracuse reported seeing a ball of fire an hour before the lights went out, and a group of men saw a ball of fire similar to the first.

Another witness was preparing to land his private plane at Hanck Field when he saw a UFO about 100 feet in diameter near the New York Power Company, which then passed over the New York Central Railroad tracks. A flight instructor reported he saw "a ball of fire of orange-red which flared up bigger than a house hovered over the high line which runs from Clay to Niagara Falls for about 10 seconds."

Two witnesses in Somerville, New Jersey, reported seeing "a very large light, larger than the evening star" moving to the northeast moments after the lights had gone out.

UFO researchers have collected more than 100 cases of local blackouts caused by the electromagnetic effects of UFOs. On September 25, 1965, a tropical resort in Cuernavaca, Mexico, suffered three consecutive power failures in less than one hour. Company officials were baffled. Several tower operators at the international airport had spotted UFOs.

On December 2, another power failure in New Mexico and Texas blacked out four important military bases and the lights of two million people. President Lyndon B. Johnson ordered a federal investigation. On December 5, another massive power failure in the southwest left 40 million homes in darkness.

In November 1953, in New Haven Connecticut, a glowing orange-red object suddenly snapped down trees and the lights in houses dimmed out. In 1957, three glowing UFOs in MogiMirim, Brazil, enveloped the houses beneath their path in complete blackness. That same year in Tamaroa, Illinois, there was a huge power failure that lasted until a huge, hovering UFO move away from the town.

On August 17, 1959, a well-documented case occurred in Minas, Gerais, Brazil. During the night, the instruments at the power company indicated some sort of temporary power flow interruption. The officials at the various locations began phoning each other, because their circuit breakers were opening automatically as UFOs moved slowly at low altitude.

In September 1952, NATO naval forces were in maneuvers off the European coast when a silvery round object appeared in the sky. Six British meteor jets gave chase, but were quickly outpaced.

On June 19, 1978, a UFO sighting near Arcalaon, France, triggered the photocells that control the lights for the whole town. At 1:30 in the morning, a witness stopped to repair the turn signal of the car when all the lights in the town suddenly switched off. At the same time, a powerful rumble like an earthquake was heard. Then the witness saw an object that was oval, red and surrounded by white flames. In the following month, the witness noted that the vegetation was affected when UFOs were present because the weeds were taller.

Major blackouts occurred around the world on November 9, 1965, into 1966. Power failures simultaneous with UFO sightings were reported in the northern states. The sudden failure knocked out house lights and appliances. Many residents reported UFOs near the major highways. The objects gave blue and orange flashes. The major power failures around the world coincide with the heaviest concentration of UFOs. All of southern Italy lost power for up to two hours. Over a million people were affected in Naples. Two successive two-hour power failures crippled the states of Nebraska and Missouri in July of 1966.

However, many events are not known to the vast majority of people, such as the one in mid-June of 1966 during the Vietnam War. A sergeant in the Army said, "In a camp of 40,000, men went into panic while they were watching a movie when a real bright light came from out of nowhere. At first we thought it was a flare, which are going off all the time. It came from the north and was moving from slow to fast speeds. Some of the soldiers said that the UFO was at 25,000 feet. Suddenly the UFO dropped right toward us and then panic broke loose. It stopped dead at 300 to 500 feet up. The valleys and the mountains looked like the middle of the day. Then it went up for two or three seconds. The shocking thing is that all generators stopped. Planes readied to take off and their engines stopped. No cars, tractors, planes, trucks and eight bulldozers that were working close by moved for four minutes. A whole plane full of big shots came from Washington to investigate."

The United States Air Force knows of many incidents like this, but they don't want to release the information to the public because they don't want to start a panic. One of the most frightening events happened in Brazil on November 3, 1957, on a beautiful and quiet night in a town named Itaipu. A garrison of soldiers were asleep when suddenly a new star burst into brilliance in a cloudless sky. Two soldiers on guard duty watched in amazement. They realized it was not a star but a luminous flying object rapidly approaching. The soldiers noted that it was not a plane because of its tremendous speed. Within seconds the UFO was over the fort, where it hovered 120 to 180 feet above the highest tower. The UFO took a while approaching, then the nightmare began. Something hot touched the soldiers' faces. Then they were struck by a very strong wave of heat. The object was large and disc-shaped surrounded by an eerie glow. One soldier said it was "like a fire burning all over the clothes." The air filled with the UFO's humming sound. Panic overwhelmed the sentries and one started screaming. His loud cries woke up the garrison and everything was in confusion. Suddenly the electricity went off. Elevators, emergency systems, communications—everything—was out. The electric clocks set to ring at 5:00 a.m. went off at 2:30 a.m. The garrison was helplessly in panic. One of the sentries was unconscious and the other was crying and mumbling, hiding in a corner. The two guards were badly burned, one still unconscious and showing sign of peripheral vascular failure. The other was in deep shock. The nightmare lasted three minutes. The lights came on and some of the soldiers saw an orange light climbing vertically above the fort. The following day, American officers arrived to investigate.

As we see in all these incidents, UFOs had the means to interfere with our most important and basic human technology. It may be intentional or simply the electromagnetic effects of the UFOs.

In 1954 a test pilot for the French Fonga aircraft company tried to approach a hovering UFO in the lower Pyrenees. He was forced to turn away because of the intense heat that built up in his cockpit.

UFOs seem to be observing our power plants. More than 100 sightings were reported in a three-week period in 1977 at the Indian Point nuclear power plant 30 miles north of New York City. UFOs may have caused New York's "Big Blackout" of 1977. According to several observers, 10 minutes before the blackout, strange UFOs were sighted near the World Trade Center. In minutes the city was in darkness.

UFOs have flown as low as 100 feet over areas where
nuclear weapons are stored. They flew over Air Force
bases in Michigan, North Dakota, New Hampshire, and
Canada between October 28 and November 12 in 1975.

A recently declassified Air Force document revealed
that thousands of people saw UFOs observing the atomic
proving grounds at Los Alamos, New Mexico. There were
an amazing numbers of UFO observations during 1948-
49, but they never interfered. There was a mysterious
crash of an Air Force plane in which UFOs were involved
on April 1, 1959. At 6:29 p.m., a C-118 transport plane
with a crew of four took off on a local training mission
from McCord AFB in Tacoma, Washington. About an
hour later, the pilot radioed, "We have hit something
or something has hit us." He then called "Mayday," the
international distress signal, and reported he was headed
for the base. Sometime later came the cryptic message,
"This is it," and the C-118 crashed five miles southwest
of Summer, Washington. A witness reported the plane
was shredded almost beyond belief; it was smashed to
bits. Three bodies were found, two nearly buried in the
ground.

CHAPTER 7

THE SUPERNATURAL, POLTERGEIST, GHOSTS AND UFOS

"Nothing belongs any longer to the realm of the gods or the supernatural. The individual who lives in the technical milieu knows very well that there is nothing spiritual anywhere. But man cannot live without the sacred. He therefore transfers his sense of the sacred to the very thing that has destroyed its former object: to technology itself."

— Jacques Ellar

Since the beginning of human history, human beings have looked to the stars for answers to their mortal destiny. Anthropologists have discovered that the Neanderthal man was buried in such a way that it shows some abstract thinking and fear of death. This fear is one of the causes of the origin of religion and the idea of immortality of the soul.

Primitive man saw dead relatives and friends in his dreams, which is how the idea of the immortality of the soul was born. However, the idea of immortality revolutionizes *Homo sapiens*, making him the center of the Universe because he is no longer "the little monkey" coming out of the trees into the valleys and walking upright.

However, there is nothing in human biology that can make us think that we are immortal. The ancients, including the Greeks, believed the soul was located in the liver. Today the location of the soul is believed to be the heart. The idea of the soul has been in accord with the development of race, culture and society. The great philosopher Bertrand Russell said, "It should be said that the old distinction between soul and body has evaporated, quite as much because matter has lost its solidity as because mind has lost its spirituality. Psychology is just beginning to be scientific. In the present state of psychology, belief in immortality can claim no support from science."

We can say without a doubt that Bertrand Russell was one of the great minds of the 20th century, but that doesn't mean he was infallible. Another writer with deep thoughts about human existence was Ernest Haeckel, who said, "The theological proof that a personnel creator has breathed an immortal soul into man is a pure myth. The cosmological proof that the moral order of the world demands the eternal duration of the human soul is a baseless dogma. The teleological proof that the higher destiny of man involves the perfecting of his defective earthly soul beyond the grave rests on a false anthropism."

William James, the great American philosopher and psychologist, gave his opinion about the immortality of the soul theory: "The soul theory is a complete superfluity, so far as according for the actually verified acts of conscious experience goes. So far no one can be compelled to subscribe to it for definite scientific reasons."

Another famous psychologist, Professor John B. Watson, wrote in his book, *Behaviorism*, "No one has ever touched a soul, or has seen one in a test tube, or has in any way come into relationship with it as he has with other objects of his daily experience. Nevertheless, to doubt its existence is to become a heretic, and once might possibly even had led to the loss of one's head. Even today a man holding a public position dares not question it."

Moreover, Professor Ernst Haeckel wrote, "The ontological proof that the soul, being a simple immaterial, indivisible entity, cannot be involved in the corruption of death is based on an entirely erroneous view of the psychic phenomena; it is a spiritual fallacy." Further, says Haeckel, "The moral proof that the defects and the unsatisfied desires of earthly existence must be fulfilled by 'compensative justice' on the other side of eternity, is nothing more than a pious wish. The ethnological proof that the belief in immortality, like the belief in God, is an innate truth common to all humanity is an error of fact."

The belief in the immortality of the soul is a matter of faith; there is nothing in science that proves the existence of this ethereal substance. However, in the history of the human race there are phenomena that transcend our logic and common sense, like the phenomena of poltergeist and ghosts. How can we explain these phenomena when we know that nothing in our physiology can cause it?

THE POLTERGEIST PHENOMENON

The poltergeist is considered one of the most baffling of supernatural phenomena. For example, one of the earliest accounts about poltergeist and haunting goes back to the first century AD when the great Roman orator Pliny, the Younger reported that his house was haunted by a spirit that "rattles chains." We don't have an explanation for this phenomenon. The most common and acceptable thought is that the soul of the dead is looking for some earthly comfort. The fact is that we don't know the origin of the phenomenon.

The most accepted theory of the poltergeist is that it is caused by a teenager, in most cases a girl, whose sexual energy produces the movement of objects. However, there is no evidence whatsoever; it is just an easy way to explain the unexplainable.

Paranormal phenomena have been reported since the beginning of history, and every culture in every age has stories about it. In the United States, modern spiritualism began in March 1848, with Kate and Margaret Fox, age 12 and 15, respectively. The two girls heard mysterious rapping on the wall of their house in Hydesville, New York. Interestingly, Joseph Smith had his visions of the angel Morony not far from the girls' home. The girls developed a system of yes/no answer to communicate with the entities responsible for the knocking on the wall.

Before the Fox family moved into that house, the family of Mitchel Weekman lived there. His family was afraid of the knockings on the door and wall. His eight-year-old daughter was caressed a few times by an invisible and cold hand while she screamed in terror.

Such phenomena exist in every culture. In Haiti, they practice voodoo; in Brazil, spiritualism; in Africa and the Caribbean, Santeria. The American Indians had a magician called "Shaman." In the year 1609, an early French explorer named Samuel De Chaplain was in the Quebec wilderness joining a war party of Algonquins, where he witnessed a supernatural ceremony. A small tent was built and the shaman started mumbling to the spirits. His voice became louder and more frantic. The tent bent and swayed back and forth as he screamed and shouted in a variety of voices. On another occasion in a shaman's consultation with the natives, the natives suddenly called out with a loud cry, pointing to the top of the tent as sparks came from the vent hole. The shaman responded with a loud screaming, and again fiery sparks appeared floating above the tent. The tent swayed and shook strongly while the sound of numerous voices, barking dogs, and screams and sobs of despair, anguish and pain were heard. Amazingly, clear speech was also heard, which sounded human, but in a tongue unknown to any of the people present. In some instances, the shaman was tied up. Nevertheless, various voices and cries from humans and animals were heard while sparks flew.

In another session with the shaman, a strange voice came from the top of the tent. After the shaman talked to the strange voice, he could answer questions from the native about hunting and fishing. He became very agitated, swinging backward and forward in plain view and there were voices unlike any human being at the same time a number of objects appeared like little stars.

The spirits contacted by the shamans were anthropomorphic beings of their native mythology, usually an animal species. In North American Indian culture, the spirit of Mikinak, the great turtle, serves as a medium between the medicine man and other spirits. Mikinak talks in a nasal voice like Donald Duck and is a clown that tells jokes to the audience. However, now and then spirits of the dead are present. Their messages are similar to those when seances are held. The spirits of the dead say they are happy in a beautiful country and they are never hungry, thirsty or suffer pain. They also said not to hurt anybody, and to do what is right and someday they will see their dead relatives.

The most famous cases of poltergeist in the history of the supernatural happened from 1817 to 1821 and went into history, like the case of the Bell Witch, an invisible entity that tormented the Jones family. On one occasion, the family was awakened by a very loud crash in the kitchen, and when they went to see, everything was on the floor, including the salt shakers, vases, cups, saucers made from fine glass. The odd thing was that nothing was broken. Everything had been in multiple cabinets, so multiple crashes should have been expected, but there was only one crash. The family saw strange dog-like animals that walked like humans. On another occasion, a family member asked the poltergeist for hazelnuts, which materialized in her hands. She said she couldn't crack the nuts, and within minutes all the nuts were cracked.

Poltergeists have known about things happening far away and have predicted events. They have had personal information about strangers that came into the house. Legend says that on one occasion, the famous general Andrew Jackson went to investigate with a witch layer, and tried to shoot the invisible being, but the gun wouldn't fire. The witch said, "Now it is my turn, look out you old coward, hypocrite, and fraud. I will teach you a lesson." Amazingly something invisible slapped his face. He was dragged around the room and his nose was bleeding. On another occasion, the poltergeist wanted sex with one of the family members.

Up to this point, I have described supernatural events that are matched by UFO events. For example, it is well known that UFO entities can become invisible, like the famous "Men in Black" (see Chapter 13). There is plenty of documented evidence that UFOs can go through walls, doors, and other solid objects. The little stars seen in the shaman seances are a very known UFO phenomenon. On January 16, 1974, in Bedfordshire, England, a witness was having dinner in her house when suddenly she felt an urgent need to go to the window and to her surprise saw "a red, bright light moving in a peculiar form, then suddenly dropping like a stone and disappearing." On another occasion, a witness woke up for no apparent reason and looked out the window and saw a glowing ball of whitish light hovering over the meadow, which was bouncing back and forth across the field and flashing wildly. After this spotting of a UFO, a full attack of poltergeist began. The TV functioned abnormally, the car's engine suddenly died, and the phone went haywire. The family received up to ten phantom calls a day. Two months after the initial sightings, the witness recalled a terrible smell like something dead rotting. The witness said, "I never noticed this before, or since. I woke my husband. The smell was not from the meadow. It made me want to vomit. My husband noticed the odor also."

Many witnesses claimed to smell sulphur or industrial oil accompanying UFO sightings. In 1967 a witness saw a UFO, a huge silvery football-shaped craft hissing like air escaping from a tire. The witness called the rest of the family to watch the strange craft. After the sighting, the poltergeist activity began. One of the family members awoke thinking someone had called her name. As her mind cleared, she saw a shadow-like entity escape the room. When she looked back, it had disappeared. The witness also heard footsteps pacing the house when no one else was home. This event is a great example of phenomena that for centuries have been called ghosts or spirits in haunted houses. In this case, the UFO has the switch to create this reality. The family moved to another house, but the visits from the poltergeist continued. They were disturbed by rapping sounds on the walls and windows. The family cat acted strangely as though in the company of an invisible presence.

In the spring of 1966, a witness in the rural area of Woodstock, New York, started to see strange greenish lights about six feet in diameter shining from the fields. Sometimes the objects would fly to investigate passing cars. When the lights began to focus on the house, the poltergeist began, with funny garbled sounds coming from the wall like the cartoon character "Tweetie Pie," then sounds like a voice mice would make if they could jabber. The witness looked all around the house and saw nothing. However, when she went to the field, she saw a bright green light and a red light. She also heard human voices and the sound of someone walking. This shows a type of supernatural phenomenon consistent with the idea of "haunted ghosts and roaming spirits."

The UFO phenomenon manipulates reality and our dreams and nightmares. As a consequence, we create a myth: the belief in the immortality of the soul. For example, in the spring of 1956, hundreds of thousands of people in the United States were in a very deep spiritual crisis when evidence of the immortality of the soul was supposedly found when businessman and hypnotist Morey Bernstein recorded the life after death of an Irish medium in his book, *The Search for Bridey Murphy*. It was Bridey's experience in the world of ghosts and spirits that became the evidence of the immortality of the soul. Bernstein's book mentions an apparent case of reincarnation. However, investigative reporters for *Life* magazine and the *Denver Post* cast doubt on the validity of Bridey's claim. No record of her school or obituary notice could be found. In other words, nothing of her claims could be verified. Even after Bridey's claims were exposed as a fraud, many people believed that the reincarnation and the immortality of the soul were true. Sadly, a 19-year-old boy committed suicide because he wanted to prove the mysteries of reincarnation.

Another supernatural belief is in witchcraft. Many lives were lost during the persecutions of alleged witches in the 16th and 17th centuries. Scholars believe that approximately 200,000 to 1,000,000 lives were taken. During the witch-hunt in Salem, Massachusetts, women were burned at the stake accused of witchcraft. In fact, the women had symptoms of food poisoning that made them seem possessed.

At the end of the 15th century an interesting feature appeared in witchcraft: the celebration of Sabbat. The first specific reference to a sabbat was in 1475. The most fantastic tales were accepted as true occurrences by ecclesiastical and secular tribunals. The sabbat usually took place at midnight on Thursday and was held in cemeteries, ruined churches, and fields. The legend said that the so-called witch was surprised to see all her friends and neighbors, whom she had not previously suspected to be witches. With them were scores of demons to whom they bound themselves in an infernal pact.

The master of ceremonies was the devil, who appeared as a big, black, bearded man, or more often as a stinking goat, and occasionally as a great toad. They all worshiped and danced around the devil to the sounds of macabre music made from curious instruments like horse skulls, human bones, and oak logs. The participants kissed him under the tail if it were a goat or on the lips if it were a toad. By their own admission, thousands of men and women made secret pacts with the devil. The question is whether these events have a remote chance of being factual or are just unsubstantiated legends.

The UFO phenomenon presents us with a variety of phenomena that can prove any legend or myth. In UFO literature, there are records of sightings of creatures that look like the devil. For example, on September 12, 1952, in Flatwoods, West Virginia, a group of children were in a playground when a UFO that looked like a red ball of fire appeared close by. The children said that the UFO had landed on a hill close to the house of Mrs. Kathleen May, who said, "Up on the hill I could see a reddish glow." A 17-year-old named Gene went with her to investigate. After half an hour of walking through the brush, the teenager saw a monster and screamed in terror. They fled in a panic from the horrendous sight. The monster was described as an immense man-like figure with a blood-red face and eyes like glowing green spots blinking out from a pointed hood. Behind the monster was a glowing ball of fire as big as a house. Mrs. May described the monster as having "terrible claws" and they were in agreement that it wore dark clothes, something like a bark green. The witnesses said the monster was between seven and ten feet tall and smelled like sulphur, a smell associated with the devil in religious folklore.

In another example, in 1995, rumors were spreading from Puerto Rico of a monster called "Goatsucker" or "Chupacabras." (UFOs had been seen in Puerto Rico for more than 50 years.) A witness said that the "Chupacabras" jumped like a kangaroo and smelled like sulphur. Another witness said it "was ugly as a demon and flew through the air." Still another said it "looked like a vampire." A construction worker about 20 miles from San Juan swore he saw it said, "It was about four or five feet tall with huge elongated eyes. A pointed tongue came out of his mouth. It was gray, but his back changed colors. It was a monster." Many people who saw the "Chupacabras" were so affected that they were taken to the hospital. (See the following chapter on the relationship between the UFO phenomenon and monsters.)

One of the most important pieces of evidence that the UFO phenomenon is a mental, spiritual, and psychological phenomenon is an event that happened at 8:00 in the evening on February 23, 1967. The daughters of the Clyde McDonald family were playing with a Ouija Board, which told them the day and time a UFO would appear. The parents of the children were seated watching TV waiting for the UFO to appear. The girls were outside waiting. The UFO suddenly appeared and the girls said, "Mother, you'd better hurry. It will be gone before you get there." The father looked up and hollered, "Oh, Tammy, there it is" and they ran outside barefoot. The family reported, "It was a big light. We just stood there and watched it, and we about froze. We were barefoot and everything, but we didn't want to come back and lose it. It was kind if an orange ball, orange to red, kind of a circle."

The most important evidence that shows the complex mental, spiritual and supernatural nature of the UFO phenomenon is that of August 10, 1975, when a witness sited a UFO about 11:00 p.m. After watching television, she went to sleep and woke up to find two beings wearing silver suits by her bed. They had slits for eyes, mouth and nose. The beings communicated with her telepathically and asked her to come with them. She said she felt very calm. She saw the house, the garage, the stars, and finally a hovering UFO. She had a sense of beauty. Suddenly she was blinded by a white light. A month after the sighting, the witness was staying with a sister in Industrial City, California, when she suddenly fell to the floor as if someone pushed her down. She was severely beaten by an invisible entity. Her sister said, "She was turning and spinning on the floor, hitting obstacles." The victim spent six days in the hospital. This event is the strongest evidence that the UFO phenomenon is behind the poltergeist and haunting supernatural phenomenon. It is similar to the famous case of the 19th century "Bell Witch" that I mentioned earlier in this chapter.

In the 1980s, a Russian pilot flying a supersonic jet responded to a call to look for a target. He couldn't see the target, so he was ordered to return to base. For three days the pilot chased the ghost target but found nothing. However, one of the pilots was walking with a friend after the chase when a powerful blow knocked him down and flung him off the road. His friend helped him to his feet. The pilot was in pain. A short and lean man dressed in black warned him that "there may be another energizer strike." The man in black was telepathic. He squatted down and touched the pilot's legs with the palm of his hand.

Instantly the pain and delusion vanished. Interestingly, the man in black paid no attention to the pilot's friend. In this event we see similarities to the Bell Witch, Men in Black, and poltergeist phenomena, giving us the only reasonable conclusion that the UFO phenomenon is the source of the supernatural phenomenon.

In the so-called supernatural, there are many cases of monsters, invisible beings and poltergeist. A witness on February 6, 1974, in Fayette County, Pennsylvania, was watching television in her home in an isolated area. She heard the sounds of rattling cans coming from the porch. Thinking they were dogs, she got a shotgun to scare them. When she opened the door, she was confronted by a seven-foot tall ape-like creature similar to "Big Foot." She shot the creature, thinking it was going to leap at her. The creature instantly raised its hands in the air, and, to her amazement "just disappeared in a flash of light, just like taking a picture." In this event we see the amazing and unbelievable nature of this phenomenon.

Again, in the '90s, a teenage girl and her family were harassed by an invisible entity. The children were scratched. They also heard a baby and a doll crying with real tears. (The crying doll is a phenomenon that also has been seen as a religious phenomenon called "miracles." The Virgin Mary and even Hindu images have been seen crying.) The children said that the entity looked like Big Foot and was saying "vulgar things."

In Port Isabel, Pennsylvania, in the fall of 1968 about 10:00 p.m., a witness heard a noise outside the farmhouse "like something hitting metal." He got a flashlight and saw a monster ten feet tall and four feet across the shoulders, which were long, like an ape's. The monster's hairy body was tanish in color and its eyes glowed. Its teeth were prominent and protruding and its ears pointed. The creature put the witness in a sort of trance. He got a shotgun and hit the monster, which screamed and vanished in a white mist. He looked for the monster, but there was no trace. Here we see another connection between Big Foot and the UFO phenomenon. (See the following chapter on monsters and UFOs.)

In another event, two gas station workers saw a large, glowing white light in the sky. The UFO moved close to the station and suddenly disappeared, leaving the strong smell of sulphur. This smell had nothing to do with the devil because the UFO phenomenon and the devil and the angel are the same thing.

In November of 1966, a witness and her friend were watching the sky when flashing lights suddenly appeared. One of the women became immobile with her head down. The two women heard a voice talking to them. The witness's family also experienced poltergeist phenomenon, like glass objects moving around and breaking without any known cause, strange noises being heard throughout the house, and telephone and television sets working abnormally. Interestingly, all these experiences happened after a UFO sighting.

In February 1976, in the woodland area of Cincinnati, two policemen witnessed large, hairy creatures. On April 16, 1976, a witness called the police after midnight to report that she was frightened by "screaming, screeching, and growling" in a ravine below her hillside home on the north side of the San Francisco Bay. The police immediately dispatched two officers to the site. The officers later said, "When we got there, we heard the sounds, too. They were high-pitched sounds." With guns drawn, they hiked the area. One of the officers reported, "I heard heavy breathing ahead of us, then there were crackling noises, as if some thing were approaching." One of the officers said he saw a large, "dark-colored thing. It was walking on its hind legs. I saw it climb an eight-foot retaining wall and disappear into the brush." The officers returned and found a thick trail of blood. Following it through the brush, they came upon a slain deer, its neck broken, the body disemboweled and badly mangled. I would refer readers to the section about UFOs and monsters, where I mention the experience of former president Theodore Roosevelt. He mentioned the same experience, which he had heard from other hunters and Wild West adventurers.

On October 25, 1973, a witness and 15 other people saw a "large red ball" descend toward a pasture near their farm. The witness ran into the house and got a .30-60 rifle and, in the company of a couple of neighbors, proceeded by truck up a dirt road. The three people walked up a hill, and saw an object that appeared to be 100 feet in diameter and made a loud sound like a lawn mower. It was illuminated and they saw two ape-like creatures with glowing eyes making crying-like sounds. The smell of burning rubber was in the air. A patrolman was dispatched to the site and saw "a glowing white light. It was light enough to read a newspaper." They reported that as they investigated, they heard a noise in the woods following them. According to police, the witness became hysterical and they all returned home. A team of professionals—a retired U.S. Air Force major, a physics instructor, a sociology professor and a photographer—went to investigate.

The team checked for radiation, and found a bull in a nearby farm that seemed scared. The witness's dog began tracking something in the same direction. Suddenly, one of the team members started "rubbing his face and shaking as if he were going to faint." The man, over six feet tall and 250 pounds, began to breathe heavily and growl like an animal. He pushed two people to the ground and went crazily around the field, swinging his arms and growling before suddenly collapsing face down on the ground. Another investigator felt light-headed and collapsed, and a third had trouble breathing. The air was strong with the smell of sulphur. Probably the ape-like creatures came from a volcano-like world. If we give it a label like heaven or hell, it is just a human affinity for explaining the unknown.

All these incidents show the connection between the UFO phenomenon, poltergeist, ghosts, haunting, and "weird monsters." On another occasion, a witness was in her home watching television. All of a sudden a bright light flashed through the window and the electrical power failed. The witness walked to the door to look outside for the source of the disturbance and saw a basketball-size ball of light hovering just above the ground about 50 feet away. She tried to walk toward the object, but she couldn't move as a tingling sensation swept through his body. She was in some kind of trance as she watched the light rise and disappear over the barn, leaving an odor of sulphur or burned rubber.

Readers, there is nothing to fear from this smell. We should not expect an alien form of life to smell like an Obsession or Old Spice perfume.

Up to this point, the reader can see the connection between Big Foot, poltergeist, the supernatural and the UFO phenomenon.

Many UFO abductions include reports from witnesses claiming to have been carried through walls, like in the 19th century case of the "Bell Witch." In many poltergeist cases, material objects appear and disappear. In 1926, saliva from a poltergeist bite was examined and was found swarming with micro-organisms. In the same vein, the tears and blood of statues of the Virgin Mary were analyzed and shown to be human. It is clear to me that the intelligence behind the UFO phenomenon is responsible for these supernatural incidents. The most important clue is the lights, present in every poltergeist, seance, and UFO phenomenon. However, it is in the 19th, 20th, and 21st centuries that the UFO phenomenon presented itself as interplanetary, extra-terrestrial or inter-dimensional phenomenon, rather than as a religious, supernatural or weird occurrence as in earlier historical times.

The following event explains the relation between the UFO phenomenon and the devil and the best evidence of the relationship of the idea of "evil" and UFOs. In the summer of 1968, about 4:00 p.m., a British woman and a friend were driving near Stratford when they saw a shining disc in the sky. They stopped to watch it dart, as did another car. After it disappeared behind the trees, during the drive home, she experienced amazing insight on the nature of reality. After supper, she encountered a strange apparition. The light in the room shone in an arc of about 10 feet around the window. She reported, "In that area, I saw as soon as I came to the window, a strange figure. My perception of it was heightened by the state of frozen panic it produced in me. It was for me without any doubt a demon, or devil, because of my western-oriented interpretation. It had dog or goat-like legs. It was covered in silky, downy fur, dark and glinting in the light. It was humanoid and to my mind malevolent. It crouched and stared at me with light, green, grape eyes that had no pupils. The eyes shone and that was the most frightening thing about it. I think it was trying to communicate with me, but my panic interfered with any message I might have received. It was four or five feet tall, had pointed ears and a long muzzle. It gave the impression of emaciation. It's hands and fingers were as thin as sticks."

In this event, we see a UFO followed by an apparition, which establishes the connection between the UFO phenomenon and the supernatural. We see a goat-like creature that is well known in mythological literature. In Greek and Medieval mythology there is mention of a goat-like creature called Pan, sucubis and incubus. The Christian scholar Saint Augustine wrote in AD 420, "There is, too, a general rumour which has been verified by their own experience, or which trustworthy persons who have heard the experience of others corroborated. The sylvans and fauns, who are commonly called "incubus and incubis," had assaulted women. In the following event we see the similarity with the UFO phenomenon with what we call legend.

In September 1971 in Los Angeles, California, a couple purchased a house that was six years old. The master bedroom was located up a short flight of stairs. The couple slept with the door open, but one night something woke the wife up and she saw a red light, which seemed to be at least five feet tall and three feet wide, moving up the stairs. She became frightened and woke up her husband. Suddenly the light disappeared. After this incident, her little son sometimes would look up from what he was doing and ask, "What, Daddy? What, Daddy?" as though his father were calling him, but his father was not at home. In this incident we see the light, a very important component of the UFO phenomenon. Also, the house is only six years old, and there is no way that we can blame ghosts for this phenomenon. The father was not at home and the entity replicated the voice of the child's father. In UFO literature it is common that UFOs and their entities can take on any form of life, and recreate reality in accord with a determined witness.

In the next case, a famous psychological researcher was testing a medium who produced a communication which was supposed to come from someone named Gordon Davies, one of the researcher's boyhood friends, who he believed had been killed in the first World War. The Gordon Davies personality appeared to control the speech organs of the medium and spoke of experiences that he and the researcher had shared. He described in detail a house Davies once lived in, including the view from the house, various pictures of a piano, china and other objects. However, about 18 months later, the researcher was shocked to find Davies living in the house that the supposed Davies entity had described, even though he had not moved to that house until sometime after the researcher's seance with the medium.

This amazing event shows the game of "make believe" that the intelligence behind the UFO phenomenon was playing with humankind. It seems to me that they have a switch to our psychological reality and that they appear wherever they chose. Moreover, they make us believe that we are immortal, and at the same time important. How many thousands of people have been fooled through the ages thinking themselves immortal? In UFO literature there are many cases in the file that show that entities aboard UFOs can make themselves invisible. Also, it means they can penetrate any object and take possession. I mentioned before a case of the Ouija board that announced the apparition of a UFO. The UFO phenomenon is an integral part of the human psyche and also the source of religion. At the same time it is deceptively playing a game of "make believe" with the human race. *Religion makes us believe we are special and the supernatural phenomenon makes us believe we are immortal.*

LEVITATION

Levitation is another supernatural event for which science has no explanation. It has been known to occur to saints, mystics, and during exorcism. When levitation occurs to saints and mystics, people think that God is behind the phenomenon, and when it occurs during exorcism, people think the Devil is behind it. The fact is that nobody knows the real cause, which is why he or she uses God or the Devil to explain the phenomenon.

For example, in 1483 hundreds of people went to the visit the Kingdom of Naples to see Saint Rito of Cascia. The king had been amazed to see the saint floating in mid-air and glowing with light. In 1608, in another event, a witness saw St. Bernardino Realino levitate and said a great radiant light was coming from the room where the saint was staying. He said the light was so intense that he thought it was on fire. So he opened the door and saw the saint raised up two and a half feet in the air.

There are hundreds of cases of levitation on record, but physiologists don't have an explanation. I believe the intelligence behind the UFO phenomenon is responsible for levitation. Why? Because the only concrete evidence we have comes from witnesses abducted by UFOs. We don't have any evidence that either God or the Devil is creating this phenomenon. However, we have plenty of evidence that people have been levitated by UFOs. So, another supernatural event that has been explained as divine or diabolic is explained by UFOs. We know that UFOs cause poltergeist and it is the same agent that causes levitation to occur. St. Theresa of Avila wrote about her experience in her autobiography: "When I tried to resist raptures, it seemed that I was being lifted up by a force beneath my feet so powerful that I know nothing to which I can compare it, for it came with as much vehemence as any other spiritual experience, and I felt as if I were being ground to powder. It is a terrible struggle, and to continue against the Lord's will avails very little, for no power can do anything against it."

CHAPTER 8

BIG FOOT, THE CHUPACABRAS (THE GOATSUCKER), OTHER WEIRD CREATURES AND THE UFO CONNECTION

"These objects are conceived and directed by intelligent beings of a very high order; they probably do not originate in our solar system, perhaps not even in our galaxy."

**— Dr. Hermann Oberth,
German Rocket Expert, 1954**

Since the beginning of history, monsters of all types have walked throughout this earth and as a consequence, one way or another, they have become part of legends and folklore. They have served the purpose of filling in the void that otherwise we would feel if human imagination were left without stimulus or challenge. The skeptic will call anyone who mentions this subject a crackpot, even though these thoughts make us human in the sense of our wonder at the mystery of life.

THE LEGEND OF BIG FOOT

Many of these monsters are not a figment of our imagination, but an essential part of our mental structures. The most famous example is "Big Foot." The legend of Big Foot has been part of the folklore of the United States and

Canada for more than 200 years. The native Indians in the Pacific Northwest on the Washington-Oregon border as well as those in Florida and Canada have legends of a monster that looks like Big Foot. Kwakiut Indians of British Columbia have a legend of the "wild man in the woods" called Butnas. The face of this creature appears on totem poles. The Seminole Indians in Florida have recorded sightings of this creature. The Yurock Indians mention a benevolent monster.

For centuries, North American Indians have had legends of monsters called by various names—Ohma, Sasquatch, Bukwas, Gilwyk, and Selahtik—but they all fit the same description as Big Foot. Although different tribes gave Big Foot different names, he was perceived as both good and evil.

The late Theodore Roosevelt first mentioned the legend of Big Foot before he became the president of the United States. Roosevelt had been a frontiersman who wrote about his experiences in a book called *Wilderness Hunter*. He wrote down stories heard in bars and told by older people. One was about Frank Bauman, a trapper who was setting up beaver traps with his partner in 1852 at Salmon River. The first night they saw a creature walking on legs like a man. One night while they were sleeping, the creature returned and one of the men shot at it. The creature escaped, leaving a bad odor. The men went out the next morning and came back to find their camp had been completely destroyed. The two trappers saw clear footprints of the creature. The story goes that before sunset that same day, the creature came back again and killed Bauman's partner, crushing him and breaking his neck. Roosevelt believed the story, writing, "Frontiersmen lead lives too hard and too practical and have too little imagination to create such yarns out of nothing."

The story is very important because it is told by someone of great moral stature. Skeptics will say that legends are only legends, but legends are a reflection of reality, distorted or factual. Legends talk about past or actual phenomenon that are lived by individuals in a certain period of history and country.

For example, in the 1960s in California, a girl had been babysitting and was coming home late at night. The first thing she noticed was that her dog was hiding and barking. Then she noticed something moving in a nearby field. She walked a few meters and suddenly a hairy, giant man appeared emitting "a powerful and awful smell." She ran into the house in a panic, crying desperately. Her parents were shocked by her story when she told them that she had seen "a creature eight to ten feet tall, hairy all over, with a wild look in its eyes. A creature that looks more like a man than an animal." A former deputy sheriff interviewed her and said he believed her.

The list of people who claim they have seen Big Foot is very large. Although there are many questions about Big Foot, like why we haven't found a complete skeleton or captured one alive. This supports the connection with UFOs, which is simply that during UFO history, there have been creatures that look like Big Foot with a special smell. There are multiple witnesses who testify about the smell of sulphur coming from Big Foot and from creatures that came out of UFOs.

In the 1970s there were many reports of monsters and baboon-like creatures in the mountains of Pennsylvania. UFO researchers had 118 documented creature sightings up to June 1974, so probably by now (2004) there is more evidence about this creature. The major part of this report in the '70s came from the counties of Allegheny, Beaver, Fayette, Indiana, Somerset, Washington and Westmoreland.

On October 25, 1973, at 9:00 p.m. a witness and 15 other people saw a large red ball descend toward the pasture. The witness ran into the house and got a .30-60 rifle. In the company of neighbors, he proceeded by truck to see where the object had landed. As the object approached, the lights in the trunk went out. The object was bright and appeared to be 100 feet in diameter and made a loud sound like a lawn mower. The craft was illuminated. The men could make out two tall creatures with glowing eyes that were making crying sounds and the smell of burning rubber filled the air. The witness fired several shots over the heads of the creatures, which didn't stop them. The witness then fired three more rounds into one of the creatures and there was a whining sound. The one that was hit raised its arms and moved off into the woods and the UFO disappeared.

In the fall of 1968, a witness and two of his neighbors heard a sound around his farmhouse like something hitting metal. He got his flashlight and saw a monster ten feet tall and four feet across the shoulders, its arms long like an ape. The hair was a tanish color, its eyes glowed, its teeth were prominent and protruding, and its ears pointed. The monster put them in a trance. One of the witnesses used his flashlight and fired at the creature with a shotgun. It screamed. Then, before the disbelieving eyes of the three men, it was suddenly enveloped in a white mist. Less than a minute later, the mist vanished and the creature with it. The three men searched, but found no trace.

All these examples show the complexity of the UFO phenomenon. However, we can see that monsters like Big Foot are very common with UFO sightings. The interesting thing is that during the 1960s and '70s, there was a wave of UFO sightings. The question is why we haven't found a skeleton of Big Foot. The answer is because Big Foot is not a creature of this world and probably not of this dimension. The reason the intelligentsia that travel in those UFOs has this strange wild life is to amuse, create a sense of wonder, and in some cases, frighten us, like in the case of the Chupacabras (Goatsucker).

There is also a good chance that they are the real entities that fly the UFOs.

On March 14, 1971, a witness was transported to a hovering aircraft. He remembered driving that evening into the desert near Superstition Mountain and standing alone watching a flying object overhead. He experienced a "pulsating, pulling feeling" that lifted him upward into the UFO. There he met very horrifying creatures which he described as having "gray skin like that of a crocodile or a rhino, with a thick patch of hide over the front torso. The beings were seven feet tall and looked like a combination of earth animals. They had three fingers and a thumb over to one side." The last thing he remembered was a bad odor like "rotten socks" someone had been wearing for 20 years.

Another famous case happened on the afternoon of October 11, 1973. Two shipyard workers, Charles Hickson, 42, and Calvin Parker, 19, were fishing in the Pascagoula river when they heard a buzzing sound. They looked behind them and saw a large, oval, glowing object about ten feet wide with blue lights hovering a few feet above the riverbank. The two men were frozen in fear at the sight of the UFO. Then three strange beings appeared from nowhere and began moving toward them. The creatures didn't seem to walk but to float. They didn't move their legs. They were about five feet high, had bullet-like heads with no necks, slits for mouths and where the ears and noses would be, had thin cone-shaped appendages that stuck straight outward. They had no eyes, round feet and clawed hands. The skin was wrinkled and grayish. Hickson claimed that the two men were floated to the UFO and found themselves in a very bright room were they were examined and then brought back to where they had been. The following day this incident was in every newspaper in the country.

In 1973 there was a great wave of UFOs and their entities all over the world. A writer called 1973 "the year of the humanoids." In 1964 about 11:00 p.m., a couple suddenly caught sight of a figure moving across the field near the farm where they lived. When they turned the lights of their car on it, the figure was coming toward them in what seemed to be big leaps. The witness said, "The thing moved through three strands of barbed wire. All I can remember, even after it happened, was the feeling like I was being hypnotized by the creature's glowing eyes. I couldn't hear anything and I think I tried to scream, but I am not sure if I did or what. It felt like a time lapse or like I was living in another time. I just remember its eyes focused in mine." Suddenly, the creature changed into another form right before the two witnesses. "But this thing just crouched down, its hands became paws and it went out on all fours. And it happened like a slow motion movie, Then it was gone, vanished into thin air." The witness said the creature was six feet tall with wide shoulders that narrowed down to the waist. "The body was upright and covered with a yellowish fuzz. The head was horrible. It was pointed at the top and narrow at the chin, the ears large like a pig's. The eyes glowed orange, the teeth were like fangs and the skin wrinkled." The two witnesses were in shock for a long time. This experience was beyond anything that we call our daily routine life.

In July 1974, dozens of witnesses saw a UFO crash into Lake Okeechobee in the Florida swampland. Six months later a security guard at a housing development site said that he shot six bullets at a huge, hairy and very smelly monster. So again we see the great relation between UFOs and "big hairy and smelly monsters that fit the Big Foot description.

THE CHUPACABRAS OR GOATSUCKER

Another new kid on the block is the famous "Chupacabras" or "Goatsucker." In 1995, rumours were spreading from Puerto Rico that animals had been found dead with two punctures in their necks, drained of their blood and, in some instances, without their internal organs. Most of the animals were farm animals like chickens, pigs, and, sometimes, dogs and cats. The Chupacabras became an icon. It has been seen around Los Angeles, San Francisco, San Antonio, and on Long Island, but its favorite hangout seems to be Puerto Rico. Coincidence or not, UFOs have been seen in Puerto Rico for more than 50 years. Some UFO researchers suspect that there is an alien base on the Island. On the subject of UFOs, nothing is impossible. The *New York Times* of Friday, January 26, 1996, printed an article about the Chupacabras with a picture of a sheep with two punctures in its neck.

A witness in Canovanas, Puerto Rico reported, "It jumped like a kangaroo and smelled like sulphur." Another witness said, "It was ugly as a demon and flew through the air." Another said that it "looked like a vampire." In South American culture, and Spanish culture in general, the association is well known between the devil and sulphur, and the similarity between this creature and the legend of the devil is more than a coincidence. The worldwide representation of this legend is exactly like the Chupacabras. The only conclusion is that most legends and religious symbolism are based in actual events created by a superior intelligence. What would man be without myths and legends?

A construction worker about 20 miles from San Juan swears that he saw a Chupacabras. "It was about four or five feet tall with huge elongated red eyes, a pointed long tongue came out of his mouth. It was gray, but his back changed colors. It was a monster!" Many people who saw the Chupacabras were so affected that they were taken to the hospital. The authorities said that stray dogs were to blame for the deaths of the animals, that the deaths of cows in the '70s were blamed on the "Vampire of Mocha" and that this mass hysteria was nothing new. The only coincidence is that UFOs were seen all over the world, and monsters came out of the UFOs.

In August 31, 1990, in Caboroso, Puerto Rico, many witnesses reported seeing five small alien creatures that were gray, very thin with large heads, pointy ears and a slit-like mouth, small nose and large, white, almond-shaped eyes. One of the witnesses tried to get close and a "blinding bright light emitted from the being's eyes, forcing him to stop." In August 1991, in Cuesta Blanca, Puerto Rico, a witness had a daylight encounter with a creature with a large head and large black eyes. The purpose of all these apparitions is to simply frighten us, to create a sense of wonder in our mental structure, otherwise our lives would be dull. Also, they can disguise themselves as monsters to map our psyche.

THE MONKEY MAN

These are not the only cases of weird creatures. All over the world there are sightings of monsters that are not part of our every day reality. In India in 2000, people were being attacked by a monster called the "Monkey Man." In Delhi dozens of men carried tridents, bamboo poles and iron rods late at night. The witnesses claimed that the beast looked like a slinky cat with tawny eyes or like a bear. Most often it was described as half monkey-half man. Witnesses said that it leapt along rooftops, scratched with long, poisoned metal claws, and vanished into thin air. A 16-year-old witness said, "I saw it with my own eyes. When the ladies started shouting on the ground floor, we went to the roof and saw a small black creature hiding in the corner and suddenly it just disappeared." The witness carried a sword for self defense. A pregnant woman fell from the stairs of her home as she fled in terror. Another man fell from his roof as he tried to escape the Monkey Man. Both the man and the woman died. The authorities said that it was "only their imagination," but to say that what people see is "only their imagination playing tricks" is to insult our common sense and the reliability of our cognitive mental-sensorial faculties that define us as human.

There is information in UFO history that mentions monsters like the Monkey Man. In 1954 in Caracas, Venezuela there were many reports of hairy creatures coming out of UFOs. On one occasion a sleeping horse trainer was awakened by a tug on his pillow. Then his arm was grasped tightly. He tried to sit up, but a strong arm encircled his neck almost choking him. He screamed for help and the creature ran out of the room and the employees found the trainer with scratches on his neck, back and chest. A half an hour later the horse was kicking and prancing, so the trainer and employees went to check on the horse and saw a small creature about three and a half feet tall. It zoomed out of the stable and the witness described it as an orangutan or monkey. The horse was nervous for several days and lost its appetite. Folklore is full of creatures that many people think are products of overactive imagination, but that is not true. Every story is based on facts.

THE NEW JERSEY DEVIL

Another example of a legend that many people think is a product of the imagination is the "New Jersey Devil." It looked very similar to the Chupacabras or any of the other monsters that populate the UFO literature. The Jersey Devil appeared in 30 different towns in one week in 1909. From January 16 to 23, thousands of people saw the Jersey Devil's footprints. His natural habitat is the Pine Barrens area of New Jersey and witnesses have described him as a kangaroo horse, flying death, flying horse, etc. People in the towns where the Jersey Devil was seen were so fearful that factories and schools closed. A witness reported, "I heard hissing sounds and some thing white flew across the street. I saw two spots of phosphorous like the eyes of the beast. There was a white cloud like escaping steam from an engine.

The postmaster of Bristol saw the Jersey Devil and described it: "I awoke about two o'clock in the morning and finding myself unable to sleep, I rose and wet my head with cold water as a cure for insomnia. As I got up I heard an eerie almost supernatural sound from the direction of the river. I looked out upon the Delaware and saw lying diagonally across what appeared to be a large crane, but which was emitting a glow like a firefly. Its head resembled that of a ram, with curled horns and a long thick neck was thrust forward in flight. Its front legs were shorter than its long thin wings. The monster made an awful sound like a whistle very high and piercing."

Many residents in Bristol saw their backyard covered with hoof prints. The residents organized hunts, but curiously dogs refused to follow the tracks. Another witness looking out his bedroom window at 2:30 a.m. saw the Jersey Devil for ten minutes. "It was about three feet tall with a head like a collie dog and a face like a horse. It had a long neck and wings about two feet long, and their back legs were like those of a crane with horse hooves. It walked on its back legs." Another witness said, "It was about three feet high. Long black hair covered its entire body like a monkey, a face like a dog, split hooves and a tail a foot long." Yet another witness said it "looked like a kangaroo with a long neck." We see that there is not much difference between the Jersey Devil, the Monkey Man, or the Chupacabras.

There are more but less famous monsters. On July 26, 1984, in Port Henry, New York, a tourist witnessed something strange in Lake Champlain. "I thought it was a lake loon. It made a noise like a loon, but very loud. It was a quarter of a mile away and was big."

More than 200 people have claimed that they saw something swimming in Lake Champlain. The list of claimants started with Samuel Champlain, who reported he saw the monster in 1609. He wrote in his journal, "The monster was eight to ten feet long with silvery scales and dangerous teeth." Another witness said, "It looked like the head of a huge snake. It just rose out of the water and slid back in. It looked black."

The phenomenon is similar to the Loch Ness Monster many people swear to have seen but can't find—like all the others monster apparitions. We can't capture them because the intelligence behind this phenomenon wants to keep us guessing and wondering about the world. It is very hard for me to accept that an alien intelligence has a monopoly on our dreams, fantasies and nightmares, but everything seems to point to an alien intelligence behind everything that we call "supernatural."

Stories about monsters and weird creatures have been part of humanity's folklore, since man has been on this planet. After a devastating plague in 774, before the reign of the Byzantine-Greek Emperor Leo IV, monsters appeared and killed many animals and men. They were not afraid and went into houses and took children with them and killed and devoured cows. They looked like wolves, but their muzzles were small and long, and they had great ears, like those of horses. Their skin resembled the bristles of pigs, and stuck straight up. The monsters

appeared in the region of Arzanene, south of Armenia on
the borders of Assyria.

In the year 1955, a farming family in Kentucky saw
a UFO land near their property and five "tiny goblin"
creatures emerged and harassed the family for a couple of
hours. The family shot at the creatures and they seemed
unhurt. One of the entities peered in through the window
and when one of the farmers went outside "a silvery hand,
brushed the man's hair." The family called the police
and when the police came, the entities disappeared. But
when the police left the entities came back. The police
found the story credible because the family was in panic
and there were bullet holes in the walls. Some said that
after the incident the family disappeared or moved away.
Nobody knows.

In the city of Zafra in Spain in 1968, there was a
report of an alien six and a half feet tall with long arms
and glowing green clothing. In Arizona in 1971, two men
claimed to have been captured by creatures eight and a
half feet tall operating a device which appeared to be
for medical purposes. The men claimed they were taken
aboard the UFO and examined with a probe linked to a
giant computer.

In England in February 1855, a perplexing mysterious
event shocked people. Clawed feet or hoof marks of a
biped, not a quadruped, were found at huge intervals
in a garden of a cottage on a moor, on house tops, on
vertical walls and in open fields. The tracks were found
in the snow and on both sides of the wide estuary of the
river Exe, and also in a wide area of Devon. The sight
caused terror. Many people of the villages followed the
tracks to the woods, but the dogs refused to enter the

trees. The animals were frightened by something unseen and unknown. The *Illustrated London News* of February 24, 1855, reproduced in the newspaper some prints which looked like horses hoofs that were sketched on the site in the Devon countryside. In March 1840, similar mysterious prints, like those of a great horse, were found in wild Scottish glens and high mountains. In Galician, Poland, marks like these were seen in the snow every year and sometimes in the sand on the hill. In October 1866, the Maoris of New Zealand were perplexed to see the sudden appearance of a huge and hairy animal with antlers in a desert of mud. The animal was unknown to them, because in New Zealand there are no deer.

The descriptions of these weird animals come amazingly close to the description given by witnesses of the New Jersey Devil. Many witnesses in the 19th century described the Jersey Devil as "a ram with curled horns and a long thick neck; it had long thin wings, the front legs shorter than the wings." Other witnesses said that it was emitting a glow like a firefly and making a supernatural sound. Again, as in the previous case, residents organize a hunt, but dogs refused to follow the tracks.

As I have shown, UFO researchers have on file hundreds of cases of monsters coming out from UFOs that show the connection between the two phenomena. Another aspect of this phenomenon is that it takes on psychological reality, like miracles, poltergeist and monsters. The UFO phenomenon is very complex and everything of the invisible world is created by the UFO phenomenon.

Chapter 9

The Mystery of Cattle Mutilation and the UFO Phenomenon

"I have lived in this country all my life and worked on ranches and seen plenty of dead animals, but never did I see an animal with its face mask removed like that and the reproductive organs also removed."

— A witness in Montana, October 2001

Cattle mutilation is another mysterious part of the UFO phenomenon that is still without an answer. UFO researchers can't find a meaning or sense to this alien activity. The first case of cattle decapitation that UFO researchers have on record happened in 1897 in Leroy, Texas. The witness was Alexander Hamilton, a member of the U.S. House of Representatives, who reported:

"We were awakened by a noise among the cattle. I arose, thinking my bulldog was performing some of his pranks, but upon going to the door, saw to my utter astonishment an air ship slowly descending upon my cow lot about 40 rods from the house. Calling my tenant, Gid Heslip, and my son, Wall, we seized some axes and ran to the corral. Meanwhile the ship had been descending until it was no more than 30 feet above the ground and we came within 50 yards of it.

It consisted of a great cigar-shaped portion, possibly 300 feet long, with a carriage underneath.

The carriage was made of glass or some other transparent substance alternating with a narrow strip of some material. It was brilliantly lighted within and everything was plainly visible. It was occupied by six of the strangest beings I ever saw. They were jabbering together, but we could not understand a word they said.

Every part of the vessel which was not transparent was of a dark reddish color. We stood mute with wonder and fright, when some noise attracted their attention, and they turned the light directly upon us. Immediately on catching sight of us, they turned on some unknown power, and a great turbine wheel about 30 feet in diameter, which was slowly revolving below the craft began to buzz and the vessel rose lightly as a bird. When about 300 feet above us, it seemed to pause and hover directly over a two-year-old heifer, which was bawling and jumping, apparently fast in the fence. Going to her, we found a cable about half inch in thickness made of some rare material fastened in a slipknot around her neck, one end passing up to the vessel, and the heifer tangled in the wire fence. We tried to get it off, but could not, so we cut the wire loose and stood in amazement to see the ship, heifer and all, rise slowly, disappearing in the northwest.

We went home, but I was so frightened I could not sleep. Rising early Tuesday I started out by horse, hoping to find some trace of my cow. This I failed to do, but coming back in the evening I found that Link Thomas, about three or

four miles west of Leroy, had found the hide and
legs in his field that day. He, thinking someone
had butchered a stolen beast, had brought the
hide to town for identification, but was greatly
mystified at not being able to find any tracks in
the soft ground. After I identified the hide as my
brand, I went home, but every time I wanted to
sleep, I would see the cursed thing, with its big
light and hideous people. I don't know whether
they are devils or angels, or what, but we all saw
them, and my whole family saw the ship and I
don't want any more to do with them."

As a member of the House of Representatives and
other high social-political circles, Alexander Hamilton
staked his honor upon the truth of the story in an affidavit
signed for the most important people of his town. Some
skeptics will say that it is a lie, but why would a man of his
political position lie? I don't see any reason for that.

The interesting thing is that they didn't find any
tracks, which is exactly what is happening now. Many
people find mutilated cows, but no tracks around them.

Probably there are more cases as old or older, but
I haven't seen any earlier ones in the literature. In the
20th century, the first case we heard about was not a
cow, but a horse. The case received a lot of publicity. On
September 9, 1967, near the King Ranch in the San Luis
Valley, Colorado, a horse named Snippy didn't show up
so the owners started looking for him. They found him a
quarter of mile from the ranch. The horse was dead and its
condition was shocking. From the neck up, it was without
flesh. The rest of the carcass was intact and there was no

blood for evidence. The area to the front of the shoulders was also without flesh. It looked like it had been cut with a surgeon's scalpel. Using test areas, the investigators found radiation beyond normal counts. As in the Hamilton case in 1897, there were no tracks of any kind within 100 feet of Snippy's carcass. Bushes 150 feet from the horse appeared to have been crushed by something coming from above. In the two days, neither insects nor predators had touched the carcass.

Coincidence or not, UFOs were seen in the area and in the '60s there were sightings of UFOs all around the world, especially in the U.S. Many theories about the death of Snippy were proposed: lightning, coyotes, wild dogs, wolves and bad people from a secret cult. None, however, met the criteria for this mysterious death. Furthermore, in the mid-1970s stories of cattle mutilation were in the major newspapers in Minnesota, Wisconsin, Kansas, Nebraska, Iowa, South Dakota, Colorado, Texas, Arizona and California. The cattle mutilations were done very professionally, like a surgeon had done them. The ears were removed, tongues were cut out, udders, sex organs, and anuses were sliced out with surgical skill and the blood drained. Again, no footprints or vehicles tracks were found near the carcass. The phenomenon had been going on for more than 30 years and no explanation had been found, no perpetrators, no cults. Like the case of Alexander Hamilton in 1897, nobody found any tracks near the carcasses of the dead cattle.

The most shocking case is related by UFO scholar Dr. Jacques Valle in his masterpiece, *Messengers of Deception*. The event happened on July 6, 1975, at the entrance of a North American Air Defense Command (NORAD) installation near an unmarked road that doesn't show on maps. The entire area is a military installation where every few feet there is a warning that "Violators will be prosecuted to the full extent of the law." However, cows were found dead with sex organs removed and many of the carcasses seemed to have been dropped from the air. They found a bull with all four legs broken. Other animals were found in a pasture with a *padlocked gate*!

In Colorado, there were cattle mutilations near very sensitive and sophisticated military installations. NORAD in Cheyenne Mountain is the agency's operations Center. Its installations are a monumental work of engineering; 45,000 cubic yards of rock had to be blasted out to accommodate its buildings. Some of the buildings are three stories tall. The purpose of this fortress is to detect and analyze anything that enters or crosses United States air space. However, on Tuesday, October 21, 1975, a 1,500-pound female buffalo carcass was found mutilated without udder or ears, and the vagina had been removed. This incident raised eyebrows because it was so shocking. If UFOs and their occupants are capable of make themselves so invisible that the most sophisticated human technology can't detect them, it means we are dealing with a civilization probably hundreds, if not millions, of years old. They are like gods!

In the *New York Times* of October 17, 2001, an article titled: "Unsolved Mystery Resurfaces: Who Is Killing Cows?" Eight cow killings were reported in Montana similar in form to the 1970s cattle mutilation. Some law enforcement and veterinarians said they had never seen anything like that. A witness said, "I have lived in this country all my life and worked on ranches and seen plenty of dead animals, but never did I see an animal with its face mask removed like that and the reproductive organs also removed."

I think the intelligence behind UFOs is responsible for this phenomenon and the purpose is to frighten us and to make us wonder. It also shows the cold personalities of these creatures, indifferent to pain or suffering in animals or humans. The great UFO scholar, Bob Pratt, said it shows how in Brazil, very poor peasants are terrorized by UFOs. The peasants already are suffering in an environment of scarcity and want. Why would the UFOs terrorize this people? This shows that are not here to help us. I think we are part of cosmic game in which we are both actors and spectators.

CHAPTER 10

THE UFO PHENOMENON IN LEGEND AND HISTORY

"We don't know what it is. We don't know where it came from. But we do know it's like nothing we've ever seen before. This may be the biggest thing that's ever happened."

— It Came from Outer Space, 1953 movie

Legends and history are many times so intermixed that we don't know where one ends and the other begins. One very famous example is the battle of Troy, which was immortalized by the famous Greek poet Homer in his masterpiece *The Illiad and the Odyssey*. This event was considered a myth until 1870 when the amateur archeologist Heinrich Schlieman found ancient sites in eastern Turkey that showed that the battle of Troy really was an historical fact. The Greeks and Romans had never heard of the ancient city of Ur until the 20th century when the ancient Sumerian city was discovered. Another example is the legend of women warriors, the Amazons, mentioned many times by the Greeks. Just recently archeologists have discovered burial grounds that give light to this legend. The famous legend of the Biblical flood was considered a myth for centuries until the 20th century when scientists discovered that at the end of the last Ice Age, a natural disaster of giant proportions struck most of the planet. There are approximately 80,000 legends around the world that mentions the great flood.

Scientists now know that such a flood happened because of the sudden extinction of 50 million animals in the United States alone. The whole world was turned upside down.

As long as human kind has been in this world, many sightings of what we call UFOs have occurred around the world, but were described with different names. The description goes with the level of development at a particular time and space of a society. For example, in 332 BC, "flying shields" were reported over Tyre, a city besieged by Alexander the Great. The flying shields dived on the Macedonians as they were crossing a river in India, stampeding the soldiers and elephants with darts of fire. In this description, the witness is relating what we call in modem times a UFO, but his society wasn't at a technological level to use the word UFO, so he called them "flying shields" instead. Further, in 234 BC, while the Gauls were invading Italy, three moons appeared over Rimini. Again this is the best description they could use because they were unfamiliar with this phenomenon. The famous Roman historian Livy reports that in 218 BC, "Phantom ships had been seen gleaming in the sky. In many places in the district of Amitemun, apparitions of men in shining garments had appeared in the distance, but had not drawn near to anyone."

Obviously, this is a description of UFO entities that have been seen through centuries. In 217 BC, Hannibal invade Etruria. The Romans were routed in the bloody battle of Trasimene. Apparitions of ships were seen in the sky, dreadful earthquakes shook the ground. The historian, Lycosthenes, mentions this incident. In the same year at Caperne, "two moons had risen in the daytime."

As we see, the ancient cultures employed words that are familiar to them in the natural landscape. In 214 BC, Livy mentions that "at Hadria an altar was seen in the sky and about it the forms of men in white garments." These kinds of sights are very common in UFO sightings. "In 152 BC in many places in Rome, apparitions of men in togas were seen, On approaching they vanished from view," (*Livy, Book XXXIV*)

Plutarch in 103 BC reported that "at night there had been seen in the heavens 'flaming spears and shields' which at first moved in different directions and then clashed together, assuming the formation and movements of men in battle and finally some of them would give way, while others pressed on in pursuit and all streamed away to the west."

As we see, this sighting is very similar to those that witnesses in the 20th century claimed to have seen. Pliny in *Book XXXIV* mentions, "In the consulship of Lucius Valdrius and Gaius Marius, a 'burning shield' scattering sparks ran across the sky at sunset from west to east." This is a great description of a UFO. Even if we don't want to use that word, the description is similar to modern UFOs. The Roman historian, Obsequens, tells us that in 93 BC, "At Volsivii a flame seemed to flash from the sky at dawn after it had gathered together. The flame displayed a dark grey opening and the sky appeared to divide. In the gap, tongues of flames appeared."

In 91 BC, the same historian wrote, "At sunset a glove of fire in the northern region rushed across the sky emitting a tremendous sound. In Spoletion a gold coloured fireball rolled down to the ground and, growing larger, rose from the earth towards the east becoming large enough to blot out the sun."

This is the most amazing description in ancient times of a UFO. Researchers of UFOs have known hundreds of reported cases that fit this event. As we can see, what we call UFOs have been present since the beginning of history and are responsible for the development of consciousness in every historical epoch. It seems to me that UFOs have been involved in our mental and religious development. As we are going to see, many of our religious ideas came from the struggle to explain UFO sightings. In 83 BC when the Roman dictator Sulla invaded Italy near Apollonia, a satyr was caught (a satyr was a being that was half human and half animal). "He was asleep and brought to Sulla, where he was asked through many interpreters who he was. When at last he uttered nothing intelligible, but with difficulty emitted a hoarse cry that was something between the neighing of horse and the beating of a goat, Sulla was horrified and ordered him out of his sight."

The satyr looks like the god Pan, who appears in the works of many sculptors and painters. Again, what we see is the struggle of the ancients to explain an alien entity and finally made him a god. The creature looks like the Chupacabras and the New Jersey Devil. In ancient times there were no "Men in Black." So, alien entities appeared in a grotesque form and people named him "the God Pan," even though it was only an alien like many million in the universe. The event is very significant because it shows how the UFO phenomenon has influenced and altered our consciousness and the idea of reality. The Etruscan god, Tages, sprang from a furrow in a field. In ancient times a legend said that satyrs, also called elfin, haunted the forest.

In the following account we see that in ancient times the UFO phenomena were very bold in their appearances. In 73 BC, Plutarch writes, "The consul, Luculilus, led the Roman legions against the king, Mithridates, who was laying waste to Asia Minor. The king's army of 120,000 footmen, 16,000 horsemen and 100 Scythian four-horse chariots were charging the 35,000 infantry and 25,000 cavalry. The king's army was going to destroy the Roman legions, but as they were on the point of joining battle, with no apparent change of weather, all of a sudden, the sky burst asunder as a huge flame-like body was seen to fall between the two armies. In shape it was most like a wine jar and in color like molten silver. Both sides were astonished at the sight and separated."

The consequences of this event are far reaching in modem history because if King Mithridates had destroyed the Roman army, there is a chance that the Roman Empire would never had reached the influence in the world as we know it. However, that was not the plan of the intelligence behind the UFO phenomenon. In 480 BC, a great light flamed over Salamis watching the Greeks smash the invasion fleet of Xerxes. In 384 BC, there was a celestial beam over Nidus and the Spartans were defeated at sea to lose the empire of Greece. For a decade globes of fire followed Hannibal ravaging Italy; probably that is the reason they never tried to invade Rome.

"In 66 BC, in the consulship of Gnaeus Octaviust and Galus Scrib Scribonius, a spark was seen to fall from a star and increase in size as it approached the earth, and after becoming as large as the moon, it diffused a sort of cloudy day light, and then returning to the sky, changed into a torch. It was seen by the proconsul Silenusn." (Pliny)

What we see in this phenomenon is its versatility to change form. I think this event is most extraordinary in the history of the supernatural and UFO phenomenon. Legend says that in 49 BC, Julius Caesar hesitated in crossing the river Rubicon, the frontier between Gaul and Italy. An apparition of superhuman size and beauty was seen sitting on the riverbank playing a reed pipe. A party of shepherds gathered around to listen and when some of Caesar's men broke ranks to do the same, the apparition snatched a trumpet from one of them, ran down the river, blew a thunderous blast and crossed over. Caesar exclaimed, "Let us accept this as a sign from the gods and follow where they beckon in vengeance on our enemies. The die is cast." Gaius Suetonius wrote about this incident.

Plutarch in 48 BC wrote, "Furthermore, during the morning watch a great light shone out above the camp of Caesar which was perfectly quiet and a flaming torch rose from it and darted down above the camp of Pompey. Caesar himself says he 'saw this.'"

This incident proves that the influence of supernatural phenomenon in human history is very real. As I am going to show, Joan of Arc was influenced by the supernatural and changed history.

It is said that as Caesar's body lay on its ivory couch awaiting cremation, two divine forms, Castor and Pollux, appeared and set fire to the couch with torches. It is hard to believe, but in the UFO and supernatural phenomenon everything is possible.

In the legend of Brutus, it is said that in the night before the crossing of the Hellespont with his army into Thrace, he was in his tent lost in meditation. Suddenly he heard a noise at the door, looking toward the lamp, almost extinguished, his eyes suddenly beheld a strange and monstrous apparition of a man silent at his side. Terrified, Brutus asked fearfully, "Who art thou of gods or men?" The phantom replied "I am thy evil genius, Brutus, and thou shalt see me at Philippi. Brutus replied, "I shall see thee." Brutus fell on his sword. The great Roman historian Gaius Suetonius mentions this event in *Caesar, Book LXXIX.*

We see in this incident a phenomenon that had been happening since the beginning of history. It has been called various names, like ghost, apparitions, and now "Men in Black."

In the year 776 AD, the Saxons built a scaffolding to storm the castle where the Christians lived. Suddenly, "The Glory of God appeared in manifestation above the church within the fortress. Those watching outside said they beheld the likeness of two large reddish shields in motion above the church and when the pagans who were outside saw this sight, they were thrown into confusion and terrified and they began to flee from the castle." Here we see a clear case of bias, since the UFO phenomenon is clearly siding with the Christians because they best fit their plans of future conquest. A luminous cross was seen in 1188 between Gisors and Neautles-San-Martin. A cross carved in stone still marks the spot. A similar event took place in Thaun Alsace, where a chapel was built in 1160 after three lights had been observed over a fir tree. As we see, the presence of UFOs right away creates a religious feeling with a sense of wonder, and our consciousness is neatly manipulated to see a reality that is not real, only a projection of a higher intelligence. Willian De Newburgh in his *Historia Anglicana*, Volume 1, writes that during the reign of King Stephen in Suffolk, "there emerged from a ditch in a field two children, a boy and a girl, green all over their bodies, clad in garments of unusual colors and unknown material." Many witnesses claimed they had seen UFO entities three feet tall, so it is no surprise that many people called them children by mistake.

On October 11, 1492, Christopher Columbus thought he saw a "light glimmering at a great distance." Columbus immediately called Pedro Gutierrez, a gentleman of the king's bedchamber, who also saw the light. After a short time it vanished, only to reappear several times during the night, each time dancing up and down in sudden and passing gleams. The light was seen four hours before land was sighted. This phenomenon has never been explained. As we see, in many important historical events, UFOs have been present, but people are unaware or misled by the phenomenon.

In Central America in Mexico, the Aztecs had the legend that their teacher was Viracocha, and the Mayan's legend mentions Quetzalcoatl as their master. The legend said Viracocha, Lord of the Sun, Moon and Stars, created the human race from stone. Another tradition said he built Tiahuanaco, and came from Lake Titicaca. Quetzalcoatl's emblem was the feathered serpent and his name means "Winged Serpent." He arrived in a serpent airship. Viracocha also had a winged serpent as an emblem. Curiously, in the history of UFOs, there had been contactees who claimed to have seen alien entities with the winged serpent emblem.

In the early 1960s, a lawyer was abducted from a small town in Wisconsin. He was arriving home at midnight, after a business meeting. Suddenly, he saw a flying object hovering over the highway. When he passed, he noticed static on his radio. He saw some shadowy figures walking toward his car. The attorney said that they seemed friendly. Their heads were thinner and elongated. They had a large chest and were extremely muscular. Their uniforms had the insignia of a snake with wings. When he returned home, he heard a funny sound in his living room similar to a buzzing of bees. (Interestingly, the sound of bees was heard during the apparition of the Virgin Mary, which we will discuss later.) The contactee didn't remember anything until he went into hypnosis.

This event is very important because it shows that these alien races are very familiar with terrestrial fauna. The snake has many meanings in human culture, and in religion it has been revered and venerated as God. Wherever this alien civilization came from, they are responsible for many of the religious and cultural manifestations of human kind. So Quetzalcoatl wore a winged serpent as an emblem for a reason. He saw it on somebody with god-like powers. That is the only reason to follow the customs. The interesting thing is that here on earth we think of the snake as evil. However, alien entities are beyond good and evil, because we are the ones that give meaning to their actions. The Dogon tribe in Mali, Africa since time immemorial had worshiped a star known today by astronomers as Sirius B. The Dogon tribe knew its precise elliptical orbit and how long it took to revolve around its parent star, Sirius. The orbit of Sirius was discovered in the 20th century. Again the only explanation is that this information was given to the Dogons by space travelers. I don't how a primitive culture could figure out where the star was situated without a telescope.

In a famous case in September 1961, Betty and Barney Hill were abducted and given a star, 86.1. There was no star catalog that had the information. No astronomer between 1961 and 1964 knew that star 86.1 was where Betty Hill pointed to on the map given her by the aliens. This event shows that what we call legends and myths are real experiences that are transmitted in every culture. It seems incredible, because at the time that the legend or myth first appeared, the particular society was primitive.

In the Second World War, Allied, German and Japanese planes were followed by balls of light. The Germans thought they were secret American weapons and vice versa. An explanation was never found, but this was the beginning of the UFO wave in the 1940s. Also, a modern legend was born, "The Legend of the Foo Fighters and UFOs." As we have seen, UFOs had been present in every major event in human history.

CHAPTER 11

JOAN OF ARC, THE SUPERNATURAL AND THE UFO PHENOMENON CONNECTION

"Air Force, Navy and commercial pilots have revealed to me when a UFO would fly right off their plane's wing. Highly secret government UFO investigations are going on that we don't know about."

— Senator Barry Goldwater

The birth of Joan of Arc, scholars believe, was in November of 1412. There is uncertainty because birth records were not kept. She was born in the town of Domremy, an autonomous state outside the jurisdiction of France. A peasant and illiterate, she was very devoted to church and confession. Joan's mother was a very strong influence in her Catholic beliefs.

Joan's real name was Jeannette, but she went into history as Joan of Arc. She became a heroine in the 19th century and Napoleon made her a figure of nationalistic and political greatness. She was canonized in the 20th century. Joan worked on her parents' farm spinning, plowing, and keeping the cattle healthy. She was a sweet soul and gave alms to the homeless, who at the time were many in the streets. She made pilgrimages to sacred places, including Notre Dame and the Hermitage and went to mass every day to confess her sins. She was good, chaste, simple, pious and brought up fearing God. She was a real Christian and real human being.

The first time Joan heard the voice was when she was 13 years old. She said in her trial of condemnation, "When I was 13 years old, I had a voice from God to help me govern my conduct. The first time I was very fearful, and there came this voice, about the hour of noon, in the summertime, in my father's garden; I had not fasted on the evening preceding that day. I hear the voice on the right-hand side, towards the church; and rarely do I hear it without a brightness. This brightness comes from the same side as the voice is heard. It is usually a great light."

The voice told her two and three times a week to go to France and not to tell her parents. She continued, "The voice told me to raise the siege laid to the city of Orleans."

It is perplexing that God was directly involved in an historical event while millions of peasants were dying of malnutrition and lack of shelter. Probably if this intelligence behind the light and voice that directed Joan of Arc to raise the siege of Orleans never had spoken, France never would have become a country. The historical background of the siege of Orleans was that the Treaty of Troyes in May 21, 1420, disinherited the Dauphing Charles Vl and Isabeau Catherine whose sister Michelle was married to Phillip, the Duke of Burgundy, under whom a so-called dual monarchy was established in France, with France and England uniting under the English crown. Historically, if this event had not happened, the remaking of Europe would have been dramatically different. As a consequence, we would have had a world more unified and probably all the destructive wars of the following centuries would not have happened.

Moreover, Joan didn't know anything about war or being a soldier. Suddenly she knew how to ride a horse and fight a war. At the trial, she was asked how she knew that the voices were from a good spirit, and she answered that Saint Michael had told her.

The prosecutor asked her, "How do you know it was St. Michael?"

Joan answered, "1 believed firmly that they were angels. I had the will to believe."

St. Michael told her that St. Catherine and St. Margaret would lead her and that Joan should believe because it was God's order. One of the prosecutors asked her a very important question: "If the devil posited himself in the form or figure of a good angel, how would you know that it is a good or bad angel?"

The question is of unprecedented importance because it shows the absolute contingency of every angel, alien, god and human. The question also demonstrates that human reality can't recognize the difference between an angel and an alien entity. The reason is that our human reality is limited by our senses and our time dimension. Joan assumed that the voice and the light came from God, but in the 20th and 21st century the lights and voices have been in the UFO phenomenon. The fact is that there is no difference between the alien reality and the divine reality; the difference is cultural. The effects like lights and sounds are the same. Joan answered that in the beginning she was afraid, but that after St Michael assured her that he was what he claimed to be, he told her to help the King of France. I don't understand how he *proved* who he was, but Joan of Arc believed him.

So Joan departed and went to see the King of France, but before she saw him, she was interviewed by the priest to find out the real reason for her visit.

When Joan met the king, she made a couple of requests. One was that if he gave his kingdom to the King of Heaven, God would do unto him like his predecessors, and would restore him to his original state.

At her trial, Joan said that she touched and hugged Saint Margaret and Saint Catherine because they appeared visible. This is remarkable because of the hundreds of cases of materialization and dematerialization in UFO cases and there is a similarity in the phenomenon.

The inquisitor asked her, "Did you kiss or embrace Saint Catherine or Saint Margaret?"

Joan answered, "I embraced both of them."

Then the inquisitor asked her, "Had they a pleasant odor?"

Joan answered, "It is good to know that they had a pleasant odor."

The inquisitor asked, "When embracing them, did you feel any warmth or any other thing?"

Joan answered, "I couldn't embrace them without feeling and touching them."

Her answers are very important because they show the reality of the phenomenon that Joan of Arc was living.

The inquisitor further asked Joan, "In what part did you embrace them—the lower part?"

Joan answered "It is more fitting to embrace them by the lower part than the higher."

Another inquisitor asked, "How do they speak?"

Joan answered, "I see their faces, their voices are beautiful, sweet and humble and they speak the French language."

In later weeks, the voices of Saint Catherine and Saint Margaret told Joan of Arc that she was going to be apprehended before Saint John's day, and that it must be, so she was not to be dismayed and to take all in good part and that God would help her.

The background of her capture is the following: On May 22, 1430, British troops in great numbers went to besiege the town of Compiegne. Joan found out about it and went into battle with 300 to 400 men. The battle was bad for the French because they were losing. The governor of Compiegne ordered the closing of the gates to the city because the British were coming.

During the skirmishes, Joan of Arc was overwhelmed and taken prisoner with a small group of men. While in prison, she tried to escape because she heard that the city of Compiegne was going to be destroyed. Besides she didn't want to be in the hands of the English. She made a very strong comment about God: "How can God let the good people of Compiegne die, who have been so faithful to their Lord?"

She tried to escape, leaping from the prison, but the voice of Saint Catherine told her to submit and said that God would help her. Joan remained in the fortress of Beaurevoir for four months until the end of November 1430.

At the trial she was asked in what form, size, appearance, and clothing Saint Michael appeared to her and Joan answered, "He was in the form of a true honest man. As for the angels, I saw them with my own eyes."

One of the inquisitors asked her, "Do you see Saint Michael and the angels corporeally and really?"

Joan answered, "I see them with my corporeal eyes as well as I see you, and when they withdrew from me, I wept and I should have like them to take me with them."

One of the inquisitors asked her why she had done all this. Joan answered, "All that I have done, I have done by God's commandments."

Another inquisitors asked her, "Have your voices told you to escape?"

Joan answered, "Yes, truly they have told me that I should be delivered, but I know neither the day nor the hour and I baldly put a cheerful face on it."

One of the inquisitors asked her about the reality of the angels and she answered, "They come many times among Christians, but are not seen and I have many times seen them among Christians."

Joan suffered very much while in prison and the voices told her to "take it all in good part, do not whine over thy martyrdom, by it thou shalt come at last to the kingdom of paradise." And the voices told her if she wanted God to help her, she must trust in Him in all she did.

She said, "I know well that God has always been the master of all that I have done." As we see, Joan of Arc was very ingenious. She believed everything the voices told her to do. On one occasion Joan asked the voices if she was going to be burned and the voices answered that she should trust in the Lord, that He would help her. On May 30, 1431, in Rouen, the inquisition accused her of witchcraft and heresy and her visions of diabolical origin, and condemned her to be burned at the stake.

When the inquisition announced to her that she must die, burned at the stake, Joan understood that it was a very cruel death. She began to cry out grievously and pitiably. She was so emotional that she pulled and tore her hair, because she didn't want to die. Joan of Arc enjoyed and loved life with the will to live that is so strong in every living being. She didn't deserve to die, even though the voices that claimed to come from God had promised to help her. While she was burning, she cried more than six times, ''Jesus, Jesus.'' The legend said that her heart didn't burn and was intact after her body was completely ashes.

As we have seen, her first supernatural experience was when she was 13 years old. The voices came with a blaze of light. In UFO history there are many cases of contactees who had a similar experience. This also happens in cases of poltergeist phenomenon, like the one in August 9, 1799, in the house of Mr. Abver Blaisdel, where a disembodied voice was heard. It was a woman's voice and she claimed she was the voice of Capt. George Butler's deceased wife. The voice had an authoritative sound. In late January 1800, the voice materialized and a witness called her "an unreal looking woman," she seemed to float and not to touch the ground. She was very white and spoke in religious terms even though the person the voice claimed to be was not known as religious. At first the apparition was a mass of light, then grew into a personal form. The glow of the apparition had a constant tremulous motion. The personal form became shapeless and expanded every way and then vanished.

However, an amazing event took place. A preacher that didn't believe in supernatural phenomenon was walking in the open field near the house where the events were happening when he saw a group of white rocks. After two or three minutes, the witness dropped his jaw in amazement because one of the rocks raised and took the form of a globe of light, shaped with a rosy tinge. As he walked to the light, it came close to him and took the form of a woman. Curiously, her size it was abnormally small, like a child of five.

The witness said, 'You are not tall enough for the woman who has been appearing to us." Immediately the figure expanded to normal size. The witness said, "She appeared glorious with a ray of light shining from her head like a halo extending clear to the ground."

The witness had conflicting emotions of fear and pleasure. The bright light that came from her illuminated the field at night and shone like a lamp in the cellars. The poltergeist ghost predicted events and knew of events happening far away.

As I am going to show, UFOs contactees have claimed that alien identities know the future and come in a ball of light and also materialize in different forms. On November 1966, Mrs. Ralph Buttler was with a friend watching flashing lights from a UFO outside her home in Owatonna, Minnesota. Suddenly her friend became immobile with her head dipped down. Mrs. Buttler heard a voice talking to her and also heard strange voices in the radio. After that experience, she had many manifestations of poltergeist phenomenon, like glass objects moving around and breaking without any known cause, strange noises being heard throughout the house, television sets and telephones having strange interference. This was after a sighting of a UFO. As we see from these two examples, the line between the UFO phenomenon and what we call the supernatural, miracles or paranormal is very thin. Now, in the case of Joan of Arc, it is very clear that she was deceived by the voices that claimed to be messengers of God. She died a horrendous death and she loved life.

Her life was an example for anybody called Christian. She didn't deserve to end her life like that.

Now the question is whether Joan of Arc's experience came from God or if it was an alien trap. If this experience came from the Christian God, why did he lie to her and make her pay with her life? The God of Christianity is supposed to be full of love and understanding, at least that is what Christians are taught in school. So if the cause of this phenomenon was not the God of Christianity, because God is full of love, who was responsible? Since there is a clear similarity between the UFO phenomenon, poltergeist, miracles and the supernatural, the obvious answer is that UFOs are responsible for this phenomenon. The similarity and common sense tells me that an advanced technology can create all the "special effects" that we see in all these phenomena.

UFO researchers have plenty of evidence that UFO entities misled the contactees. On many occasions, contactees were told lies, such as that UFOs came from Venus or Mars. A rare coincidence is that participants in many seances claim that spirits lied when asked questions about themselves. In the example of the poltergeist, the witness never found the true identity of the ghost/poltergeist, because the ghost lied about her origins. The sad thing is that ghosts, UFO entities, or poltergeists had no concern for human life. UFO researchers know of cases where witnesses died after an encounter with UFOs.

Another very important point is that most of the miracles occurred to seers who can't read or write. You don't have to be a rocket scientist to know that it is easier to make a person who can't write believe anything you want, because they don't have a critical thinking process to analyze reality. The greatest seers and prophets were illiterate, like Mohammed, Joan of Arc, Jesus, the seers of Fatima, and Mormon Church founder Joseph Smith. Many of the seers were very simple peasants. The reason for this choice is that peasants are easier to believe. However, nobody believed Joan of Arc's supernatural experience and that is why she was called a witch and crackpot, finally dying at the stake.

Since that time miracles had multiplied around the world. The most famous are the miracles at Fatima, Lourdes and Guadalupe. Nevertheless, the miracles are similar to Joan of Arc's experience, so Joan of Arc has been already vindicated. Interestingly, on June 18, 1961, in a little village of 70 homes named Garabandal in the Cantabrian Mountains in Spain, a miracle took place in the presence of four peasants girls. Their names were Mary Loli, Conchita, Jacinta and Mary Cruz. The first three were twelve years old and Mary Cruz was eleven. The girls went to pick up apples when suddenly Conchita saw "a very beautiful figure appear, surrounded by a great light" that didn't dazzle her eyes. Conchita said to her friends, "Look over there." They all were in shock. The entity was wearing a long blue robe. His face was small; it wasn't long or round, and his eyes were black. He had fine hands and short fingernails, but they couldn't see his feet. He looked about nine years old, but although he looked like a child, he seems very strong. The entity was glowing.

The girls went back home, and while they were praying, each in her respective house, all four girls heard a voice at the same time. "Do not worry. You will see me again." On one occasion the girls were going back to the village when suddenly a shining light blocked the path. It blinded them, and they were afraid and screamed in horror. The light soon disappeared. The children went into a trance and seemed to be frozen to the spot, kneeling, their faces reflecting a strange light. Suddenly, all four girls were looking in the same direction with their heads thrown back at a strange angle. Their eyes were unblinking and staring at the heavens.

One of the children asked the vision a question that she had been told by the priest to ask: "Who are you? Why have you come?" But the vision didn't answer. The children would go into a state of ecstasy any time during the day or night. During the rapture, they were insensitive to pain, and burns, unaware of their surroundings. Many times they were pricked very hard, but they didn't react at all. Sometimes they fell to their knees, with a tremendous force, but no show of pain was seen from the girls. On one occasion Mary Loli fell and hit her head on the edge of a step made of cement. The noise produced was so strong that many bystanders screamed in horror, said a witness. After Mary Loli came out of the rapture, the bystanders asked her if she had felt anything and she answered that she felt a sensation of pins and needless all over. Many UFO abductees have reported feeling the same sensation.

On another occasion, doctors put a strong spotlight in their eyes, but when they were in a trance; nothing could make them wake up. Sometimes when the ecstasy took place at night, their vision was as bright as daylight.

On another occasion the children were waiting for the vision, and the light appeared and in its midst the entity. Beneath him were some letters and Roman numerals. The children asked the entity the meaning, but the he smiled without saying anything. The children were talking to an invisible being, but they had to undergo a physical change in which they seemed to be anaesthetized to any stimuli of the external world. One Sunday a big crowd was waiting for the miracle, among them five priests and one doctor. When the children were in ecstasy, they became very heavy. The doctor tried to lift Conchita, but he couldn't and fell smashing her knees. Her brother tried to break the fall, but he said that an invisible force kept him in check. The girls were examined after the raptures, the doctor didn't find anything. On another occasion, the girls were followed by a crow, eleven priests and several doctors to a stone enclosure. Suddenly the Virgin appeared accompanied by two angels; one was St. Michael and the other unknown. Both wore the same clothing and the children said that "they looked like twins." On the Virgin's right, they could see a square of red fire framing a triangle with an eye and some writing. The letters were in an odd oriental writing. Some of the witnesses believed that the bright square was a symbol of the concept of God.

On occasion, the virgin brought the baby Jesus. The infant was a year old and didn't talk, but he was laughing. Sometimes the Virgin allowed the children to play with the baby Jesus. The crowds observed how the children held baby Jesus in their arms and play with him. However, the Virgin and baby Jesus were invisible to the crowds. The children had several visions in a single day. In a split second the children went from a normal standing position to kneeling in ecstasy. The children said that baby Jesus was weightless, but that their hands met an obstruction when they touched him.

We see in these so-called miracles of Garabandal that the experience of the children was similar to that of Joan of Arc. In both events, an invisible being took control of the seer and lights were seen. However, Garabandal visions went from 1961 to 1965, the decade of the greatest UFO wave around the world. Moreover, the kind of ecstasy and trance that the girls were forced to experience by an invisible force happened in the 18-century as well. Jansenism was founded in the early 17th century, but it was at odds with the Catholic Church. When the Jansenite deacon named Francois De Paris died, it precipitated a supernatural reaction on the part of his followers. One of the reasons Jansenism became popular was because its leader performed miraculous healing. Many followers began concentrating around his tomb and many diseases were cured including paralysis, cancer, arthritis, fever and blindness. Also, the mourners began to experience strange involuntary spasms or convulsions. They made the most amazing contortions of their limbs and quickly the seizures spread like fire to men, women and children. Everyone was twisting and writhing.

It was in this state that the *convulsionaires* show the most amazing feats. They took any kind of pain, such as severe beatings, blows from heavy and sharp objects and even strangulation. The most amazing thing is that they didn't show signs of injury, wounds or bruises. The phenomenon was witnessed by thousands.

It is in the public record that in 1732 more than 3,000 volunteers were needed to assist the *convulsionaires* to ensure, for example, that women didn't get exposed. Thousands of people of every social condition flocked to see them. On one occasion a 20-year old named Jeanne Maulet leaned against a wall and "a very strong man" volunteer from the crowd delivered 100 blows to her stomach with a 30-pound hammer. The *convulsionaires* asked to be tortured because of the excruciating pain of the convulsion. On another occasion a woman asked that a 50-pound stone be allowed to fall on her stomach many times, and the woman was unaffected.

An investigator, a member of the Paris Parliament named Louis Basile, witnessed enough miracles to fill four thick volumes, which were published in 1737 under the title, *La Verite Des Miracles*. Nothing could hurt these people—no blows, chains, metal rods or timbers. The strongest men could not choke them; others were crucified and showed no signs of wounds. The most mind-boggling is that they could not be cut or punctured with knives, swords or hatchets. Some of the *convulsionaires* were heard saying, "Oh, that does me good. Courage, brother. Strike twice as hard, if you can."

Some had clairvoyant powers and they could see hidden things with their eyes closed. Levitations were seen, too. All these traits had been seen in the miracles. One of the levitators was lifted into the air and witnesses tried to hold him down, but they couldn't keep him from rising off the ground.

The niece of the philosopher Pascal cured a severe ulcer in her eye as the result of a Jansenist miracle. The great philosopher David Hume wrote, "There surely never was so great a number of miracles as credited to one person as those which where lately said to have been wrought in France, upon the tomb of Abbe Parish." King Louis XV closed the cemetery and the Catholic Church said that the devil was responsible. Voltaire said, "God was forbidden by order of the King to work any miracles there."

The similarity between these phenomena and the miracles that I mentioned before is that both have levitation, insensitivity to pain, and clairvoyance, with an invisible force that is behind all of them. In the 1960s there was a wave of UFO sightings around the world. In the afternoon of August 7, 1967, a strange being appeared in the office of a doctor in Caracas, Venezuela. The entity appeared to be four feet tall and had a strange way of walking and talked in perfect Spanish. The entity was human in appearance and was wearing a silver colored suit, which covered him from neck to feet. The doctor was alarmed to see the entity just "appear" in the office without using the door. The entity asked for a physical examination and told the doctor not to be alarmed about his high temperature because he didn't came from planet Earth. He spoke perfect Spanish. He had ten teeth in his mouth, five above and five below, arranged with one in the middle and two in each side. The ones in the middle were double like a rat's. He had no ear orifices, his heart made noises like the human fetus and his eyes were completely round. The trunk of his body was extremely long.

He told the doctor his people learned languages with the help of instruments. He couldn't understand the question about age because his reproductive system was different. He said that in his world there were no wars or disease. He also told the doctor about a fissure on the earth crust under the city of Caracas, which would result in an earthquake. He said that his ship was parked outside the doctor's office, but few people witnessed a UFO outside the building. The doctor died of a heart attack the following day.

Chapter 12

Joseph Smith, the Supernatural, and the UFO Phenomenon

"We all know that UFOs are real. All we need to ask is where do they come from."

— Capt. Edgar D. Mitchel, *Apollo 14*
Astronaut, 1971

Joseph Smith, founder of the Morman Church, was born in Sharon, Vermont, in 1805. He was a great visionary, adventurer and all-American representative of the 19th century.

In 1827 Joseph married Emma Hale. In 1827 he found the plates of the *Book of Mormon.* In 1830 the *Book of Mormon* was published. In 1844 he announced his candidacy for President of the United States. Joseph became a powerful figure, founder and mayor of the city of Nauvoo, then the largest city in the state of Illinois. He was the lieutenant general of a militia of 5,000 men. He defied freedom of the press by closing an opposition newspaper.

Joseph Smith loved life, family, children and friendship. He loved dogs, horses, contests, games, parades and all of pleasures of life. Many fanatic followers were disappointed with him. He was 38 years old and his brother, Hyrum, 44 years old when they were removed from jail and murdered. The two brothers suffered a horrendous death. Unfortunately, most prophets and seers suffer a terrible death, like Jesus, the two children from Fatima, and so forth. For what purpose would God play this game? UFOs have all of the characteristics of an extraterrestrial civilization. Only an advanced civilization can create so many illusions. Even though it is hard to accept, such a civilization is the only rational and common sense answer.

The family of Joseph Smith were very religious. Joseph's father was preoccupied with religious thought and visions. His mother thought that God was thinking about them. The children were required to sing hymns together on their knees and to listen to prayers morning and night. Joseph and his brothers were raised in the fear and love of God. The family educated themselves. People were angry with the family because of their religious claims and nobody believed their stories. The Smiths were very poor and nobody wanted to associate with them.

Joseph's father claimed that he, too, had visions. Lucy, Joseph's mother said that her husband had seven visions. On one occasion, Joseph's father was walking through a field of dead timber with a spirit that told him that the field represented a world without religion. The spirit told him that he was going to find a box of food that would give him wisdom. The senior Joseph was very happy, but was kept from eating the food by a horned beast.

In another vision, a spirit led Joseph's father to a tree bearing white fruit. Praising God, he brought the family to share the fruit. Opposite the tree was an immense building in which richly dressed people stood pointing at the Smith family with the finger of scorn. The spirit told Joseph that the fruit was the love of God and the building was Babylon, which must fall.

The visions that began with Joseph, Sr. were similar to the visions of Fatima, Joan of Arc, and Mohammed. On one occasion he told his scribe "At about the age 12, my mind became seriously impressed with regard to the all important concerns for the welfare of my immortal soul, which led me to searching the scriptures, believing as I was taught, that they contained the words of God. From age 12 to 15, I pondered many things in my heart concerning the situation of the world, of mankind, the wickedness and abomination. My mind became exceedingly distressed, for I became convinced of my sins."

In 19th century Puritan America, it was very common to feel guilty and wicked with a fear of damnation. Joseph was in distress because of his parents' conflict over religious issues. His mother was going from church to church and in 1820 joined the Presbyterian Church with three of their children: Hyrum, Samuel and Jophronia. The religious meetings lasted most of the day and into the night, with music, seizures, trances, and rolling on the ground. One preacher followed another.

In New York, there was a climax of religious awakening between 1825 and 1827. On one occasion Joseph went into the woods to pray for guidance, when suddenly, "A pillar of light fell upon me and the Lord opened the heavens. I saw the Lord and he spoke unto me, saying, 'Joseph, my son, thy sins are forgiven thee. Behold, I am the Lord of Glory. I was crucified for the world, that all those who believed on my name may have eternal life. Behold, the world lieth in sin at this time, and none does good. They have turned aside from the gospel and keep not my commandments. They draw near to me with their lips, while their hearts are far from me and mine anger is kindling. I come quickly as it is written of me in the cloud clothed in the glory of my Father, and my soul was filled with love, and for many days, I could rejoice with great joy and the Lord was with me, but [I] could find none that would believe the heavenly vision."

On one occasion, Joseph was reading the *Epistle of James*, first chapter and fifth verse, which reads, "If any of you lack wisdom, let him ask of God." He retired to the woods to meditate about the verse, when suddenly, "I was seized upon by some power which *entirely overcame and with such astonishing influence* over me as to bind my tongue so that I could not speak. Thick darkness gathered around me, and it seemed to me for a time as if I were doomed to sudden destruction. Just at this moment of great alarm, I saw a pillar of light exactly over my head, above the brightness of the sun, which descended gradually until it fell upon me. It no sooner appeared than I found myself delivered from the enemy, which held me bound. When the light rested upon me, I saw two personages whose brightness and glory defy all description standing above me in the air. One of them spoke unto me calling me by name and said, pointing to the other, 'This is my beloved son. Hear him.'"

Joseph, very impressed with this vision, talked to a Methodist preacher who told him that visions and revelations had ceased with the apostles and that his vision came from the devil. Between the ages of 14 and 15, Joseph suffered great persecutions for his visions and he only shared the experience with his family and close friends.

On Sunday, September 21, 1823, after everyone went to bed and the house it was quiet, the 18-year-old Joseph prayed earnestly into the late hours of the night. He asked God to manifest to him. He said that he prayed with full confidence that he would receive some kind of manifestation. Suddenly a light appeared in his room, which increased until it was brighter than at noon. "At once a personage appeared at my bedside, standing in the air, for his feet did not touch the floor. He had on a loose robe of most exquisite whiteness. His whole person was glorious beyond description. I was afraid, but the fear soon left me. He called me by name and said unto me that he was a messenger sent from the presence of God to me and that his name was Moroni, that God had work for me to do."

Joseph Smith's supernatural experience was not new; every religion, legend and folklore has a similarity in the "special effects" of the phenomenon. Since the beginning of civilization there have been many reports of sightings that are similar to modern UFOs sightings. One example is from the *Bible.* In the year 538 BC as Daniel was sitting on the bank of the Tigris River:

"And in the fourth and twentieth day of the first month, as I was by the side of the great river, which is Hiddekel, when I lifted up my eyes and behold, a certain man clothed in linen, whose loins were girded with fine gold of Uphaz. His body also was like the beryl, and his face as the appearance of lightening, and his eyes as lamps of fire, and his arms and his feet in colour to polished brass, and the voice of his words like the voice of multitude. (*Daniel 10,4-6*)

A more recent example of such "special effects" happened in January of 1968 as a truck driver was traveling from the East Coast to Baraga, Michigan. It was snowing very hard, so the truck driver stopped to clean the windshield wipers. "Suddenly, I was blinded by what I can only describe as a tremendously brilliant strobe light. The area all around me lit up. My first thought was that an airplane got lost in the snowstorm. The light lasted for only few seconds, then I seemed to be in some sort of pale green cone. I say cone-shaped, because it seemed to get thinner as it went up. But it was huge, because it covered myself and the truck. I thought I was crazy. I could see it snowing, but it wasn't snowing on me or the truck. That is when I noticed the sudden warmth.

"That's all I remember for a while. The next thing I recall I was standing about 20 feet away from the truck, and I don't know how I got there. It was still snowing heavily and, although the snow was at least five to seven inches deep, there was not one track that showed that I had walked that distance. Also, I was completely dry and warm.

"Briefly, I really thought I was loosing my mind. I walked back to my truck, which had in the meantime stalled. This is weird, because I had a 335 Cummins diesel engine and a diesel just doesn't up and stall. When I got back in the truck and restarted, I found the temperature of the engine was zero. To get cold it normally takes about three hours. I checked my watch, thinking that I had been out of the truck for only a few minutes and I was shocked to see it was 5:00 a.m. I was baffled: I had lost nearly five hours! After I got back in the truck, I had a severe headache and developed nausea that stayed with me for about four days."

This event is a typical case of abduction with the missing time. Many abductees don't remember any episode until they are treated to a hypnotism session. According to Les Krantz, about 10,000 people per year reports UFOs, 3.75 million people in the United States believe they have been abducted, and 25 million people had some kind of encounter with the supernatural.

On one occasion, Joseph tried to jump a fence and fell and the name "Moroni" appeared surround by light. On May 15, 1829, Joseph and his friend, Oliver, went into the woods to pray for enlightenment about baptism. They wanted to know about a question of authority for baptism. In Joseph Smith's account, while they were praying, a messenger from heaven descended upon them in a cloud of light and laid his hands upon Joseph, saying, "Upon you, my fellow servant, in the name of Messiah, I confer the priesthood of Aaron which holds the keys of the ministering of angels and of the gospel of repenitence, and of baptism by immersion for the remission of sins."

In June 1829 Joseph and three friends had a revelation while they were in the woods praying. "All at once a light came down from above us and encircled us for quite a little distance around and the angel stood before us. He was dressed in white and spoke and called me by name and said, 'Blessed is he that keeps His commandments.' A table was set before us and on it the records were placed."

While they were viewing them, the voice of God spoke out of heaven saying that the book was true and the translation correct. This event refers to the translation of the book of Mormon. Then Joseph Smith had a vision. His face became brilliant white, transparent and it seemed to be illuminated. He spoke each sentence slowly and distinctly, with a pause between them long enough for it to be written.

On Christmas Day of 1832 came the most important revelation after the *Book of Mormon*, The Civil War Prophecy: "Verily, thus saith the Lord, concerning the wars that will shortly come to pass beginning at the rebellion of South Carolina, which will eventually terminate in the death and misery of many souls; and the time will come that war will be poured out upon all nations, beginning at this place, for behold, the southern states will call on other nations, even the nation of Great Britain, as it is called, and they shall also call upon other nations and then war shall be poured out upon all nations."

In my opinion this part of the prophecy predicted the alliance between the United States and Great Britain in the war against Iraq in the 21st century. Obviously, this prophecy goes beyond the Civil War and into the 21st century.

The prophecy continues, "And it shall come to pass after many days, slaves shall rise up against their masters and thus with the sword and by bloodshed, the inhabitants of the earth shall mourn, and with famine and plague and earthquake and the thunder of heaven and the fierce vivid lightening. Also, the inhabitants of the earth shall be made to feel the wrath and indignation and chastening hand of an almighty God, until the consummation decreed hath made a full end of all nations."

I see this part of the prophecy as relating the final apocalypse. In the life of prophets and contactees there are always prophecies and revelations about the end of the world and calamities to come, but these revelations about the Civil War and the Iraq invasion are very exact and the final part has the possibility that it will became reality.

In 1831, Joseph said that God had revealed to him that plural marriage was a correct principle, but that the time had not yet come for it to be taught and practiced in the church. To preach plural marriage is against Catholic doctrine, but the entity was teaching something unacceptable in the entire Christian religion. On one occasion, three members of the church spoke in tongues while church was in session.

On October 2, 1966, at 8:20 p.m., a witness was going to retire to sleep, but she had a feeling of being watched, so she went to look out of the window. To her surprise a UFO was hovering over the lawn. She saw a brightly-colored, oval-shaped object with portholes. The craft was approximately 75 feet in diameter with red, green and white lights rotating around the rim. The witness recalled a strange odor that made her sick and it was all over the house. (Many UFO witnesses report the odor of sulphur or an industrial chemical odor.) The dogs in the neighborhood were barking.

Suddenly, a smaller object was ejected from the craft. The witness said it looked like a red ball that wobbled, bounced and made erratic movements. Then in a gliding motion, it came toward the house without a sound. The red ball shot a white ray of light over the house and then passed 75 to 100 feet directly overhead. The witness said that the underside of the UFO was like aluminum foil, smooth and shiny. It was bigger than the cottage and yard combined. After the sighting, the witness retired to bed and suddenly her room was filled with a brilliant white light. She was in shock. The room was bathed in light from wall to wall and from floor to ceiling. It was so bright that the furniture stood out and there were no shadows. Next, the light slowly flicked out and in the darkness appeared a globe of the same intensity of light as that at the foot of her bed. (As we see, this phenomenon is beyond our wildest dreams.) Inside the globe, the witness said, she saw a television screen with five non-humans with hairless heads and oval eyes "sunken like skull eyes." All the heads were the same. They had slits instead of noses and no mouths, no necks, bodies or arms. The witness received a message telepathically that said, "We have made contact." The witness got hysterical and went to a doctor for nervous disorder, and received shock treatments for two years.

What this event, the so-called religious experience, the UFO phenomenon, and even the so-called supernatural phenomenon like poltergeist, haunting and ghosts have in common is the same mechanics, like balls of light, voices and sounds that seems from another dimension. There is often the odor of sulphur, which is believed to be the smell of the legendary religious figure called the devil.

As we go through time, records show that the experience of Joseph Smith is not a singular one. In the 20th century, we have similar phenomena, but the coincidence is that UFOs were all over in wave after wave. The same encounters that Joseph Smith was experiencing were happening in others part of the world. For example, in France in 1846 in La Sallett in the French Alps, two shepherd children witnessed a figure assumed to be the Virgin. Neither Melanie Calvat, the older seer, nor the boy, Pierre-Maximin Giraud could read. They both saw a bright light. Melanie said that the light whirled and seemed to turn on itself, rising to the height of a person.

(The light is similar in appearance to the light seen by other witness in 1966.)

Melanie began to make out an oval face and hands inside the light, but she couldn't see clearly. She cried out "Oh my God " and dropped her shepherd's stick. Maximin grabbed it and said that he would give the figure a "good whack" if it tried something against them. Melanie and Maximin could make out a person in the light that seemed to be seated. Suddenly, it stood up and folded its arms across its breast. Melanie said it looked like a woman, because of the hands and face, but the dress left them puzzled. The figure came near the children walking as if she were following the brook and she began to speak. "Come near, my children. Don't be afraid. I am here to tell you great news." The apparition began to speak in French. Melanie didn't understand the French word "potatoes" and was going to ask Maximin, when the woman said, "You do not understand, my children; I will say it in a different way" and she began to speak the local dialect.

The figure gave the children a prophecy," If you have wheat, it is not good to sow it. All that you will sow the beasts will eat, and that which remains the beasts will not dare to eat. In the upcoming year it will fall into dust. A great famine will come. The children under seven years of age will be seized by trembling and they will die in the hands of those who hold them. The others will do their penance in the famine. The walnuts will be worm-eaten and the grapes will rot. If they are converted, the stones and rock will become heaps of wheat, and the potatoes will sow themselves in the fields. In the summer only some old women go to mass on Sunday and the rest work, and in the winter the boys only want to go to mass to mock religion. No one observes Lent, they go to the meat market like dogs."

The prophecy came true. The potatoes rotted before Christmas. The 1840s had seen a famine in Europe that by the fall of 1846 reached southeastern France, bringing food shortages and high prices. Francois-Melanie Mathieu or Melanie Cavat was born on November 7, 1831. She was a farmer and a shepherd. Melanie could not read, spoke only the dialect of the region, and understood French only imperfectly. Pierre-Maximin Giraud was born on August 26, 1835. He also could not read. His father said that he taught him a few prayers with great difficulty. The two young seers didn't meet until one or two evenings before the experience that made then famous. The event happened while the cows were pasturing. The children had taken a nap for an hour, and when they woke up, Melanie saw a bright light. She called Maximin's attention to it and he saw it too.

In 1858 at Lourdes, in the foothills of the Pyrennees, Bernardette Soubirous (Marie Bernarde) had a vision or so-called miracle. She was born at Lourdes on January 7, 1844. Her early childhood was one of misfortune and poverty. She worked as a laborer and lived in a "foul, somber hovel" in a courtyard of trash and poultry manure. The supernatural events happened in public and in a series. The first happened when she was gathering bones along the shore of the river with a friend, Jeanne Baloume and her sister Marie (Toinett). She heard a very loud rustling in the hedge above the grotto called Massabeille. She looked up and saw the hedge moving and something white behind it. It had the shape of a young girl who Bernardette called "Aquero." In the local dialect it means "that one." She stared at it for a moment and then she knelt down and began to pray. Aquero smiled at her then disappeared into the grotto. When Bernardette's companions appeared, she asked them if they had seen anything and they answered no.

Bernardette's next experience happened on Sunday, February 14. She and other friends returned to the grotto. They knelt down and were saying the rosary when Aquero appeared to her. She wanted to ask Aquero if she came in behalf of God or the devil, but the figure disappeared. On February 18, Bernardette and two other friends went to the grotto and recited the rosary. Bernardette had described the figure of her vision as being about her own age, wearing a white dress with a blue waistband and carrying a rosary. One of the friends of Bernardette thought that the apparition fit the description of a little girl that died a year before. About six o'clock in the evening, Bernardette walked toward the grotto carrying a candle. She knelt down to pray the rosary. Bernardette was stiff and unmoving during her ecstasies, her eyes open and fixed on a spot just above the grotto. Her lips sometimes moved as if to speak and sometimes she moved forward to salute her vision. Sometimes she smiled and her eyes were moist, her body immobile and her gaze fixed. When making the sign of the cross, she did it with grace.

On February 25, Bernardette crawled on her hands and knees and dug in the ground. When asked why, she answered that Aquero told her about a spring of water. Some people dug deeper. Aquero told her to tell the priest to build a chapel. During the apparitions of March 3 and 4, Bernardette asked Aquero to tell her name and to make the rosebush bloom. Aquero only smiled and requested a chapel. Some witnesses said that a dove had hovered over Bernardette's head during her ecstasy. Others said that her embrace of a child had restored her sight; others said that she healed a child's arm that was paralyzed.

Bernardette asked Aquero many times who she was and on one occasion, she answered, "I am the Immaculate Conception." Belief in the Immaculate Conception had been common in many parts of the western church since the late Middle Ages. It was not until 1854, four years before Bernardette's experience, that the doctrine of the Immaculate Conception, through a proclamation of Pius IX, became an official and obligatory dogma of the Roman Church.

On another occasion, a group of women went to the grotto and saw a white rock and then suddenly, a little to the right of the rock, the form of a woman of ordinary height carrying a child in her left arm. The woman had curly hair falling to her shoulders, with something white above her head, and she smiled most of the time. She wore a white dress. The following day another group of witnesses saw a white figure, vaporous and vague, and the sight made them weep and tremble.

Another visionary, Marie Courrech, reported appearances of the Virgin at the grotto from mid-April through December 1858. Marie went to the grotto to recite a rosary and there appeared a person 15 or 16 years old dressed in white. By the spring of 1858 about 50 people had seen visions. On another occasion a seer and more than 100 people had gathered near the grotto for 45 minutes and every one was silent. The seer suddenly announced he would recite the rosary. He recited a decade, but suddenly exclaimed, "Ave Maria!" He then put his rosary in his pocket and walked to the base of the grotto with his arms open as if to grasp what he was seeing. He ran back and forth as if chasing something, emitting little cries of joy and moving so quickly that the others crowded into the small area had difficulty following him. Once he slipped and fell on the wet rocks, but he didn't seem aware that he had fallen. He rose quickly and continued moving with astonishing deftness. When the object of his pursuit seemed to stop on a rock near the miraculous spring, the seer cried out "Ah, Ah, Ah" with his arms extended as if he had before him an object of ravishing beauty. He then put his thumb and forefinger together as if he had seized something and turned to the crowd as if to show them. He exclaimed, "The rose bush of Mary," but the people saw nothing. In the meantime five or seven seers from Lourdes arrived and staring in the same direction exclaimed "Ah, Ah, Ah" in unison. They knelt, then they rose and went farther into the grotto, and the crowd heard them weeping and lamenting.

Later, a seer took a child with a bad arm and healed him. One of the seers told the cure (a parish priest) to add the phrase, "Sancta et Immaculate Conception, Beatae Mariae Virginis." The cure did so, dumbfounded, for a child poorly dressed and barefoot could barely speak the dialect.

Some of the messages that the seer reported seemed inspired by a rivalry between the towns. A resident said while she was with the seer a voice came from within the grotto, a very high voice like that of an affected child, saying, "In the valley of Batsurguera and specially at Ossen there are worthy people, at Lourdes there are only scoundrels." The woman reported that she did not believe that this was the Virgin. She said, "The one who speaks is more the devil than the devil himself."

Abbe Peyramale was skeptical about the ecstasies. He noted that the children sometimes made crazy twirling motions and their visions were taking place in circumstances "bizarre and burlesque." As we see in these so-called miracles or apparitions, it is hard to understand that these kinds of visions would come from God. The children were doing very weird moves, apparently without sensitivity for the rest of the people watching the so-called miracle. Further, there is no way for anybody to know the essence of these phenomena and call them divine. Why would God use innocent little children in a clown-like performance? There are no messages of any kind to the human race in these apparitions just as many of the UFO contactees are approached by alien entities without purpose or reason, yet we called them divine or supernatural.

In the years from 1964 to 1981, the seer Rosa Quattrini witnessed supernatural events. She was born on January 26, 1909, in the province of Piacenza in north central Italy. She worked and went to school. On September 29, 1964, she was home in bed with her aunt, Adele. Around noon a young woman came to the house. Rosa described her as about 25 years old, very beautiful, more blond than brunette, and dressed in poor clothing. She wore a bluish-grey dress and carried a black purse, and said she came from far away. The woman talked first to Adele, Rosa's aunt. Rosa said that she was seeking a contribution of 1,500 lire. Adele replied that they were poor and that they had only 1,000 lire, which they had borrowed. The woman insisted on the contribution. The aunt said that Rosa was ill. The woman wanted to see her.

She entered the room and asked her what was wrong. Rosa said she had been sent home from the hospital because there was no hope. Then the bell rang. The woman told Rosa to get up. Rosa answered that she couldn't get up. The woman told her to hold her hand. She still could not rise, so the woman told her to hold her two hands. Grasping both hands, Rosa said she felt "a great shock." The woman told her again to get up, and this time she arose. Rosa began to exclaim, "I am healed. I am healed."

The woman told her to be quiet and to recite an Agnus Dei, and five Paters and five Aves. After she recited the prayers, the woman placed her hands on Rosa's wounds, and the wounds were healed. The woman also asked for a glass of water and put in it five grains of holy earth, an olive leaf and a bit of a candle consecrated on the feast of the purification of the Virgin on February 2. The woman told Rosa to drink a little of the mixture and to place what was left on the window ledge. For the next three mornings, Rosa was to rise at five o'clock, the same hour that Padre Pio said mass, and drink a little of the water.

The woman told Rosa that she was to go as soon as possible to see Padre Pio. When Rosa asked her how she could do this, since their landlord had taken all their money. The woman replied that Rosa and her aunt should find another place to live and that then she should make the trip. Rosa said that she did not have money for food, much less for clothes for the trip. The woman told her not to worry, that when the time came, she should have everything. She said she needed Rosa's aunt to give her 500 lires and she left. There were some people outside including her little boy, Pier Giorgio, who was playing. *He alone saw the woman leave.*

Rosa's Aunt Adele went into her room where there was a statue of a Madonna and she asked the Madonna to make sure that the money she had given the woman really went to Padre Pio. Surprisingly, the statue replied, "Have confidence. Your sick one will be healed."

On another occasion Rosa was sitting with a companion at the church reciting the rosary. When she had finished, she suddenly saw the strange woman. Remarkably, Rosa's companion and others standing around saw no one. Rosa said that the woman had asked her if she recognized her and Rosa had replied "yes," that she knew that she was the Madonna. She replied that she "was the mother of consolation of the afflicted." After mass Rosa found herself standing with the woman close to the altar. The "heavenly mama" opened the door that led to the sacristy and Padre Pio was waiting for her. Rosa knelt before him, but she didn't know what to think of all these events. The Padre Pio said, pointing to the Madonna, "There is the one who will confirm it for you." Then Padre Pio told Rosa to go and care for the sick.

On another occasion, Rosa said that she was leaving home when suddenly Padre Pio "appeared" to her and told her to go to the hospice, because "there is another soul to care for and to save." Rosa said that on October 16, 1964, at about 11:30 a.m. when she went to pray, that she heard a woman's voice saying "Come, come, I am waiting for you." She left the house, but continued hearing the voice calling to her. Rosa followed the voice and as she came close to the vineyard, she saw *a beautiful light*. As she came closer the "light grew stronger" and "the voice became sweeter and more penetrating." Rosa began to weep and tremble. She sat down and made the sign of the cross, asking the Madonna the meaning of the light and the voices.

Looking toward the heavens, Rosa saw *a cloud* descend with stars of gold and silver dancing and turning around it and a great shower of roses and petals, but none of them reached the ground. Rosa said that the cloud covered all the foliage of a plum tree; the only thing she could see was a little bit of the trunk. She then saw *a red globe of light* on the branches of a nearby pear tree. The *white cloud* disappeared from the plum tree and in its stead, the Virgin Mary appeared. She was wearing a white cloak and blue gown tied at the waist with a white sash. A rosary with shining, white beads hung from the sash on the left side and ended with a crucifix on which there seemed to be a living figure of Jesus. Circling her neck was a round necklace of shining stars.

Rosa said that the Virgin's arms were open and that luminous rays radiated from the palms of her hands. The rays struck Rosa on her face and body, and she felt to her knees and exclaimed," Oh, my mother, I am not worthy enough for you to come to me, but say a word and I will listen." Rosa said that the Virgin was beautiful, but sad. The Virgin left the plum tree and moved to the red globe in the nearby pear tree.

Rosa felt that she was just a poor, ignorant peasant and that nobody would believe her. The Virgin said to Rosa, "Listen, my daughter, I come from afar to announce to the world that it is necessary to pray, to pray much, for Jesus can no longer carry the cross. You must help him carry it." Rosa asked the Virgin for a sign and the Virgin answered that she would cause trees to flower and that everyone would see. The Virgin departed, raising about two meters and moving in the direction of the church and showers of rose petals fell from her. As the Virgin continuously moved away there was a great light.

We see in this event that all the components of a UFO experience are present: the "special effects" lights, voices and human-like entities. In the UFO experience, "the light" is a very important form of traveling and communicating with humans. Moreover, the messages are without any concrete meaning. Rosa, alone can't cure poverty and suffering in humankind. Rosa was a peasant who couldn't read or write, and she is part of a list of seers and prophets who were illiterate. The similarity of the UFO phenomenon and the so-called supernatural is in the phenomenology of cause and effect that points to a common origin. The case of miracles is interesting because what we see is an Intelligence able to mutate in every form of human need, fear, and the sublime.

The important point to keep in mind is that all these events happened during a major wave of UFOs around the world. We could say that the miracles came from God and the UFOs from the devil, but that does not make sense. The fact is that the idea of good and evil is only a social construct in accord with our convenience and purpose. The same is true of the idea of ugliness and beauty. They are only relative concepts. Now, if the UFO phenomenon is creating these events for a purpose, I think it is to make us believe that there is something unexplainable at the end of this world.

However, the most important point is that they want submission and obedience from the human race. Since the "special effects" in these events are probably something like what we are expecting to see in the "Second Coming of Christ," nobody will be able to question the phenomenon. It will look marvelous, supernatural, and you can call it divine. What is the difference between the divine and the extraterrestrial? The answer is none, because the effects of the divine and extraterrestrial are basically the same. Any superior advanced extraterrestrial civilization will look like gods to us, just as with our mediocre technological development, we would look like gods to the bushman.

On June 18, 1961, in San Sebastian of Garabandal, a small village in Cantalabria in northern Spain, supernatural events—as many 2000 apparitions of the Virgin—were reported. The apparitions at Garabandal began on Sunday evening. The witnesses were pre-teen girls: Maria Conception (Conchita) Gonzalez, 12 years old, Maria Cruz, 11 years old, Jacinta Gonzalez, and Maria Dolore. The girls were gathering apples after they decided to take a short break and sit down and pray like good Christians. Suddenly, they heard a noise like thunder. Conchita said, "There appeared to me a very beautiful figure that shone brilliantly, but did not hurt my eyes at all." Conchita was crying and suddenly the figure disappeared. After playing with her friends, Conchita returned home. While she was praying, she heard a voice saying, "Don't worry, you shall see me again."

The girls reported that as they were leaving, they seemed to be surrounded by a "dazzling light" that momentarily hid them from one another. They were terrified and began to scream, but by then the light was fading. On another occasion they were praying and they saw a large frame, but could not make out what it was and they began to cry and went into ecstasy. On six of the eight days that an entity appeared, its only communication was a smile. On June 24, Conchita said that the entity appeared with a sign beneath him. The first line began with "hay it is necessary that" and the second line contained Roman numerals.

On July 1 the entity appeared and told Conchita that the Virgin would appear at our Lady of Mount Carmel. On July 2 the girls went to the calleja and the Virgin appeared with two entities, one on each side. Conchita said that the entities looked like twins and were dressed alike. She identified one as Saint Michael; the other on the right side was a large eye that Conchita said seemed to be the eye of God. Conchita said that they spoke to the Virgin during the first meeting and Conchita told the Virgin about their daily lives, like their work in the fields, putting up hay, and being bronzed by the sun. Conchita reported that the Virgin laughed as they described their daily lives. The Virgin taught them the proper way to recite the rosary.

During their ecstasy the girls tilted their heads back, looking upward and speaking. Their faces transformed and became serene, happy and beautiful. During their ecstasies they became so heavy that it was hard to lift them even a few inches of the ground, and when pushed, they retained the positions, no matter how uncomfortable, which they had been forced to assume. Doctors came to Garabandal to examine the young seers, measuring pain and sensitivity. They pinched and scratched the girls' legs. One doctor used a strong electric light and examined their eyes and faces. A doctor said that the girls smiled saying to their vision, "What, what, they are pricking us, but we don't feel anything!"

On one occasion a number of young men in their 20s and 30s tried to lift them, but they couldn't. The boys lifted them when they were not in ecstasy. The girls walked in ecstasy and nobody could keep up with them. The witness said that their stride seemed extraordinary. They moved forward at three times the normal speed any 18- or 20-year-old man could keep up with them, and they showed no shortness of breath. Sometimes they walked backward on their knees.

Conchita said that the angel gave her communion on Friday 22, 1962. There were many people around. The angel told her that it was going to perform a miracle and Conchita asked, "What kind of miracle?" The angel replied that those gathered around them will see the host." Conchita responded that this would be a "tiny" miracle, and the angel laughed at the comment. Conchita was surprised. She didn't think the host was invisible.

A witness followed Conchita to one of her trance/ecstasy events where an entity or angel was going to give a host to Conchita. The witness was only 18 inches from Conchita trying not to miss anything, but began to feel disappointed about not seeing anything on the tongue of Conchita. Suddenly, a neat, well-formed host appeared on her tongue, and remained visible for three minutes.

Other witness reportedly saw different phenomenon. One witness reported seeing "a white shadow." Another reported a "white coating" like "a light of carbide lamp." Yet another witness reported something like a "snow flake" which the sun's rays were striking. Another witness said that he had seen "a chalice and a hand and a light."

After this experience, Conchita and the other seers were told by the Virgin to deny the experience. Two priests, Father Luis Maria Andrew and Father Luis Reinosa, traveled to Garabandal to investigate the miracle and were shocked to see so many supernatural events. On the evening of August 8, the girls fell into ecstasy and walked to the pines. Father Luis Maria Andrew followed them, and when the girls arrived, he stood close to them and he look upward and exclaimed four times, "Miracle, miracle, miracle, miracle!"

After the apparition, Father Luis left Garabandal and traveled by jeep to Cosio, a nearby town to meet with Pastor Valenin Marichalar and told him that he believed in the miracles. Then Father Luis left in a caravan of four cars. According to the driver, Father Luis was very happy. After sleeping for an hour, Father Luis awoke feeling refreshed and in good shape. About 4:00 o'clock in the morning, the caravan stopped for a rest and Father Luis spoke of his happiness and thankfulness to the Virgin. He said that there was "no reason to fear the afterlife," and concluded, "This is the happiest day of my life." According to the driver, Father Luis "raised his head and was silent and when asked if anything was wrong, he responded that he was sleepy. Then lowering his head, he coughed slightly and "his eyes rolled upwards and he died."

The death of Father Luis made a profound impression in the people of Garabandal and created great confusion and wonder. The priest was only 36 years old and had no physical or health or heart problems. Again we see in this phenomenon the lights, sounds and "stars wars" effects that are very common in supernatural and UFO events. It is beyond any human reason and logic to think that God was using little children to prove a point to the human race. Rather what we see is a senseless phenomenon without a message to human beings, only confusion.

However, these kinds of apparitions have been around for hundred of years, like in Guadalupe, Mexico, in the year 1531. Again it was to a poor peasant, Juan Diego, to whom the Virgin appeared. She asked him to build a chapel. Juan Diego couldn't write or read, joining the list of contactees and prophets who were illiterate. It seems that God needs people very ignorant to believed his doctrines or teachings.

The death of Father Luis seems meaningless, but in the UFO literature we find many cases of abductees, or seers dying without any logical reason, except that they came in contact with the UFO phenomenon or supernatural. Many theologians or metaphysicians will say that this phenomenon is a mystery from God, but that doesn't explain anything.

The supernatural events in Garabandal and with Rosa Quattrini in the 20th century and the miracles in the 19th century in La Sallette and Lourdes in France have a great similarity with the UFO phenomenon in their "special effects" like lights, sounds and images of sometimes indescribable entities. What we see is a slow evolution of the phenomenon. In the 19th century and Middle Ages, people were more religious and the UFO phenomenon interpretation was religious. The phenomenon acted on our consciousness dialectically and our consciousness acted on the phenomenon creating concepts and ideas of good and evil.

The most important point is that the UFO phenomenon expands our consciousness, creating the basis of our beliefs, fears and nightmares. We see that with Rosa Quatrilli. She had a personal relationship with entities as real as Rosa herself, proving that the phenomenon is not a product of the imagination. In the UFO phenomena, there are the famous "Men in Black" who disappear at will and make themselves invisible. Rosa mentions that when the woman appeared to her at the church, Rosa's friend didn't see her, only Rosa did.

However the most important aspect of this phenomenon is the mechanics or the structure that created the "special effects." For example, in the miracle in La Sallet, the children saw "a bright light" that whirled and turned in itself, and inside the light "an oval face and hands." I don't see a difference between these events and the experience a housewife lived through in October 2, 1966, which I mentioned earlier in this chapter. As you will recall, her room was filled with a brilliant white light, then a globe of the same intensity appeared at the foot of her bed. Inside the globe, the witness said, she saw a television screen with five non-humans with hairless heads and oval eyes "sunken-like skull eyes." All the heads were the same. They had slits instead of noses and no mouths.

We can see the similarity of these phenomena; now the question is, which phenomenon caused the other to exist? Can we say that God is responsible for both the religious and UFO phenomena?

CHAPTER 13

THE UFO CONNECTION AND THE MEN IN BLACK

"For thirty years I've held that image in my mind. What I saw was a circular object that looked like two plates put on top of each other with a golf ball on top. It was a classic flying saucer, and it shot a beam of something at our warhead."

— Lt. Robert M. Jacobs, U.S. Air Force

"Men in Black" are part of the folklore of the UFO phenomenon. We can trace it back to the first official UFO sighting by Kenneth Arnold in 1947, when afterward he felt the invisible presence in his house of entities sitting and walking in his living room. Many witnesses claim that the Men in Black are very weird looking, with skull faces and wearing old clothes from the 1940s. Many times they claim to be agents of the FBI or the government. They move like robots and their speech is very strange. They often seem out of place because they don't know the customs.

The Men in Black have appeared after UFO sightings and have harassed the witnesses with questions about the sightings. In the 1950s, they appeared in Cadillacs; now they come in black unmarked helicopters.

In the 1950s a UFO researcher was threatened by the Men in Black and told to stop for good his research on UFOs. He said that the men were pale looking and you could see through their skin. After this experience, the witness quit his UFO research. During the 1960s and '70s stories of the Men in Black were common. Witness said that they usually appeared in pairs and some of them looked Asian, four feet to 5'3" inches tall, or like androids.

One witness of a dramatic UFO sighting was in a restaurant when he was approached by a very weird looking man who sat next to him and started talking nonsense and told the witness, "You know, people that look for UFOs find problems." The witness said that the Man in Black picked up a quarter and as the quarter disintegrated, said, "You see how this quarter disappeared? I can make anybody disappear." After six months the man died of a heart attack. He was in good health and only 35 years old. In another case, a witness said that he followed the Men in Black to his Cadillac, but both vanished in thin air in front of his eyes.

In 1967 the Air Force issued a top-secret memorandum in which they acknowledged the possible existence of UFOs. It stated, "Information not verifiable has reached USAF HQ that persons claiming to represent Air Force or other defense establishment have contacted citizens who have sighted UFOs." In one reported case, an individual in civilian clothes, who represented himself as a member of NORAD demanded and received photos belonging to a private citizen. In another case, a person in Air Force uniform approached local police and other citizens who had sighted UFOs, assembled them in a school room and told them that they did not see what they saw and that they should not talk to anyone about the sighting. However, the Air Force wanted all the reports of UFOs sent to the their Office of Special Investigation.

What we see with the Men in Black phenomenon is the versatility of the UFO phenomenon to change form and adapt to any time and environment. The materialization of alien entities as the Men in Black gives us a clue to the materialization of different kind of entities in miracles, the paranormal phenomenon, etc. Not only that, if extraterrestrial entities have materialized throughout history adopting the many forms we see in mythology and religion, this is more than we bargained for because it means that these entities are responsible for our higher ideas about God and everything we call sacred and evil.

In February 1953, a weird story went around among UFO researchers. It happened in an office for missing persons where two strange, 6'2" tall men who had been working for the office disappeared. The officials of the office said that on January 20, 1953, these weird men, not well clothed, with bluish-green complexions and with prick ears like those of dogs, were given a job in the Los Angeles office. Witnesses also said that the men had strangely curved wrists and hands. Their job was to trace missing persons, and they were amazing at finding people in a fraction of the usual time. One day one of the men leaned over a filing cabinet and with his curiously curved hand made an indentation in the steel at least half an inch deep. The Federal Bureau of Investigation in Washington, DC, sent agents to investigate, but when the agents arrived, the men had disappeared. The indented steel was sent to a metallurgical chemist to examine and the results were mind-boggling. Their report said that to produce such an indentation would require a force of one ton to the square inch. It also said that traces of more than a dozen unknown elements were found. As a UFO researcher it is difficult for me to believe everything I read, but with the UFO phenomenon anything is possible.

On November 10, 1953, a newspaper in Bridgeport, Connecticut, reported that "three men in black, believed to be FBI agents forced a man to shut down a journal named *Space Review*, a publication of an organization called International Flying Bureau. They closed the organization, too. The newspaper article said that the director of the organization were so frightened that he didn't eat or sleep, and that he wanted to quote the very famous French doctor and astronomer, Nostradamus, who predicted that "a third world war would break out soon and that a big spaceship would land to aid terrestrials."

As we see in this case, information about the future of humankind exists here and there, but we can change the future if we want to.

Chapter 14

The Bermuda Triangle, Vanishing Planes and People, and the UFO Connection

"Cuban military installations reported a bogey approaching the Cuban landmass from the Northeast. Two Mig-21 interceptors were scrambled. Cuban air defense headquarters ordered the wing leader to arm his weapons and destroy the object. Seconds later the wingman began screaming that the wing leader aircraft had exploded. Within hours we received orders to ship all tapes and pertinent intelligence to the National Security Agency, and were told to list the incident in the squadron files as aircraft loss due to equipment malfunction."

> **— Testimony from a member of the 6947th Security Squadron. Boca Chica Naval Air Station, charged with the monitoring of Cuban military communications**

The disappearance of planes, ships and people is something that has puzzled everyone in the last 50 years. The Bermuda Triangle has become a legend for such disappearances.

First, however, let's look at the relationship between UFOs and the disappearance of planes. One classic case in UFO literature is the Kinrose case. On the evening of November 23, 1953, radar at Truaux Air Force Base picked up a blip over a restricted airspace. An interceptor jet F-89 piloted by Lt. Felix Moncla, Jr. was sent to investigate. The UFO hovered and headed into Lake Superior. The gap on the radar narrowed and the plane closed in on the UFO. The radar detected the two blips merging and after they hung together, a single blip flashed out on the screen. The Air Force initiated an intense search, but not a single oil slick of the plane was found. The plane was equipped with survival tools to keep afloat. I would say that a technology that can make a plane simply disappear is beyond our wildest dreams.

As I write, this phenomenon is still going on in the Bermuda Triangle. However, there are more places on planet Earth where ships and planes disappear. For example, in the Great Lakes in the U.S., the Sea of Japan between the Manam Island and the East China Sea, and Australia.

In 1947 in St. Maries, Idaho, about 12 people saw a puzzling event. A fleet of eight skimming platters were coming at full speed. Suddenly they slowed and then fluttered like leaves to the ground. The mysterious part is that no one could see where they landed. Although they fluttered down into the timber, they didn't do anything to the trees. We see in this event that the UFOs and their occupants can make themselves invisible.

In 1967, a contactee, an attorney, was told by alien entities that they have spaceships capable of traveling at the speed of light. Some of the entities like to stay in the pure energy form and just by thinking, they can go anywhere because they are pure energy and the universe is open to them. They told the contactee that they are able to enter any being, plant, animal or solid rock and that when they enter our atmosphere with the spaceship, they become invisible.

According to the entities, they can manipulate the brains of humans, and they record the conscious, subconscious, and memory banks of each individual. The entities are interested in this planet and for some reason, humans seem to fit neatly into their plans. The contactee saw that they spoke through an antenna, in broken English, and they said that they are able to speak any language on the planet.

The contactee also said that they have powerful devices in the form of light beams that allow them to scan a house or building anywhere in the world. They have bases all over the world and an underwater base off the coast of Florida in the region known as the Bermuda Triangle, and another off the coast of Argentina. They also have two bases in the United States, and on Venus and other planets. Curiously the insignia in their uniform was a winged serpent.

What can we make of this witness's story? Is it just a crackpot or lunatic? The best way to answer this question is to compare what the witness said with facts that we know are on record. For example, we know that the Bermuda Triangle is a fishing alley for UFOs. Ships, planes and people disappear and we suspect this has gone on for at least 100 years—we know for sure for the last 50 years. So is it possible that an alien race has a base there, because UFOs have been seen in the area? Since they said that they are pure energy, that seems possible. We don't know all the different kinds of life forms that exist in the universe.

The entities said that they are able to penetrate any animal, vegetable or solid rock. We know that the phenomenon of possession is real and the most accepted theory is that it is the devil possessing the body of a person. The fact is that we don't know. I don't find it impossible to accept that an alien intelligence can possess bodies. There is plenty of evidence that they can make themselves and their machines invisible, which is well known by radar operators.

In June of 1963, an interceptor from Otis Air Force Base with a crew of a pilot and a radar officer flew about 1,500 feet from a UFO and the engine stopped and the entire system failed. The pilot called the ground operator, saying that they were going to bail out. The pilot parachuted and landed near the backyard of a house. The owner of the house heard the pilot calling the radar operator, but he couldn't be found. The pilot had a hard time convincing the owner of the house that his plane had crashed because the owner hadn't heard anything. The plane should have crashed near the pilot, but it was nowhere to be found. The area was combed, both on foot and from the air, for three months without finding a thing. The aircraft and the radar operator were never found. The area was very populated with pleasure and commercial watercraft. The plane had a full tank and it was the tourist season. If the plane exploded nobody heard it. No wreckage or fuel slick. The navy dragged the bay from end to end without any success.

One of the most frightening events happened in Australia. On October 21, 1978, Frederick Valentich, a 20-year-old pilot with the Australian Air Training Corps left Moorabrin Airport in Victoria at 6:20 p.m. for King Island. His flight path would take him across the Bass Strait Triangle, where planes and people have disappeared just like in the Bermuda Triangle. Valentich had heard rumors of strange disappearances, unexplainable mechanical failures and magnetic anomalies. People had found planes crashes and shipwrecks with no bodies. There have been lots of UFO sightings in the Strait.

Valentich was about 45 minutes into his flight when he contacted the air tower near Melbourne about a speeding aircraft which seemed on a collision course with his single-engine Cessna-182. According to tower controllers, the radar screen was clear. The tower control transcript goes like this:

Valentich: Melbourne, this is Delta Sierra Juliet [Valentich's call sign]. Do you have any known traffic below 5,000 feet?

Tower: Delta Sierra Juliet, no known traffic.

Valentich: I am seeing a large aircraft below 5,000.

Tower: What type of aircraft is it?

Valentich: I cannot affirm. It is four bright lights. It seems to me like landing lights.

Tower: Delta Sierra Juliet?

Valentich: Melbourne, the aircraft has just passed over me at least a thousand feet above.

Tower: And it is a large aircraft. Confirm.

Valentich: Er…unknown due to the speed it's traveling. Is there any aircraft from the air force in the vicinity?

Tower: No known aircraft in the vicinity.

Valentich: It's approaching now from due east toward me. It seems to me that he's playing some sort of game. He is flying over me two, three times at speeds I could not identify.

Tower: Confirm you cannot identify the aircraft.

Valentich: It's not an aircraft as it's flying past. It's a long shape. Cannot identify more than that it has such speed. It's before me right now. Melbourne, it seems like it is stationary right now. What I am doing is orbiting and the thing is just orbiting on top of me. Also, it's got a green light and is sort of metallic like. It's all shiny on the outside. It's just vanished again.

Tower: Confirm the aircraft just vanished.

Valentich: It's now approaching from the southwest. The engine is idling rough. I've got it set at 2324 and the thing is coughing. That strange aircraft is hovering on top of me again. It's hovering and is not an aircraft!

This was the last transmission of Frederick Valentich. The day was beautiful. The search was done in a 50-mile radius in sea, air and land, and continued for five days, 24 hours a day, and the daylight search continued for three weeks before they called it off. Valentich had four life jackets. No debris or oil slick was found. Nothing.

Valentich's father still visits the airport where his son was last time seen, hoping he will come back. He believes that his son is still alive.

In 1953 during test flights from the local military airfield over Kunashir Island, an airplane vanished as observers watched it, first on radar, then visually. Ships were sent to search and found nothing. The area had experienced many UFO sightings. In 1982 in Byelorussia, a Mig-21 disappeared during a routine test flight in a militarized zone. UFOs were seen after the disappearance. In 1992 in Russia, radars were following the flight of the new Soviet SU-27 fighter plane when it suddenly vanished from the screens. The Russian air defense reported a UFO in the vicinity. A search proceeded for one month, but no traces were ever found.

The Bermuda Triangle has been an evasive mystery for more than 100 years. Writer Gian J. Quasar reported in his masterpiece *Into the Bermuda Triangle*, "In the last 25 years alone, some 75 aircraft and hundreds of pleasure yachts have inexplicably vanished despite the fact that GPS is now extensively used, that communications systems are powerful and reliable, and that searches are immediately launched."

A frightening incident happened on June 28, 1980, near the coast of Puerto Rico. Jose Torres, the pilot of an Ercoupe, signaled that a "weird object" in his flight path was forcing him to change course. Despite all his evasive maneuvers, the object continued to cut him off. That's not all. He reported his equipment was on the fritz, and he was lost. "Mayday, Mayday," he continued to call. That is a distress call. Then astounded controllers watched the plane vanished from their screens. The plane, Torres and passenger Jose Pagan disappeared of the face of the earth. Minutes later an object reappeared on the scope and disappeared. A search of the area was launched, but found nothing. This incident was reported by Quasar in his book.

This is the most famous disappearance of all time and this event gave the Bermuda Triangle its fame. On December 5, 1945, five planes disappeared on a routine training mission. The famous "Flight 19" had a crew of five officer pilots and nine crewmembers, two to each plane. The planes were Navy Grumman TBM-3 Avenger torpedo bombers and each carried enough fuel to travel 1000 miles. The temperature was 65 degrees, and there was sunshine, a moderate wind and no clouds.

Flight 19 left their base at Fort Lauderdale at 2:00 p.m. Lieutenant Charles Taylor with over 2,500 hours of flight was the commander. About 3:15 after the bomber training, the planes continued east. The radioman at the Fort Lauderdale Naval Air Station tower received an unusual message from the flight leader. The record shows the following:

Flight Leader (Lt. Charles Taylor): Calling tower. This is an emergency. We seem to be off course. We cannot see land...repeat...We cannot see land.

Tower: What is your position?

Flight Leader: We are not sure of our position. We cannot be sure just where we are...We seem lost.

Tower: Assume bearing due west.

Flight Leader: We don't know which way is west. Everything is wrong...strange. We can't be sure of any direction—even the ocean doesn't look as it should.

About 3:30 p.m. the senior flight instructor at Fort Lauderdale picked up a message from someone calling Powers, one of the students flyers requesting information about his compass reading.

Powers answers. "I don't know where we are. We must have gotten lost after that last run." The senior flight instructor managed to contact the Flight 19 instructor who told him "Both my compasses are out. I am sure I am in the Keys, but I don't know how far down." The senior flight instructor advised him to fly north.

In the search for Flight 19, unexplained lights in red, green and white described as "streaking or dancing" were seen from as far as the Keys to the Atlantic Ocean off Jacksonville. The same phenomenon is seen to this day after a disappearance, but their sources are still inexplicable.

One of the pilots reported, "We have just passed over a small island…No other island in sight." It became increasing difficult to hear messages from Flight 19 because of static. The gyro and magnetic compasses in all the planes were going crazy, showing different readings.

During this time, the powerful transmitter at Fort Lauderdale was unable to make contact with any of the planes, although the inter-plane communication was fairly audible. By this time the personnel at the base were very worried and dispatched a twin engine Martin Mariner flying boat patrol with a crew of 13 men from the Banana River Naval Air Station. The Martin Mariner reported strong winds at 6,000 feet. This was the last message received from the rescue plane. A message was sent to all the search planes that there were now six planes missing.

The next day, Thursday, one of the greatest searches ever in U.S. history was launched. It involved 307 planes, 4 destroyers, 18 coast guard vessels, several submarines, search and rescue cutters, hundreds of private planes, yachts, boats, and additional PBMs from the Banana River Air Naval Station and help from R.A.F. and Royal Navy units. Nothing was found. The search included a daily average of 167 flights, flying about 300 feet above the water from dawn to dusk, an inspection of 380,000 square miles of land and sea, including the Atlantic, Caribbean, parts of Gulf of Mexico and Florida. The air-search totaled 4,100 hours. Nothing was found, no rafts, wreckage or oil slick. The beaches of Florida and the Bahamas were checked daily for several weeks without success for any flotsam from the lost planes.

Another baffling disappearance happened on December 28, 1948. A DC-3 passenger plane chartered for a flight from San Juan, Puerto Rico, to Miami vanished within sight of Miami. The weather was excellent, the pilots were experienced and there were no signals of mechanical problems. The plane had 27 passengers, including two infants. The captain of the plane contacted the Miami control tower stating that they were approaching the field from 50 miles south and were waiting for landing instructions. Whatever happened to the DC-3 was fast and decisive, so quick that there was no time for a distress call. The tower sent the landing instructions, but there was no response that it was received. The plane was almost within reach of the airport and simply vanished. A massive search was launched without any luck. Again, no oil slick, no life jackets or debris, simply nothing.

We know that UFOs have been responsible for the disappearance of planes. This is not fiction, because is on record with the civil and government agencies. On September 10, 1971, a Phantom II, Sting 27 jet fighter was on a routine mission out of Homestead Air Force Base south of Miami. It took off at 8:05 and its last radar return was at 8:22. There were others Phantoms in the area and the coast guard cutter, *Steadfast*. The Sting 27 vanished without a trace. According to a report, minutes later another Sting 29 dropped down 1,500 feet to get a closer look at an area of disturbance in the ocean and described it as "an area of water discoloration oblong in shape, approximately 100 by 200 feet with its axis running North/South."

When the coast guard cutter *Steadfast* arrived, there was no trace of the discoloration. The area was searched with sonar in a five-square-mile radius, but no trace of the fighter jet was found. It is clear that what the pilot saw was a UFO.

On February 11, 1980, the Beech Baron 58 left St. Thomas and headed for Miami. The pilot's last message reported at 150 feet altitude was that he was descending to ditch, but was completely disoriented in a *strange cloud*. Nothing was ever heard again from the pilot and plane.

On October 11, 2001, the cruise ship *Celebrity* was near Bimini. Four people were looking at the stars between midnight and 1:00 a.m. when suddenly one of the stars started to move. The object began to circle, moving in clockwise and counterclockwise motions. After approximately 15 minutes, it started moving close to the ship. It seemed to be checking the ship out. All of its movements were deliberate. One of the witnesses said, "Three rows of lights in the form of a triangle became visible on its underside with blue, white and red lights. It then receded to the sky, again looking like a star." Two of the witnesses were a corporate lawyer and his wife, a doctoral student

There is no doubt that UFOs have created this environment to kidnap not only humans, but also technology like state of the art fighter jets. Today this phenomenon does not come in waves like in the '40s, '50s,

'60s, and '70s. It operates in rural areas. It seems that they don't want publicity. I believe there must be a purpose for all this kidnapping that has been going on for decades. They know something that we don't know and the clue probably is in everything the abductees have been told through the years.

The most famous case of abductees happened in September 1961. Betty and Barney Hill were traveling near the White Mountain in New Hampshire when they were abducted by a UFO and unable to account for several lost hours on the road. For three years they suffered nightmares. Finally, Barney and Betty Hill decided to submit to time-regression hypnosis and discovered that they had undergone an extensive medical examination. The entities showed them a star map and they were told that there were trade routes and paths of exploration. In 1964 under post-hypnotic suggestion, Betty Hill drew the star and three grade school teachers in Oak Harbor, Ohio, isolated the specific star. The teachers built a model within 60 light years of the sun to try to match Betty Hill's map. It was in 1972 after six years of intensive work that the teachers were able to locate the background of stars that Betty Hill's map showed. In 1964 when Betty Hill made the drawing, Star 86.1 was not listed in any earthly catalogue. "No astronomer on earth between 1961 and 1964 could have known that the triangle of background stars existed in its present geometric position," said the famous now deceased astronomer Dr. J. Allen Hynek.

Scholars Dr. Stanton Friedman and B. Ann Slate said, "What this implies is that the Reticular II crew, using Einstein's time-change factor, a one-way trip at 80 percent of the speed of light at a constant velocity would take them 22 years. At 99 percent of the speed of light it would take them five years and two months and at the speed of 99.9 percent of the speed of light it would take them 20 months to reach our solar system."

However, it wouldn't take much time at all for a civilization originated in another dimension to travel between universes. A civilization a million years more or less ahead of us in their technology is beyond our comprehension. Our civilization was founded in slavery and is still primitive as long as our only worries are to defend, to copulate, and to eat.

Another, famous abduction on November 5, 1975, took place in Arizona's Mogollon Rim. Travis Walton was driving home from work in his pickup truck with six other coworkers when they saw a hovering, glowing object near the road. Walton jumped from the truck to look closer at the UFO. Suddenly, a flash of light from the UFO hit him in the chest and he was thrown into the air ten feet away. His friends fled after a couple of minutes in a state of shock. They came back to look for him, but he was no where to be found. When Walton woke up, he was lying on a metal table in great pain aboard the UFO, and three entities were looking at him. They were five feet tall, hairless with large heads, chalky skins, tiny mouths and huge black eyes. Later another alien that looked human led Walton out of the UFO to a hanger where more UFOs were parked. Here he saw more aliens that looked like humans. They led him to a table where they put a mask on him, and when Walton woke up he was on the side of the road. Later Walton found out that he had been missing for five days. This case was well documented by famous

UFO researchers Dr. J. Allen Hynek and James and Coral Lorenzen. A movie with James Gardner was made about it. UFO abductions have been very well documented by UFO scholars like John Mack, Bud Hopkins, and David Temple.

CHAPTER 15

THE MIRACLE OF FATIMA AND THE UFO CONNECTION

"In a funnel-shaped space there were innumerable little lights gleaming ranged step fashion over one another; and they shone so brilliantly that the eye was dazzled. Now whether this was a pandemonium of will-o' the wisps or a company of luminous creatures, I will not decide."

— Goethe, Autobiography, 1768

The cult and myth of the Virgin Mary evolved with the birth of civilization in Sumeria and near East more than 3,000 years ago. The Great Mother was known in the ancient world, but with different names like Aphrodite, Ishtar, and Demeter. She was the goddess who grieved for the unhappiness of mankind and often interceded with other deities. For example, in the myth of Isis, the sister and wife of Osiris conquered death with love. She was the female principle of creation, which shows the leadership of woman in the beginning of civilization. The Egyptians worshiped her with special fondness and piety, and raised up jeweled images to her as the mother of God.

The priests praised her in sonorous matins and vespers. In mid-winter of each year, coinciding with the annual rebirth of the sun towards the end of our December, the temples of her divine child, Horus (Sun-God), showed her in holy effigy nursing the babe that she had miraculously conceived in a stable. The poetic legends of the Near

East had a great influence on the birth of Christianity and its rituals and theology. Early Christians sometimes worshiped before the statues of Isis and the infant Horus sucking the breast.

We see in this myth that women where the female principle, creator of all things and mother of God. The Romans called her Venus, in Greece she was Astarte, the Jews called her Asshtoreth. The Virgin Mother was the creative principle everywhere. Prehistoric cave art findings of figurines of females known as the "Willesdorf Venus" have been dated at approximately 2,3000 BC.

These findings point to an early fertility cult of females as goddesses. The great Sumerian scholar Zecharia Sitchin mentions in one of his masterpieces that archeologists had found a wall sculpture in Ishtar Templo in Ashur. The goddess Ishtar is shown with a decorated helmet and with earphones and antennas, and she is wearing goggles. Archeologists believe that the sculpture is 5,000 years old. However, miracles and supernatural phenomenon had been happening since the beginning of history. For example, ancient Romans and Greeks wrote that statues cried, talked, and on some occasions bled. In one instance, when the statue of the Goddess of Cybele was removed from the palace of King Attalus on her feast day, she said in Latin *"Ipsa peti novi; ne sit moramitte volemtem; dignus roma lucus quo dens omvis eat,"* which means in English, "I want to be carried off; take me quickly away; Rome is worthy to be the home of every god."

The Roman historian Livy mentions that statues of idols often talked or cried. In modern times, the great German philosopher Friedrich Engels in his masterpiece *The Peasant Wars* mentions that peasants claimed to have seen the Virgin. In the 1980s in India in the Temple of the Elephant God, she was seen pouring milk from her eyes. What at the beginning of history was only a cultural component of ancient society materialized in the miracles of Fatima, Lourdes, and so forth. The legend or myth materialized through the intervention of the intelligence behind the UFO phenomenon.

The miracle at Fatima began in the year 1915, when a child name Lucia Dos Santos and two cousins were tending sheep on Mount Cabeco in Portugal. Following their Christian tradition, after lunch they started to recite the *terco* or the third part of the rosary. As the children were praying, they suddenly saw a strange *cloud*, whiter than snow *hovering* above the trees. The mysterious object was transparent and had a human form. As we know *clouds* don't *hover* above trees, but there are thousands of eyewitness accounts of UFOs hovering above the trees. Lucia saw the cloud with human form three times and said, "It looked like somebody wrapped in a sheet, there were no eyes or hands on it." In 1916, Lucia and her two cousins Jacinta and Francisco Marto were tending the family flocks in a field east of Mount Cabeco and around noon when a very fine mist began to fall. Lucia and her two cousins decided to find refuge among the boulders hidden behind an olive grove. It was the first time the children had played there. After the rain ended, they decided to remain there playing. After a few minutes, the children heard the rumble of a "powerful wind." They were surprised because the day had been calm.

A "powerful wind" is often mentioned by witnesses of the UFO phenomenon. For example, a witness was driving his truck along the highway when suddenly the lights went off and a strange object came down over the truck with a "sizzling-wind-blowing-sound."

Further, the children saw at a distance a "very strange light, whiter than snow." The light came moving at fast speed toward them, and in the center of the light was the form of a young man. The entity in the light was "whiter than snow" and transparent, gleaming brilliantly, like a crystal of great beauty that the sun's rays glistens. Lucia recognized the figure seen three times before and she described it as a human-like youth of 14, "its beauty surpassing anything human." The children were silent and the entity spoke, "Do not fear. I am the angel of peace. Pray with me." Kneeling, he prostrated until his forehead touched the ground. Lucia and Jacinta were moved by a supernatural impulse to imitate the entity. They were in shock and afraid to talk about their experience.

In the hot summer of 1916, the children were playing in the garden when suddenly beside them the entity appeared again, asking, "What are you doing?" He then told them, "You will thus draw down peace upon your country. I am an angel guardian, the angel of Portugal. Above all, accept and bear with submission the suffering which the Lord will send you." Lucia recalled that on another occasion, after the children had finished lunch, "An extraordinary light shone upon us. The entity appeared holding a chalice in his left hand, with the host suspended above it, and some drops of blood fell into the chalice, leaving the chalice suspended in the air." (Mohammed had the same experience in a cave. In his case, the entity claimed, its name was Gabriel.) The entity gave the host to Lucia and shared the blood from the chalice with Jacinta and Francisco. Not long after the two cousins suddenly

died. The entity also prepared Lucia for a meeting with
the Virgin, but she was afraid to see her, because the girl
thought she was the devil in disguise. Lucia's mother
never believed the visions. The three children were raised
in a very Catholic home with the fear of God and the
devil.

On another occasion, the Virgin showed hell to Lucia,
who said, "The lady showed us a great fire that seemed to
be under the earth. Plunged in this fire were demons and
souls in human form, like transparent burning embers,
all blackened or burning bronze floating about in the
conflagration, now raised into the air by the flames." It
is unthinkable that God or a Supreme Being full of love
would frighten little children. Even on the human level,
it is unacceptable. Only an alien intelligence can explain
these strange events.

On Sunday, May 13, 1917, the Virgin gave to the
children a prophecy divided into three secrets. The first
secret predicted the First and Second World Wars. The
prophecy said, "The war is going to end, but another war
will break during the pontification of Pio XI." It also said,
"When you see a night illuminated by an *unknown* light,
know that this is the great sign given by God, that he
is about to punish the world for its crimes, by means of
war, famine and persecution of the Church and the Holy
Father." Interestingly, the only "unknown lights" that we
know are the lights of the UFO phenomenon.

Shockingly, the Virgin didn't give warning about the
coming holocaust of the Jews. If this vision came from
God, why didn't he stop the slaughter?

The supernatural events in the lives of the three
children continued. Interestingly, Francisco couldn't hear

the angel's voice, only Lucia and Jacinta. About the third apparition Francisco said, "I love to see the angel, but the worst of it is that afterwards we are unable to do anything. I couldn't even walk. I don't know what was the matter with me." Francisco asked Lucia, "The angel gave you Holy Communion, but what was it that he gave to Jacinta and me?" Not long after this vision Francisco and Jacinta died mysteriously.

Francisco was very inquisitive and always questioned the nature and origin of the apparitions. On one occasion Francisco was tormented by the vision of a monster. He was screaming and Lucia asked him, "Where are you? What is wrong?" Francisco trembling in fear replied, "It was one of those huge beasts we saw in Hell."

On another occasion, the children were in the Cova Iria playing when suddenly they saw a *flash* of *light*. The children thought that a storm was coming. Then there was another *flash* of *light* and the lady appeared dressed in white. Lucia said, "She was more brilliant than the sun and radiated a light more clear and intense than a crystal glass filled with sparkling water, the rays of the burning sun shining through it."

The Virgin asked Lucia to come to the same place for six months. Then the Virgin began to raise the light that surrounded her and seemed to open a path before her in the firmament. Lucia was surprised to see flashes of light without thunder. The lady told Lucia," I will take Jacinta and Francisco to heaven." I think it was unnecessary to take the lives of the two children, because they loved life. Jacinta and Francisco were happy on this earth. Ironically, there were twelve attempts on the life of Hitler, but he survived.

On another occasion, the lady appeared in a luminous *cloud* and a *strong wind* and a flash of light. The lady was standing on the top of the branches of an oak tree. The children heard a very faint voice or the *buzzing* of *bees* and others heard the same sound.

In the UFO literature, it is well known by many witnesses that UFOs produce those sounds. For example, in May 1966, a group of British scientists saw a strange *cloud*. The white mass appeared and rose close to the ground, an estimated altitude of 600 feet. The mass was approximately 100 feet across and was moving very slowly and pulsating expanding and contracting. Also, a noise was coming from the *cloud* like the *buzzing* of a *gigantic swarm of bees*. Further, a dark tube emerged from the *cloud* and started inspecting the snow on the ground.

Another witness in the 1960s said she was driving to her home when she suddenly noticed a brilliant glow, a red light that covered everything. It was 50 or 60 feet in diameter with red and green lights. A strange noise came from the object, a low humming sound like the *swarm of bees*. In another event a witness said, "The object was hovering above the road. There was a strange humming sound coming from the object, like a *cluster of bees.*"

Betty Hill, the most famous abductee said of her experience that the beings aboard the UFO "had a sort of flat face and very large wraparound eyes, almost no nose, just a slit for a mouth. When they talked with each other, it sounded like the *hum of insects.*" In another event in Lima, Peru, a witness heard a noise like the *buzzing of bees*, and looking outside saw an object 10 to 15 feet in diameter. In another event two teenagers walking to school, witnessed a UFO that was "dull metallic and silver shaped" and "made a sound like a *humming of bees*."

On July 13, 1917, the children and a priest name Manuel were present at Cova Iria. They were praying, when suddenly the Lady appeared. The priest saw a little *grayish cloud* resting on the oak tree. Now remember, clouds don't rest on trees. A breeze came from the tree, then "a *buzzing* sound, like a mosquito in an empty bottle." Lucia was kneeling, frightened. A witness said that from the tree of the apparitions came a sound like an explosion or underground thunder and small *light-cloud* like smoke rising from the tree. It ascended very high and very far in the direction Lucia was pointing. At the Lady's departure, a *buzzing* or *humming* sound, a decrease in both the sun's glow and in the heat of the small *whitish cloud* above the tree of the apparitions, and a loud noise were reported.

In the village where the children lived, nobody believed them, so Lucia asked the Virgin for a sign for all to see. The Virgin promised to give a sign on Thursday, October 13, 1917. Some 70,000 thousand people saw it, thousands in the Cova Iria area alone. Many witnesses—journalists, priests, policemen, military atheists—saw the sun get dimmer and dimmer, fading to a degree that some people were able to see the moon and the stars. Lucia, exclaimed, "There she is, I see her," as a *globe* of *light* was coming, *gliding* slowly down the valley. The *globe* shone brightly, and as it was moving toward the children, Lucia said, "I still see it, I still see it." The globe came and rested on the tree of the apparitions.

A *white cloud* formed about the tree and out of the cloudless sky a shower of mysterious shiny white petals began to fail. The mysterious downpour of what at first seem like brilliant petals of flowers seemed to come in a jet of light. The big beam of light seemed to come from high in the sky, and as the rays approached, they seemed to broaden. The crowd was amazed and perplexed as they watched the marvelous show of lights. They tried to touch the shiny, white petals, but they disintegrated at contact with their hands. In the luminous globe was the Lady from Heaven. The white *cloud* disappeared in a *flash of light*.

Lucia said, "Look at the sun," and the lady appeared and opened her hands, turning her palms upward, toward the center of the sky. From the lady's hands, rays of light were reflected and a *spinning disc of brilliantly glowing silver* got the attention of the children. The attention was on the Virgin who was beside the *silver glowing* object. The Lady stood to the right of the sun. She is all light and clothed in a dress of *glowing* white and a mantle of blue. Further, the people watched in terror the silver *glowing object*, which was a *whirling* mass of *flashing lights.* The silver disc turned rapidly on its own axis and cast off beams of colored lights in all directions. Shafts of red lights came from the object and it seems to color the clouds, the people, and the trees with colors like violet, blue and yellow, like the rainbow.

Seventy thousand people saw the phenomenon in amazement and fear. The witnesses agreed that the color of the object was close to white or silver. It was more like a *disc* or *flat plate* than a solid ball, and it *rotated* at terrific speed upon itself. The color of the spinning disc differed from the moon because of its silvery appearance. The object was very bright and shiny with a rim of colors clearly seen surrounding it. The beginning of the rim was red and there was a great contrast with the silver color of the object.

Curiously, the sun appeared like a gigantic spinning wheel that seemed to be rotating in its own axis. About three times the sun seemed to dance and rotate with great shafts of lights coming out in colors like red, violet, blue, and yellow. However, on the third rotation the sun seemed loose and falling from the sky. The crowds watched in amazement as the sun plunged in a zigzag fashion toward the earth. Horrified and in panic, the spectators watched the sun staggering downward, getting bigger and warmer as it got closer to earth. Suddenly, it stopped its downward fall and reversed its course, back to heaven, shining with a golden *glow*. The event had been witnessed at various places, including by reporters. Interestingly, no astronomical observatory seemed to detect the phenomenon.

The most amazing and shocking thing about it was to see the "Lady from Heaven" appear on the right side of the sun. A change of light took place and she appeared in a garment hard for Lucia to identify. The Holy Family was present, Saint Joseph and the child Jesus at the right side, both dressed in red and both blessing the world. Jesus made signs of the cross with his hand to the crowds.

As we see in the miracle, the lights, the silver object, the change of weather patterns, all had been seen in the UFO phenomenon. For example, On December 27, 1980, over a period of a week between Christmas and New Years near Rendlesham Forest in England, U.S., UK and NATO forces sighted a UFO. The animals on a nearby farm were agitated and making noises. The military police saw a *small flashing light* between the trees. As the light moved from the trees, it was red, but with multicolored lights like a rainbow. The light imploded in an enormous *flash of light,* and the machine appeared to glow in spectacular form. Some of the witnesses said that it was like an eye winking. The witnesses also saw up to five lights in the sky that looked like half moons, then shockingly turned into full circles. The object appeared silvery and beams came out of it after a big flash of light and an icy blast of wind hit the witnesses. One of the witnesses was in such shock that he lost consciousness. The military police used a Geiger counter and found a little bit of radioactivity where the indentations were.

Earlier, I discussed the relationship between miracles and UFOs. The USAF released information, under the Freedom of Information Act, which said, "Early in the morning of December 27, 1980, the USAF security police patrolmen saw unusual lights outside the back gate at RAF, Woodbridge. Thinking an aircraft might have crashed or been forced down, they called for permission to go outside the gate to investigate. The on-duty flight chief responded and allowed three patrolmen to proceed on foot. The individuals reported seeing a strange glowing object in the forest. The object was described as metallic in appearance and triangular in shape, approximately two meters high. The object illuminated the entire forest in a *white light.* Also, the object had a pulsing *red light* on top and blue lights underneath. The object was hovering or on legs. As the patrolmen approached, the object maneuvered through the trees and disappeared. At the time, the animals on a nearby farm went into a frenzy.

The object was briefly sighted approximately an hour later, near the back gate."

On October 15, 1973, in Wisconsin, a witness was awakened by a "high-pitched sound." A bright, orange glow bathed his bedroom. Right in front of him were three frightening creatures three or four feet high with rounded heads, large ears and grayish white wrinkled skin. The witness said that their movements were unnatural, mechanical like robots. The witness passed out.

In New York State on November 5, 1957, a shiny silver UFO hovered and moved from side to side, emitting a slight trail. At the same time but at a different place, a witness described a UFO as round, silvery, orange and egg-shaped. The same month a group of railroad employees saw a silvery, elliptical object passing overhead at high speed. On July 20, 1952, in Chicago, the U.S. Rocket Society president wired the Defense Department and President Truman urging them to restrain pilots from shooting at UFOs. Should they be extra-terrestrials, such action might result in the gravest consequences. Navy scientists wired President Truman expressing similar views. I will end this chapter with what Dr. J. Allen Hynek said about UFOs:

> "I had started out as an outright "debunker" taking great joy in cracking what seemed at first to be puzzling cases. I was the archenemy of those flying saucers groups and enthusiasts, who very dearly wanted UFOs to be interplanetary. My own knowledge of those groups came almost entirely from what I heard from blue book personnel: they were all crackpots and visionaries. It was useless to

remonstrate with the staff of blue book personnel; it would have been a clear-cut case of fighting city hall. My transformation was gradual, but by the late sixties it was complete. Today I would not spend one further moment on the subject of UFOs if I didn't seriously feel that the UFO phenomenon is real and that efforts to investigate and understand it, and eventually to solve it, could have a profound effect, perhaps even be the springboard to a revolution in mankind's outlook on the Universe."

CHAPTER 16

THE UFO PHENOMENON AND THE BIRTH
OF THE JEWISH RELIGION

"Receiving a visit from outer space seems almost as comfortable as having a God. Yet we shouldn't rejoice too soon. Perhaps we will get the visitors we deserve."

—Dr. Jacques Vallee

Until the time of Abraham, the predominant forms of religion in the Near Eastern ancient world were animism and totemism, which is the normal psychological path followed by human civilizations.

Historians and scholars know that the Jewish religion is a recollection of all the known ancient myths and legends of the ancient Near East cultures. The Jewish people were ruled by the Egyptians, Babylonians, Romans and Assyrians, so they assimilated and were assimilated by those cultures. The *Bible*, for example, mentions The Flood, but it is mentioned first in the Sumerian epic *Gilgamesh*. Historians also know that circumcision was learned by the Jews in Egypt, the first country in the Near East to have practiced this custom.

Historians and scholars know that the monotheist religion of Yahweh is the repackaging of the monotheist religion of the Egyptian Pharaoh Akhenaten, who lived in approximately 1335 BC. He created the first monotheist religion in the world. He believed that the sun was the creator of the universe and that all other gods were false. He went into every temple and destroyed the images of all the false gods. His religion lasted only 17 years after which the polytheistic religion was reinstated. Akhenaten said in a famous prayer, "Oh living Aten, who initiates life…Oh sole God, without another beside him!…You create the Earth according to your wish. You are in my heart and there is none who you except your son." This was a beautiful prayer more than a thousand years before Christianity.

Let's start with the origins of the Jewish god, Yahweh. The Hebrew god had different names. In some parts of the *Bible* the word Elohim is mentioned, which is the plural form and means "gods." The Hebrew god was also known as "Elion" which means "exalted one." The word Shaddai came from the Babylonian Saddan and means "mountain." Other words used in the *Bible* are Adon and Adonai, which mean "master or lord."

The early forms of the Jewish religion were naturism and animism. The phenomena of nature were considered "deities." Yahweh was basically a god of "thunder and lightning," a volcano god. Many scholars believe that it was to Moses that God made Himself known as Yahweh. Before that, he was known as "El Shaddai." In *Exodus 6:3*, Yahweh said to Moses, "I am Yahweh; I appeared to Abraham, Isaac, and Jacob as "El Shaddai," but I did not make myself known to them by my name Yahweh." It is only in Moses' revelation that God uses the name Yahweh.

On the other hand, "J" document claimed that Yahweh was not a new god, but well known to the Hebrew people since the times of Enoch. *Genesis 4:26* said, "Seth in turn had a son born to him whom he named Enoch. It was then that men began to call upon the name of Yahweh. In *Exodus 3:15* Yahweh said to Moses, "Thus shall you say to the Israelites, Yahweh the god of your father, the god of Abraham, Isaac and Jacob has sent me to you. This shall always be my name and this my designation throughout the ages."

In the "E" document there is confusion about the time Moses called God Yahweh instead of Elohim. The "P" document claimed that the name for God from the beginning was Yahweh. The Kenite hypothesis claims that Yahweh was originally the tribal god of the Kenites and was entirely unknown to the Hebrews, until introduced by Moses, who learned the name from his father-in-law, Jethro.

The name Yahweh had its origins in nature, derived from "Hwy" which meant "to blow." Many scholars claim that Yahweh was a storm-god. The Old Testament indicates that Yahweh was a storm-god and that his habitat was in the southern Negeb Desert. The most famous song in the *Old Testament* is by Deborah in *Judge 5:4*, "Oh Yahweh, when thou camest forth from the steppes of Edom, the Earth quaked, the heavens also shook. The clouds too dripped water." This is a beautiful explanation by Deborah about nature and origins of Yahweh.

Deuteronomy 33:2 says, "Yahweh came from Sinai and rose up from Se'ri. He shows forth the mountains of Paran, and advanced from Meribath Kadesh, with his lightning-bolts at his right hand. The mountains rocked at the presence of Yahweh, the god of Israel." Yahweh originally was not a god of a settled land, because when the Hebrews were in Egypt they had to travel a three days journey into the desert to visit his shrine. (*Exodus 3:1,5:3.*)

Many scholars believe that the Jews took one of the gods from Canean called Yahu and recreated him as a warlike and vindictive god. Interestingly, a coin was found with a picture of Yahweh which bears resemblance to the South American god Quetzacoatl. Although the Jewish odyssey began with Abraham, many scholars doubt that he ever existed, it was so long ago. However, there is the possibility someone called Abraham existed, and that the experience of hearing a voice that told him what to do was real. Why? Because in recent historic times, the same event happened with Joan of Arc. She was told to go and help the King of France. If the voice haven't told her to help liberate France, there would not be a country named France (see the chapter about Joan of Arc).

Many scholars also doubt that Moses ever existed. Others like Sigmund Freud believe that Moses was an Egyptian because "Moses" is a short form from the Egyptian name "Ahmose." Moreover, some scholars believed that the Exodus never happened. The English historian, Egyptologist and archeologist William Petrie accepts the Biblical figure of 430 years for the stay of the Jews in Egypt with their arrival about 1650 BC and their exit about 1220 BC.

The Egyptian historian Manetho wrote in the third century that the Exodus was due to the desire of the Egyptians to protect themselves from a plague that had broken out among the destitute and enslaved Jews. He also said that Moses was an Egyptian priest who went on a missionary mission to help the Jews with leprosy and gave them laws of cleanliness modeled upon the Egyptians clergy. In his book *Against Apion*, Manetho said, "After the blasts of God's displeasure broke upon Egypt, a Pharaoh named Toumosis negotiated the shepherd people, the people from the east, to evacuated Egypt and go whither. They would go unmolested and they left and traversed the wilderness and built a city in a country now called Judae and gave it the name Jerusalem."

Others think that probably the Exodus happened in the years 1440-1433 BC. The Jewish people were nomadic Bedouins who believed and feared the djinns or spirits of the air and worshiped rocks, cattle, sheep and the spirits of caves and hills. The cult of the sheep, lamb and bull was also popular. The Egyptians worshiped the bull and the snake. Moses is known to have owned a brazen serpent, a sacred phallic symbol of virility, and worshiped in the Temple until the time of Hezekiah (720 BC). The Baal was symbolized in conical upright stones much like the "linga " of the Hindus, which was venerated as a male principle of reproduction.

Many scholars believe that the Exodus and the so-called miracles in it are just explainable natural events. For example, the Red Sea looked like blood because of red algae present in the water. The quail emigrated at the right time and flew near were the Jews were waiting for food and it was easy for them to catch the birds and eat them. The crossing of the Jordan River was possible because of an earthquake. The plague of locust was a normal event that still goes on in the 21st century. However, the most important event in the Exodus odyssey was the "cloud" that talked to Moses and give religion to the Jewish people. Someone named Moses guided probably 20,000 to 50,000 Jewish people throughout the wilderness for 40 years. The

Bible says that approximately 600,000 people were in the Exodus, but I think that number is unrealistic.

However, men in the 20th and 21st century have seen cloud-like formations that camouflage UFOs, as I will show. Interestingly, Yahweh didn't want to show his face to Moses, but Moses asked Yahweh to show his face. Yahweh answered, "Behold, there is a place by me and thou shalt stand upon a rock; and it shall come to pass while my glory passeth by, that I will put thee in a cleft of the rock, and will cover thee with my hand, while I pass by and I will take away my hand, and thou shalt see my back parts, but my face shall not be seen."

According to scholars, the term "kabod" is used in the books of the *Pentateuch: Genesis, Exodus, Leviticus, Numbers* and *Deuteronomy*. The kabod of Yahweh was something concrete that the people could see, but it was always surrounded by a cloud or dark fog. The prophet Ezekiel used the term to describe the divine chariot as "engulfed with a bright brilliance." The kabod of Yahweh, says *Ezekiel 10:4,* "had a luminosity that shone through the cloud that shrouded it, a kind of radiance. The Hebrew word that has been accepted is "glory" in the English translation. Kabod came from the root kbd whose meaning is "weighty, heavy."

The literal meaning of the kabod is "the heaviness, the weighty thing." However, when this word is used to mention Yahweh it means that of a concrete object. The *Bible* says, "beheld the Kabod of Yahweh enveloped by the ubiquitous *cloud*...The Kabod of Yahweh rested upon Mount Sinai, covered by a cloud for six days...The appearance of the Kabod of Yahweh on top of the Mount in full view of the children of Israel was like a devouring fire."

So Yahweh was the god of thunder and fire and "Mount Sinai was completely engulfed by smoke. Yahweh had descended in a fire, and the smoke thereof rose up like that of a furnace and the whole mount quaked greatly. Moses went up on the mount and the *cloud* enveloped the mount, and the glory of Yahweh rested upon Mount Sinai covered by the *cloud* for six days, and on the seventh day, he called unto Moses from inside the *cloud* and Moses went into the *cloud* and ascended up the mountain, and Moses was on the mountain forty days and forty nights."

At this time Moses received instructions about how to build the Tabernacle, including the Arch of the Convent, the wooden chest laminated with gold with two golden cherubim on top, where the two tablets of the Ten Commandments were to be kept. Instructions about marriage, eating, hygiene, morality, etc. were also given.

Some scholars believe that the cloud that guided Moses was an active volcano, which can be used as a beacon up to a certain point. But in the case of Moses, there was a very close interpersonal relationship between the "cloud" and Moses. However, a cloud hasn't changed in millions of years. A cloud in the times of the Neanderthal man, a cloud during the last Ice Age, and a cloud in the times of Moses are basically the same. Clouds are dark grey, black and sometimes they look blue. A cloud is a cloud in China or Nigeria.

The ancient people and Jews knew the difference in the natural landscape like rain, thunder and mountains. However, clouds don't talk, so if Moses said that an entity within a cloud gave him instructions, then it is not longer a cloud, it was a machine. Moreover, there wouldn't be a Jewish religion or state without either the cloud alone or

Moses alone, the two together made the Jewish religion. Furthermore, throughout human history there are events that describe cloud-like formations that talk, fly and give instructions especially in the so-called miracles. However, in the 20th and 21st centuries, thousands of people have seen UFOs disguised or camouflaged in a cloud-like appearance.

Sometimes a mist or fog surrounds the UFOs. In *Daniel 7*, "The son of man came with the *clouds* of heaven and came into the presence of God, and God gave him power and a glorious kingdom and all the people's of the Earth serve him."

In 1904 the crew of the British vessel, *The Mohican,* had a terrifying experience. A strange *grey cloud* appeared with *bright glowing* spots in the mass. It went straight to the ship and surrounded it. The ship was completely enveloped by the cloud and had a strange glow. The compasses were spinning wildly and some of the crew were praying on their knees. The captain said, "It was beyond me. I never saw anything so terrifying in the years I have been at sea." After the scare, the *cloud* went away.

On January 1996, a pilot was flying from the Bahamas to Miami. As he was approaching Bimini, a *cloud* came from nowhere and the compass in the plane started to spin and the RPM dropped drastically.

On April 23, 1976, a witness was quietly relaxing at home watching television when suddenly static interrupted the program. She went outside to find the cause of the disturbance and in amazement saw a "solid white cloud" with sharp edges hovering along the ground in her yard. The interesting thing is that the sky was cloudless. After it rose back up, she saw a nearby tree bent as if whipped by a great force. The *cloud* disappeared into the sky, joining two big lights and moving slowly north.

On January 6, 1958, the Brazilian Navy released a weather balloon that was being tracked from the ground. The sky was blue and clear and there was only one solitary *cloud* overhead. The commander of the ship was tracking the balloon when suddenly the signals from it began to diminish in intensity. The commander went outside to investigate and saw the balloon climbing to the *cloud*. Then a strange thing happened. The balloon seemed to be sucked toward the *cloud*. The balloon reappeared ten minutes later and resumed its rapid ascent, but without its instruments. They were never found. Soon after the balloon reappeared, a *silver object* left the *cloud*. The crew described it as a "silvery object, with a color like polished aluminum" coming slowly from behind the *cloud*.

In August 1991 over Chechnya in the former Soviet Republic, seven UFOs appeared and they were surrounded by a "bright greenish transparent cloud." The silent *cloud* had a perfect elliptical shape.

In 1992 Army radar were following the flight of a new fighter plane, an SU-27, when it suddenly vanished from the screens. The air defense reported a UFO and an intensive, month-long search was launched, but no trace of the plane was found.

In Russia in 1997, one thousand Krihnna members were performing a religious ceremony when suddenly a "pulsating oval cloud" with defined edges appeared in the sky.

On August 19, 1959, in Trenton, New Jersey, a witness saw an object like an elongated cigar, very bright and surrounded by a bluish green "haze" with orange in the center. The witness said that during the first 25 minutes of observation it made eight to ten right angle turns. Later five shining objects flew around the cigar, then all vanished. On October 17 and 27 of 1952, a witness reported seeing "a *cloud* of strange shape, like a cigar, with a plumed cylinder puffing out smoke."

On September 14, 1954, in the town of Vendee, France, a group of farmers watched a thick layer of what looked liked a "storm cloud" suddenly discharge a patch of blue-violet luminous "mist" in the shape of a "cigar or carrot." The luminous cloud appeared rigid and its movements had no connection with the movement of the clouds themselves. It seemed to be a giant machine surrounded by mist. It came down to an altitude of perhaps half a mile above the farmers, then quickly rose and disappeared.

On August 10, 1809, the scholar John Staneley wrote in the *Journal of Natural History and Philosophy* of what he saw in a thunderstorm: "I saw many meteors moving around the edge of a *black cloud* from which lightning flashed. They were like dazzling specks of light, dancing through the clouds. One particular light increased in size till it became of the brilliance of Venus on a clear evening. I saw these strange lights for at least an hour, and they played in and out of the *black cloud*. They also increased in size and then seemed to descended." In 1809, people had no idea of UFOs and they called them meteors.

On March 22, 1870, a captain of a ship witnessed a strange phenomenon. He wrote, "My crew reported a strange object in the sky. I saw it. It was a *cloud* of *circular* form, with an included semicircle divided into four parts and a central shaft running from the centre of the circle and extending far outward and curving backward. The thing was traveling against the wind. It came from the south and settled right into the wind's eye. It was visible for half an hour, much lower than other clouds."

On July 31, 1981, two tourists were going home in a motorboat in Finland. Suddenly a *black cloud* appeared in the sky not too far from them and it headed toward the boat. It looked like a ball of *fog* or *mist*. One of the witnesses felt paralyzed. The *black cloud* had *two glowing lights*.

On May 22, 1966, a group of scientists from England saw a *white cloud* that was close to the ground. The mass was approximately 100 feet across, moving very slowly and pulsating, expanding and contracting. A dark tube emerged from the cloud and started inspecting the snow on the ground. A normal or natural cloud doesn't have devices of any kind.

On February 9, 1988, a witness was walking in the countryside and saw a woman and her dog playing. Suddenly, her dog went crazy running over the road barking furiously at something. The witness followed the dog to a "yellow fog" about 45 feet in diameter and "glowing." It was producing a noise like "wind rushing." The mist was going in a whirling spiral, causing the leaves to rotate like a mini-tornado. The dog ran into the fog and disappeared. The witnesses said that there was a terrible smell, vile, horrible and sulphurous and an "eerie stillness." The witness felt an electrical tingling and her hair was standing, like with static electricity.

On April 1, 1964, a family was having a picnic in upstate New York. About 6:30 p.m. they saw a very large black formation approximately one mile long. A witness took his 6x25 binoculars and was shocked to see smoke coming out of the black "cloud." Suddenly, it changed from a horizontal position to a vertical position with more smoke coming out of the cloud. At the same time it took the form of a banana, then slowly blended with the clouds. The whole family watched this phenomenon with the naked eye. After three minutes, the witness's daughter said, "There is another one."

A horizontal pencil-shaped object moved from the left of the horizon to the right. There was a flash of *white light* from the rear of it, and it shot forward with speed. Suddenly it stopped and smoke emanated from it. Then it shot forward and backward. It hovered until it appeared as a *saucer* shape, then became completely round and slowly divided into two parts, one above the other. The top object slowly became smaller, and the second object headed down. At this point, the object divide again, but the second object took the pencil shape.

A most frightening event took place in the First World War in August of 1915 when troops saw six to eight large loaf-of-bread-shaped "clouds" of a light grey color. The soldiers commented that the breeze didn't move the "clouds" and that they looked like material or solid in structure. The strange "clouds" hovered around a dry creek bed. The One Fourth Norfolk Regiment were seen marching up the creek bed to reinforce the men on Hill 60. One of the large "clouds" hovered into the path of the marching troops. The soldiers in the trenches look on in amazement as the marching soldiers never came out of the "cloud." After the last of the Norfolk Regiment marched into the "cloud," the large grey "cloud-like loaf of bread, rose into the air" and rejoined the other "clouds." The soldiers in the trenches watched again in amazement as the clouds left against the wind.

Officially, the One Fourth Norfolk Regiment was listed as having been destroyed by the Turkish army, its men captured, killed or missing in action. Upon Turkey's surrender in 1918, the British demanded that the Turks return the regiment. Turkey denied having killed or taken prisoners from the regiment. The incident was witnessed by 22 men of No. 3 Section of the First Division Field Company. The few survivors signed an affidavit testifying about the mass kidnapping.

Moreover, there are other baffling disappearances on record, such as the 4,000 troops on a march through the Pyrenees in the Spanish War of Succession and the 650 colonial troops marching toward Saigon in 1858, who vanished on the way. In 1939, 2,988 troops stationed south of Nanking vanished, leaving their camp in perfect order with their rifles neatly stacked. In 1930, a Canadian Eskimo village was found completely deserted with half-cooked meals next to the fire, along with their precious possessions.

During the Second War World, a Navy blimp with two officers patrolling the San Francisco Harbor was sucked into a "cloud." The blimp reappeared without the two crewmen.

As I have shown, UFOs are disguised or camouflaged in clouds, mist, fog or very bright lights. However, the most bizarre UFO activity is in what are called "religious miracles." For many centuries there have been events on record where floating, hovering clouds produced "miracles." The same phenomenon is described by witnesses of UFOs in the 20th and 21st centuries.

For example, on December 9, 1531, in Mexico, a peasant name Juan Diego was walking through the countryside on his way to the church. Suddenly he heard beautiful music. He stopped to listen to make sure it was not his imagination, but the music was real, though beyond anything human. A choir of birds also was heard. Juan Diego was in shock. Suddenly a "glowing white cloud" appeared to him. His name was called from the "cloud." It was a woman's voice that said, "Juanito, Juan Dieguito." After that, a lady of overpowering *brilliance* appeared. This event changed the destiny of Mexico by converting the population to Catholicism and is called "The Miracle of Guadalupe."

In 1915 in Portugal, four girls were tending the sheep, when suddenly a strange "cloud" appeared. It was whiter than snow and *hovering*. Later, in 1917, it was called "The Miracle of Fatima".

On March 25, 1976, in Betania, Caracas, Venezuela, a seer named Maria Esperanza De Bianchini had a supernatural experience. She saw a large "cloud" that came out of nowhere and *hovered* over the top of a tree. The witness said that it was an immense cloud-like smoke and someone said, "Look, Maria, look at the smoke; the house is burning." So, Maria looked at the "cloud" and the "cloud" seemed to open and the Virgin appeared. Many witnesses saw something like a pulsating sun; a *mist* covered the area where the seer was. Also, a very brilliant light was seen and an invisible choir was heard singing.

In 1846 in the French Alps at La Salette, two shepherd children saw a light that whirled and seemed to turn on itself, rising to a height of a person. The children saw an oval face and hands inside the light. On May 15, 1345, a poor crippled shepherd was watching his flock. Suddenly, a spectacular light attracted his attention. Within it was a beautiful portrait of the Virgin and it was surrounded by a number of small clouds.

On April 25, 1467, in Genazzano, Latium, Italy, the people of the town were celebrating a religious festival. Suddenly they began to hear beautiful music. The crowd was looking at the sky when a "cloud" descended and destroyed a wall of a church. The crowd was amazed. Then the "cloud" rose and dissipated showing a portrait of the Madonna.

In this event the solid nature of the "cloud" is clear. A regular cloud wouldn't destroy the wall of the church. On September 14, 1920, when the Russian army was going to invade Warsaw, it was chased away by the image of the Virgin that appeared on the "clouds" over the city. In Polish military history, this event is known as the miracle at the Vistula. Truth or legend, it is in the books. When Mohammed was a young boy and was going on a trip, a "cloud" kept him company (see chapter about Mohammed).

We can no longer believed that these events are fantasy or daydreaming because the UFO phenomenon has materialized all our myths or legends. Why? Because what we call miracles and the supernatural are similar to the UFO phenomenon. I have no choice but to conclude that the UFO phenomenon is the source of religion and the supernatural.

On July 21, 1557, in Rapallo, Liguria, Italy, a peasant was on his way home. He stopped to take a break, when suddenly the Virgin appeared in a "cloud" to give him a message. On a summer day in 715 AD, a "dark cloud" spread over the sky and all the air seemed on fire.

The Gospels mention the Second Coming of Christ and say, "There will be signs in the Sun, the Moon, and the Stars, and on Earth nations will be in dismay, perplexed by the roaring of the Sea and the waves. People will be of fright in anticipation on what is coming upon the world. For the powers of the heavens will be shaken and they will see the Son of Man coming in a *cloud* with power and great glory." (*Luke 21:25-27*)

The question is what kind of cloud Christ will ride: the same "cloud" that spoke to Moses or the "clouds" that appeared in the so-called miracles or the "clouds" that disguise UFOs? Which Jesus will come? The Nordic type or the dark colored one seen in Africa or the baby seen carried by the Virgin? The truth is that we don't know.

Further, if the UFO phenomenon had never reappeared in the 19th, 20th and 21st centuries, every supernatural phenomenon would be said to have been caused by God because He only would be the explanation for the phenomena in nature that we don't understand. However, as the UFO phenomenon shows, there is an alien civilization involved in human affairs, through religion and what is called the supernatural.

As recently as February 2005, new developments in quantum physics have led to the conclusion that magnetic fields on a microchip can produce small and compact *clouds* of atoms called Bose-Einstein condensates. The chips can be used in very precise sensors for airplanes and in quantum computing. The scientists believe that ultra-cold atoms levitate in the magnetic field. A microchip can hold and control a *cloud of atoms* suspended near the surface, creating magnetic fields.

Microchips from computers contain thousands of microscopy wires and currents flowing through the wires producing magnetic fields. Interestingly, the "clouds" hiding the UFOs have been known to produce electromagnetic effects on compasses, radar, televisions, cars and any mechanical device. As we see in this discovery, it is a matter of time before we know the origin of the UFO phenomenon.

CHAPTER 17

THE UFO PHENOMENON AND THE BIRTH
OF THE CHRISTIAN RELIGION

*"I must insist upon full access to discs recovered…The
Army grabbed one and would not let us have it for
cursory examination."*

—J. Edgar Hoover, FBI Director, 1947

The birth of the Christian religion was a major
event in human history, perhaps bigger then the birth
of the Jewish religion. Christianity caused an expansion
of consciousness and culture. Imagine a world without
Christianity. If there weren't Christianity we would have
to invent it. The melancholy and joy of listening to Bing
Crosby sing "White Christmas" make us feel the infinity
of the human spirit. In the First World War, the British
and Germans stopped fighting to celebrate Christmas.

What would culture be without Christianity? Since
the time of Constantine up to the 19th century, art has
been inspired by the Christian religion. Miguel Angel,
Leonard De Vinci, and Tizziano were all part of the
cultural "reawakening" of the human race called "The
Renaissance" following the "Dark Ages." Christianity kept
humanity in complete ignorance for approximately 700
years. Milton, Dante, Donatello, and Raphael also owed
their art to the inspiration provided by Christianity. The

most important beliefs of western civilization came from Christianity, like the idea of God, immortality and sin.

The so-called spiritual life of Western man is none other than the dogmas taught by the Christian religion since childhood. The *Gospels* were written 80 to 150 years after Jesus, and they contradict each other. For example, *Mark* and *John* don't mention the birth of Jesus from a virgin and this is not a Hebrew cultural tradition. The idea came from the Greeks and Romans. Many heroes like Plato, Alexander, Pitagoras and Julius Caesar were thought to have been born from a virgin.

The *Gospel of Mark* says that the Spirit descended to Jesus after his baptism. The *Gospels* preserved fragments of Jesus' discourses, but their selection and interpretation were arbitrary. The *Synoptic Gospels* do not make Jesus the creator of a new religion. According to these *Gospels*, Jesus never made claims of divinity. He taught that any human being could go to heaven through repentance and righteousness. However, the Catholic Church then came and made Jesus equal to God and made salvation possible only through Jesus. Although Jesus did not baptize or prescribed baptism as essential, the Catholic Church made the sacraments necessary for salvation after the mystery cults of the time. The four *Gospels* that survived probably were part of a bigger number that were lost in the first two centuries.

There are differing descriptions of Jesus in *Matthew, Mark, Luke* and *John*. The English term "Gospel" means "good news" and came from the Greek "evangelion" which means "glad tidings" that the messiah had come. The oldest extant of the Gospels go back to the third century. The original compositions probably were written between 60 and 120 AD. The original *Gospels* were exposed to two centuries of errors in transcription and to possible alterations historians called "pious lies" to suit the theology and special interests of the times.

Christian writers before AD quote the *Old Testament*. The only reference to a Christian *Gospel* before AD 150 is from Papias about AD 135. He mentions somebody named "John the Elder." He also said that Mark had composed the *Gospel* from memories from Peter. Papias added that Matthew transcribed the *Logia*, apparently an early Aramaic collection of the saying of Jesus. *Matthew* and *Luke* mention the birth of Jesus, when Herodes was King of Judea before 3 BC. *Luke* describes Jesus as being about 30 years old when John baptized him in the fifteenth year of Tiberius, AD 28-29. Probably Jesus was born in the years 2 to 1 BC, though we don't have an exact day of his birth. Clement of Alexandria mentions different opinions on the subject. Some claim Jesus was born on April 19, May 20, or November 17 BC.

Since the second century, Eastern Christians have celebrated the Nativity on January 6. In 354, Western churches, including the Roman, commemorated the birth of Jesus on December 25, the same day as the pagan tradition marking the winter solstice and which also was holy to Mithra, the rival savior of Jesus. *Matthew* and *Luke* place the birth of Jesus in Bethlehem about five miles south of Jerusalem. *Mark* has no mention of Bethlehem. Jesus' name was "Yeshua" meaning "The help of Yahweh." The Greeks made his name into "Lesous" and the Romans into "Jesus." His brothers were James, Simon and Judas.

The earliest non-Christian reference to Jesus came from the Jewish historian, Josephus, in a book named

Antiquities of the Jews. He said, "At that time lived Jesus, a holy man he may be called, for he performed wonderful works and taught men, and joyfully received the truth. And he was followed by many Jews and Greeks. He was the messiah."

The oldest known mention of Jesus in pagan literature is in a letter of Pliny the Younger asking the advice of Trajan on the treatment of Christians. Five years later Tacitus described Nero's persecution of the Christians in Rome. The historian Suetonios mentions the same persecution. He also reported Claudios' banishment of the Jews who under the leadership of Jesus were causing public disturbances. Scholars agree that the passage is similar to a passage in the *Bible* which mentions a decree of Claudios that "The Jews should leave Rome."

Scholars believe the Christian evidence for the existence of Jesus began with the letters attributed to Saul. Although some of the writings are of uncertain authorship, scholars believe that Paul existed and met with James and Peter and these two men had known Jesus. John the Baptist was a great influence on Jesus' faith. John was the son of Mary's cousin, Elizabeth. When John was imprisoned and beheaded, his followers were looking for another leader and Jesus was in the right place at the right time to take his place. Some thought that Jesus was John raised from dead.

Jesus could not perform miracles in Nazareth. Apparently the people didn't believed in his supernatural powers. Jesus never thought of himself as a messiah in changing the world and the social injustices of the poor. His moral preaching was already 100 years old among the

Jews. In *Exodus*, Leviticus, Hosea and Hillel were already teaching those principles.

Jesus only preached to Jews in Jewish cities. When a woman asked Jesus to help her daughter, Jesus said, "I was sent only to the lost sheep of Israel." It was Saul and the Catholic Church that expand the religion. Jesus said, "Go not into the way of the gentiles nor into the city of the Samaritans." After Jesus' death, the apostles hesitated to bring the good news to the rest of the world. Jesus attributed his unusual powers to the faith of the people he healed. He said, "A prophet is not without honor, save his own country and his own house." On one occasion Jesus revived the daughter of Jairus. She seemed dead, but Jesus said that the girl was not dead, but sleeping. In calling upon her to awake, he used a strong command, "Little girl, get up."

During and around the time of Jesus, there were many prophets. One in particular filled the requirements of a "saviour." He was Apollonius of Tyana. The legend said that he performed miracles, like raising a girl from dead and casting out devils. He taught about the existence of a Supreme Being and taught that the highest good is "love." His piety was so great that people thought that he was the "Son of God" and when he died, his followers claimed that he went in bodily form to heaven. He lived before Jesus and many historians believe that Christianity based the story of Jesus on the life of Apollonius of Tyana.

A Persian legend told of how a great prophet appeared many hundreds of years before Jesus, and his people called him Zarathustra and the Greeks called him Zoroastres. Out of love for wisdom, he decided to withdraw from the world and went to live in a mountain wilderness, living on fruit. The legend also said that he laughed aloud on the day of his birth and the evil spirits that gather around the birth of every person ran away in terror. He was tempted by the devil, and his breast was pierced by a sword, like Jesus. He did not complain and kept his faith for his God Ahura Mazda, which means "The lord of light." Ahura Mazda appeared to Zoroastres.

The legend said that for a long time, the world ridiculed him. Then a prince of Iran, whose name was Vishtaspa, helped him to spread the faith. There were 20 variations of Christianity by the second century AD, and at least 80 variations of Christianity by the fourth century. The competition of Christians, both among themselves and against the "mysteries religions," was fierce.

The greatest rival of the Catholic Church was the mystery religion called "Mithraism," which was similar to Christianity. Cult followers formed secret societies and called themselves "brothers." They admitted the poor to their ranks. They also performed the rites of baptism and communion and celebrated a festival for Mithra, their savior-God, on December 25. Christianity took over the day and made it the birth of Jesus. The ethics of Mithraism stressed continence and abstinence. Their dead were resurrected to go to heaven or hell; their god Mithras had made a sacrifice, which saved the human race. He was the mediator between a Supreme Being and humankind.

The idea of a savior was similar to a Greek idea called Tritos Soter. The idea of the last judgement and immortality came from ancient Egypt. The idea of God as the maker of heaven and Earth came from Babylonia. The idea of the dualism of Satan and God came from Persia. The idea of the resurrection drama came from Syria from the drama of Adonis. The worship of the Great Mother came from Phrygia. The idea of Universal Law came from Greece and Rome. The Jewish esoteric revelation of the coming kingdom and their god Yahweh enriched Christianity. Rituals like mass, incense, beads, holy water and chanting were taken from the various mystery religions.

Paul invented the idea of sin, which was not in Jewish theology and rescued the idea of Christianity from oblivion. Otherwise, Christianity would have succumbed to Mithraism, Zoroastrismo or any mystery religion of those times. However, the visions of Saul of Tarsus and Constantine made it possible for Christianity to survive and be propagated in the ancient world.

Let's start with Saul of Tarsus. Who was he? All the information we have comes from the *Bible*. Saul of Tarsus was born in the tribe of Benjamin between 15 and 5 BC, and was a citizen of Rome. He studied under the famous Jewish Rabbi Gamaliel. Saul was a tent-maker by trade. He became a rigid Pharisee and a persecutor of Christians. In *Acts 22*, Saul says, "I am a true born Jew, a native of Tarsus in Cillicia. I was brought up in this city, and as a pupil of Gamaliel. I was thoroughly trained in every point of our ancestral law. I have always been ardent in God's service as you all are today, and so I began to persecute this movement to the death, arresting its followers, men and women alike, and putting them in chains. For this I have as witnesses the high priest and the whole council of Elders. I was given letters from them to our fellow Jews at Damascus and had started out to bring the Christians there, to Jerusalem, as prisoners for punishment."

Saul of Tarsus was very radical in his religious beliefs. He was also one of the main conspirators in the stoning to death of the apostle Stephen, one of the earliest followers of Jesus. In *Acts 8:1,3,* it says, "And Saul was among those who approved of his murder...Saul harrying the church; he entered house after house, seizing men and women and sending them to prison."

It is clear that Saul was an enemy of the Christians. He thought that they were wrong in their religious beliefs. However, Saul's life changed suddenly while walking to Damascus. His conversion to Christianity was not a slow development based on belief and faith. On the contrary it was a shocking and physically painful event. In other words, he was forced to believe in the Christian religion. In modern times it would be like seeing Hitler changing to the Americans or French sides in World War II.

The *Bible* has three accounts of the event in the *Book of Acts* in Chapters 9, 22 and 26. In essence, the accounts are the same in their references to the flash of light and the voice that Paul heard. There is a fourth account in the first chapter of *Galatians.* The first account in *Acts 9:1-31* said, "While still on the road and nearing Damascus, suddenly a light flashed from the sky all around him. He fell to the ground and heard a voice saying 'Saul, Saul, why do you persecute me?' Saul answered, 'Tell me, Lord, who are you?' The voice answered, 'I am Jesus whom you are persecuting, but get up and go into the city, and you will be told what you have to do.'"

The men traveling with Saul were in shock and speechless because they heard the voice and saw no one. Saul got up from the ground, but when he opened his eyes, he could not see. So his companions led him by the hand and brought him to Damascus. Saul was blind for three days and couldn't eat or drink. In Damascus he was visited by Ananias, who cured his blindness and converted him to Christianity. Moreover, after the transcendental and out-of-this-world experience, he tried to explain to King Agrippa and said, "At midday, Oh King, I saw on the way, a light from heaven brighter than the Sun, shining round me and we had all fallen to the ground, I heard a voice saying to me in the Hebrew language. 'Saul, Saul, why do you persecute me?'" *(Acts 26:13,14)*

Historians believe that Saul's event was only an illusion or that Saul was simple an epileptic or a plain crackpot. Historians don't seem to consider the conversion of Saul worth writing about. However, as in the case of Moses, Saul of Tarsus knew the difference between the features of the natural landscape. Now if the light had been a thunder bolt, it would have killed him, and no voice would have been heard.

Another possibility is that God used a technology that was achievable to humankind after 2,000 years. Nevertheless, a technology like that would look "magical" or "divine" up to the 19th century. However, for men in the 20th and 21st century, a light like that wouldn't look miraculous because we have a similar technology. We know that light is a form of electromagnetic radiation that acts upon the retina of the eye, making sight possible. A normal light will make contact with the eyes with little force of impact. In the case of Saul, the light had such a force that he was blind for three days. Lightning is a discharge of atmospheric electricity and that would have burned Saul, and that was not the case.

So what type of light hit Saul that blinded him? Interestingly, the same experience has been happening to men in the 20th and 21st century and all through history, only with different names. In the space age, it is called "UFOs" and in past times it was called "miracles." For example, on October 21, 1957, two middle-aged couples were on a boat when they saw a luminous object hovering about 20 feet above the sea. It appeared to be revolving and the witnesses said that there were two human-like figures standing outside the object. Suddenly, one of the figures shone a very *bright light* on the boat. The witnesses said that it was so powerful that they were *dazzled* and felt weak, then the figures and UFO disappeared.

In another incident in 1957 a man walked into the police station in Nebraska, claiming that while inspecting grain at his farm, he had found something that looked like a wrecked balloon. While walking to the object, he was paralyzed by a *beam of light*. Two entities from the UFO searched for weapons and then invited him on board where five entities assured him that they meant no harm. The entities didn't say where they came from, but they did say they would announce their presence in the future. The entities and the UFO disappeared in a *flash of light*.

On May 8, 1980, a witness in Nicaragua went fishing. He said that as he started to walk back home, "I saw a lightning flash. I thought and said to myself, 'It is going to rain.' But I became filled with wonder because I did not see from where the *lightening* had come. I stopped, but I could see nothing, no signs of rain. I saw another lightning flash, but that was to open my vision and she presented herself. I saw that she blinked, that she was beautiful. There was a *cloud* that was extremely white. It

radiated in all directions, *rays of light*." In this example we
see the same pattern: a cloud, lights, rays and a very white
light—the same pattern seen in the UFO phenomenon.

On December 12, 1957, a witness was driving along a
highway to her home in Ithaca, New York, with her five-
year-old son in the backseat. About 7:00 p.m., the witness
suddenly saw a red light that appeared to be following her.
She looked through the window of the car, and found
that it was not a police car, but a weird, flying object.
Suddenly, the witness had no control of her car and her
son seemed motionless, as though in a trance. The witness
yelled to her son to brace himself, but he couldn't hear.
After a white beam of light flashed down from the UFO,
the witness heard *voices* that sounded weird, broken and
jerky.

The witness became hysterical, but her son didn't
notice her cries. The radio was off, but the voices told her
that her friend had been in an accident. The next day, the
witness found out that her friend *had* been involved in
an accident.

On April 3, 1965, two salesmen were driving home
when they saw something in the sky that looked like an
infrared lamp that *shown a ray of light* in the car. The UFO
descended right above the car, which started to shake.
Its lights went out and *a ray of light* came down. The
UFO set down in front of the car, and two entities that
looked like robots came out and began moving toward the
car. One of the men had a rifle and shot at the entities.
Suddenly, there was a terrible explosion and the two men
were temporarily *blinded*, but they heard no sound. It was
10 to 15 minutes before they could see again. However,

the UFO and the two entities were gone, with no signs of ever having been there.

On another occasion, a witness was watching television about nine o'clock in the evening, when all of a sudden a *bright light flashed* through the window and the electrical power in the house failed. The witness went outside the house to see the cause of the problem and about 50 feet away was a basket-ball sized *light* hovering just about the ground. He tried to walk toward it, but could not move. He felt a tingling sensation through his body and watched dumbfounded as the light rose and disappeared, leaving an odor like sulphur or burned rubber in the air.

On February 28, 1975, a witness was driving from Montbard to Paris and encountered a gray metallic UFO, which ejected rays causing him temporary paralysis. On December, 1972, in Pulkinnan, Finland, two young women in their twenties witnessed a UFO shaped like an egg. Suddenly a red light beam struck them, and both were paralyzed from head to toe. The two witnesses were unable to hear, scream or breathe, and only after a great struggle were they able to run away.

On May 10, 1975, a witness in Kentucky went outside his house between 9:00 and 10:00 p.m. to look for his dog. He saw an object shaped like a manta ray about 21 feet long and 10 feet wide and 20 feet high, hovering in the garden. Interestingly, the witness heard a buzzing like a *swarm of bees*, the same sound heard by the children at the miracle of Fatima. The witness said that a *light beam* came out of the UFO. The beam was a dark green, maybe olive green, and it went in and out of the bushes in the neighbor's yard. Then the light beam hit the witness, who reported, "When it hit me, it was like being hit by a bucket of cold water. I felt suddenly frozen. I couldn't move." The witness saw that the beam that emanated from the UFO was four or five inches in diameter when he first saw it. The light beam slowly spread in diameter to about four or five feet when it came toward him. The witness said that he was completely conscious through this frozen state. He tried to run, but was unable to move his muscles or blink his eyes. "It was as though I were molded in plaster. I didn't blank out, but in my mind were some strange thoughts. They were thoughts being put there. When the UFO and beam disappeared, I felt flat on my face." This example is a remarkably similarity with Saul of Tarso's experience.

Another witness was returning home when he saw an oval-shaped UFO hovering in the top of some trees. The large red object was so bright that it illuminated the road. The witness wanted to run or scream, but suddenly a big tube came out of the bottom and a *beam of light* shot out. The witness turned away as the beam hit the upper part of his arm, knocking him to the ground. His jacket caught fire and he rolled on the ground screaming with fright

In 538 BC, Daniel was on the banks of the Tigris River, near Babylonia, and saw a marvelous apparition. He reported, "On the twenty-fourth day of the first month, I found myself on the banks of that great river that is the Tigris; I looked up and saw a man clothed in linen, with a belt of gold round his waist. His body gleamed like topaz, his face shone like lightning. His eyes flamed like torches, his arms and feet sparkled like a disc of bronze and when he spoke, his voice sounded like a multitude." We see in this event Daniel's struggle trying to explain the vision.

About 12:30 p.m. on November 20, 1952, George Adamski watched a UFO land in the California desert. Out of the UFO came an entity with skin colored suntan, gray green eyes and long sandy hair. He was wearing a chocolate-brown one-piece suit with a gold-brown waistband. Adamski described the alien as handsome. We have here two visions. In the first one, Daniel thought the entity was a God and in the second, Adamski thought that it was an alien. Two men from different historical eras give different descriptions of the same phenomenon, reflecting their stage of industrial, technological, religious and cultural development.

After Paul rescued Christianity from oblivion, it would have taken a long time to become an official religion of the Roman Empire if not for Constantine's official support. It was the vision of Constantine that made it possible for Christianity to expand to the known world. The expansion of Christianity was made with the brute force of the sword and flames.

Constantine the Great was born on February 27, in the year 273 in Naissus, Upper Moesia. Unfortunately his place and date of birth are still a cause of polemics. His father was Constantius I Clorus and his mother's name was Hellena. Constantine's father came from a poor family. He was the son of a shepherd and a freedman's daughter. He joined the army and became an officer. Constantine's mother, Helena, may not have been married to Constantius I Clorus. In the year 293, Constantine married a politically connected lady named Flavia Maximiana, the stepdaughter of Maximian, and she gave him six children.

Constantine was a great commander and was the Augustus of the West and Maxentius ruled in Italy and North Africa. His military glory was proclaimed on many coins. He fought civil and foreign wars, incorporating the barbarians into the army and later giving them important government positions. Constantine wore long shoulder length hair like Alexander the Great. He covered himself with bracelets and other jewelry and wore elaborate robes with flowery designs.

He made an important innovation in his government, creating a new order of imperial companions called "comites," which were formed mostly by senators. The essential feature of the comites was that the only allegiance of this new hereditary "aristocracy of service" was to Constantine, which created the conditions for feudalism to emerge. Constantine gave huge payments in gold to the barbarian arm and his policies favored the landowners. He created a policy of binding the peasants to the soil, making it illegal for them to live in their own houses, making them hereditary, like military service. The peasants were never allowed to leave the state. If they ran away and were recaptured, they were punished severely. Peasants were treated like slaves and put in chains.

In Constantine's time, there was corruption at every level. He was a great leader and administrator who inspired his army's loyalty because he was very personal with them. In 325, he presided over the Council of Nicaea at which the church gave an edict stating that women had no souls. Some historians claim he was responsible for the murder of many friends. He killed his friend, the pagan philosopher Sopater, on the pretext that he had changed the wind to another direction and prevented food from arriving at famine stricken Constantinople.

Constantine was a very superstitious man. He executed his eldest son Flavius Julius Crispus, and followed that by executing his second wife, Flavia Maxima Fausta. She was not the mother of Crispus. His mother had been Minervina who gave birth to him in 305. It is disputed whether she was Constantine's wife or concubine. Fausta bore three sons to Constantine. He tried to banish adultery and magic, and was rather obsessed with anything sexual. He killed his wife Fausta by immersing her in a scalding bath, boiling her to death because he suspected that she was committing adultery with a slave in the imperial stables.

Constantine died in 337. His greatest achievement was the conversion of the Roman Empire into Christianity. He created the new capital of Constantinople on the site of Byzantium, which became the capital of the Eastern Roman Empire and later the capital of the Byzantine Empire. During the time of Constantine, the Christians were very well organized. However, it was Constantine's vision that made it possible for Christianity to become the religion of the Empire.

Although many historians believed that Constantine's vision was only the delusion of a crackpot, like in the case of Saul of Tarsus or Moses, the great Christian historian Eusebios wrote, "Constantine prayed to god. He asked him and besought him to say who he was and to stretch forth a hand to him in his present situation. As he prayed in this fashion and as he earnestly gave voice to his entreaties, a most marvelous sign appeared to the emperor from God. It would have been hard to believe if anyone else had spoken of it. But a long time later the triumphant emperor himself described it to the writer of this work. This was when I had the honour of knowing him and of being in his company. When he told me the story, he swore to its truth and who could refuse to believed it, especially when later evidence showed it to have been genuine."

Eusebios continued, "Around noon time when the day was already beginning to decline, he saw before him in the *sky* the sign of a *cross of light.* He said it was above the Sun and it bore the inscription 'Conquer with this.' The vision astounded him as it astounded the whole army, which was with him on this expedition, which also beheld the miraculous event. He became disturbed, asking himself what the vision meant. Suddenly, when he was asleep the Christ of God appeared to him, and he brought with him the sign which had appeared in the sky. He ordered Constantine to make a replica of this sign, and he was to use it as a protection during his encounters with the enemy."

The next morning Constantine told his friends of this extraordinary event, then got together all the people who worked with gold or precious stones. He sat among them and explained the appearance of the sign and made one of gold and precious stones. After this event Constantine resolved to worship only the Christian god, who had been revealed to him.

The battle of the Milvian Bridge was the decisive event between the new religion of Christianity and paganism, because Maxentious was the pagan general. After this victory, Constantine made the Christian religion the official religion of the Roman Empire and brought unity to the empire. Galerius at Serdina issued an edict revoking the persecution of the Christians. In every city of the empire, decrees were published in the name of Constantine that said, "Among the other things which have been ordained for the public advantage and profit. We formerly wished to restore everything to conformity with the ancient laws and discipline of the Romans, and to provided that the Christians also, who have forsaken the religion of their ancestors, should return to a good disposition. For in such way such arrogance had seized them and such stupidity had overtaken them. When we had issued this decree that they should return to the institutions established by the ancients, a great many submitted under danger, but a great many, being harassed, endure all sorts of death and since many continue in the same folly and we perceive that they neither offer to the heavenly gods the worship which is due, nor pay regards to the god of the Christians. In consideration of our philanthropy and our invariable custom, by which we are wont to extend pardon to all."

As we see, the Roman Empire had not succeeded in suppressing the Christian sects and some of them had won admiration by their courageous martyrdom. The persecutions of Christians were called off and the Christian religion accepted. However, the question is whether the vision of Constantine was real or an invention. Historians like Edward Gibbon were skeptical about the vision. I believe the vision of Constantine was true for two reasons: First, the phenomenon of the glowing cross had been seen before and in the time of Constantine. In the 20th and 21st centuries there have been reports of this phenomenon, but now they are called UFOs. Second, the emblem with the words that Jesus told Constantine to make is another phenomenon that has been happening all along since the times of Constantine and called a miracle.

In the 19th century on July 18, 1830, St. Catherine Laboure was awakened from sleep by an angel who appeared as a child of five, all radiant with light, and conducted her into the chapel. She was met there by the Virgin, who sat on the chair reserved for the director of the Sisters. Catherine was permitted to rest her hands on the knees of the Virgin. In a second apparition, the Virgin held close to her heart a small globe. Her hand was covered with rings from which beautiful rays of light came out. Slowly there appeared around the Virgin an oval frame on which brilliant letters appeared that said, "O, Mary conceived without sin, pray for us who have recourse to thee." At the same time, a voice said, "Have a medal struck from this model." A medal was made and peregrines around the world were buying the medal for healing purposes. In this case, the similarity of Constantine's experience and St. Catherine's miracle is very clear.

Now in the case of the flying, glowing cross, there are hundreds of sightings throughout history and they are called different names. We call them UFOs. If Constantine said that it was a flying lighted cross, it must be true since from before Jesus up to the 20th and 21st century, the form of the cross hasn't changed. For example, a luminous *cross* was seen in 1188 between Gisors and Neautles-Saint Martin. A cross carved in stone still marks the spot of the apparition. On November 6, 1954, a writer and diplomat in Rome saw a UFO in the form of a flying cross. He said that about eleven o'clock the morning, he noticed in the sky a formation of UFOs very high, like little white dots. Fascinated by the spectacle, he ascended to the terrace of the house to see better. Other UFOs started arriving, and there were so many after half an hour, the witness calculated at least 50 over the sky in Rome. The crucial moment of the sighting came when two perfect V formations of 20 UFOs steering one to the other from opposite directions met joining at the apexes of the Vs and forming a perfect *Greek cross.* According to the estimates of witnesses, the cross was over Vatican City.

In October 5, 1097, a comet in the form of a *cross* appeared for 15 days. In 1118, a *cross* and a moon shining white appeared in the sky at noon in England when King Richard Coeur de Lion and Phillip of France were preparing to make war on Saladin, emperor of the Saracens. In the years 1156 and 1161, *crosses* were seen in the moon in England and France. On August 9, 1186, in the village of Dunstable in England, the sky suddenly opened and the laity and clergy of the abbey saw a *cross* very long and of a great size. And there appeared on it, Jesus fastened with nails, and blood flowed, but not to Earth. In the year 1218 at Koln, Munster in Germany and at Lyden in Holland, *three crosses* appeared in the air. They were white, and the figure of a man with uplifted arms nailed at the hands and feet was hanging on them. In the year 1554, two red *crosses* were seen in the sky at Nebra, Thuringia. In 1478, *crosses* flying at terrific speed fell from the sky to the ground in Switzerland. In the years 1501 to 1503, very numerous *flying crosses* were seen all over Europe for 26 days. In 1269, a strange brightness shaped like a *cross* gave light from high in the air and shone down in the city of Krakow in Poland. In 1528, the city of Utrecht in Holland was under siege when the strange sight of a Burgundian *cross*, yellow in color, appeared high in the sky and terrified the soldiers.

On October 24, 1967, in the city of Hatherleigh, Devon, England, two police officers, Roger Willey and Clifford Waycott, were on their routine night patrol when they suddenly saw a group of bright lights in the shape of a large *cross pulsating* in the sky ahead of them. The officers drove towards it, but it moved silently away. The police officers went after the phenomenon, but the crosses accelerate away from them across the field and the police gave up the chase.

At the same time, *flying crosses* were seen in different parts of the United States, beginning on August 27, 1972, at Faith Baptist Church in Los Angeles. It was after 4:00 p.m. as everyone was leaving following choir rehearsal that one of the members saw a *glowing cross*. One witness described it as "a great gleaming golden cross shining in the window." Some people asked why the cross appeared in the window, which had been there for years and no cross had ever appeared before.

Two weeks later, a *cross* illuminated the window of the First Born Holiness Church in Apalachicola, Florida. It appeared for several days and hundreds of people saw it. The people asked why this refraction took so long to occur and why two weeks after the Los Angeles case.

The Florida case was on September 12. On September 2 and then a week later, glowing *crosses* appeared in two more churches in Florida, at a United Methodist Church in Mexico City, and at St. John's Baptist Church in Panama City. Three more cases appeared in Florida the following month. The most sensational case was at Paxton Revival Center in Jacksonville. The cross was seen shining through a window by two parishioners and later by crowds. Photographers and newsmen took Polaroid pictures and when they were developed, there was Jesus with his hands showing spikes. The phenomenon was seen in other churches of different denominations, like The Seventh-Day Adventist, Methodist and Church of God House of Worship. In Georgia the flaming cross appeared in seven churches.

In New York—more exactly in the Bronx—the cross started to materialize at Number One, 835 Trinity Avenue. Interestingly, the flaming cross appeared right after the main witness mentioned the Georgia case. There were also cases in California. In the 1970s, there was a wave of UFO phenomenon in the United States and the world along with the beginning of such phenomena as cattle mutilations, abductions in the Bermuda Triangle, Crop Circles, massive electrical blackouts, and abductions.

CHAPTER 18

THE UFO PHENOMENON AND THE BIRTH
OF THE MOSLEM RELIGION

"I saw the object coming at me. It went straight over my head, stopped in mid-air and backed right up. It then started zigzagging from left to right. It was so bright, I couldn't make out any of its features."

— Sgt. Ben Thomson, Police Officer, Waneque Reservoir, New Jersey, October12, 1966.

Arabia is the world's largest peninsula. Attached through Israel to Egypt and through Syria to Turkey, it has been the homeland of Bedouins and Quarish Arabs. Religion in Arabia before Mohammed was like the rest of the Middle East at that time. The prevailing religious belief was animism, called polydaemonism; that is, the worship of spiritual beings like the jinns or spirits that were in rocks, streams and air. It was totemist.

Mecca was a religious center before Mohammed. Here was the building called Kaaba, which means "cube," where hundreds of idols were kept. In a corner of Kaaba, there is a stone believed to have fallen from heaven (a meteorite). The legend said that in the beginning the stone was white, but because of the kissing of sinful man, the stone turned to black. The tradition also said that Adam had built the original stone, but it was destroyed by the Great Flood and was rebuilt by Abraham and his son Ishmael. Another story said that the angel Gabriel brought the stone.

The religion of Islam is the offspring of Judaism and Christianity. Some scholars believe that the Islamic religion was a heretic form of the Jewish-Christian religion. However, most of the population in Arabia remained attached to their ancient practices on the level of primitive animism, which is the normal psychological-anthropological stage in human historical evolution. The vast majority of these cults survived and fought against Mohammed's religious innovations.

The principles of the religion of Islam were borrowed from Christian and Jewish legends and traditions. In the eyes of medieval writers, Islam was not a pagan religion, it was a Christian heresy. John Damascene in the eighth century compared it with previous heretical movements and Dante regarded Mohammed as heretic. Scholars believe that Islam is a revival of Aramaic monotheism and Christianity. The one definite Arabian institution is the pilgrimage to Mecca. The religion of Islam raised Arabian and non-Arabian traditions to the level of the earlier prophets of Israel.

The Arabs are Semites, including the Jews, Babylonians and Assyrians. In Arabia, the Jews introduced handcrafting, goldsmithing, art, and the date palm. They also founded Medina. The Jews helped the Quarish convert their villages into cities, giving Medina a cosmopolitan air. The Jews, in gratitude for the hospitality, joined the Arabs in fighting the Christians who came to plunder and to proselytize.

As we see, the stage was set for a new religion, the nature worship of the Arabs, the salvation doctrine of the

Christians and the monotheism of the Jews. However, it was Mohammed who was the creator of the religion of Islam, for without his vision, it would never have been possible for Arabs to supercede the stage of polydaemonism which they were in.

Mohammed was born in the city of Mecca, approximately in 570 and died in 632. His father's name was Abdullah and he was a merchant. His mother's name was Amina. When Mohammed was a boy, his father fell sick on one of his trips and died, and his mother soon died also. A foster mother named Halina took care of him and handed him over to his grandfather, Abdal-Mutallib, who was happy to have his grandson. The grandfather was very wealthy, but sadly within two years he also died. Mohammed had to work as a shepherd because he didn't know how to write or read.

The name Mohammed in Arabic derives from the root Hamada, which means "to praise." However, when Mohammed was 25 years old, he met a 40-year-old wealthy woman name Khadija. She was very rich and put Mohammed in charge of her affairs. They got married and had six children, including two boys who died in infancy. The death of Khadija greatly affected Mohammed, as she was his true love. Mohammed then got a harem of 12 women ranging in age from 7 to 21 years old. The four daughters of Mohammed grew up and got married.

Before I explain the visions of Mohammed, I want to briefly mention the *Koran*, which has stories that appear in what Christians call Apocryphal literature. Jesus appears in 93 verses scattered in 15 Suras. For example, the *Koran* mentions that as a youth Jesus fashioned a bird of clay and breathed into it and it became alive. He also cured a leper and a man born blind. He raised the dead and created a table with food descended from heaven for his apostles. The regular *Bible* doesn't mention these events because they are hard to explain.

The *Koran* includes the *Old Testament,* which traces back to Syrian Christianity. They also adopt some Jewish practices such as Ashura, fasting on the tenth day of the first month, corresponding to the Day of Atonement, and the institution of a mid-day prayer. The word Islam means submitting oneself to God. The meaning is that "there is one God and Mohammed is his apostle." Mohammed is the last prophet and the *Koran* is the final revelation of the divine will.

However, there are differences between the *Bible* and the *Koran.* For example the Moses of the *Bible* and the Moses of the *Koran* are different. The idea that Moses died in the Jordan is not mentioned in the *Koran.* In the *Bible,* the sole objective of Moses is to get to the Promised Land. In the *Koran*, the Promised Land is not a factor. Islamic tradition regards Mary and Jesus as the only two human beings born without the evil touch that makes newborn babies cry. (I don't understand this superstition.) Also, in the Islamic tradition, Mary is among the most beautiful women along with Khadija, Fatima and Asiya. The *Koran* is approximately the size of the *New Testament.* It is divided in 114 chapters called Suras.

When researching the life of Mohammed, I was shocked to discover that a cloud like the ones described in the chapters about the Jewish and Christian religions was also present in his life. The legend says that when Mohammed was 12 years old, he was on a trip with his Uncle Abu Talib near the city of Bostra. The Meccan caravan always stopped near a monastery where Christian monks lived liked hermits. When one monk died, another took his place. One of the monks, Bahira, had old manuscripts. In one of them, it mentioned the coming of the prophet of the Arabs.

The legend said that Bahira had seen caravans before, but this one was special because there was a small hanging "cloud" that moved slowly above their heads between the sun and the two travelers. The monk was fascinated and amazed when the cloud suddenly stopped and remained stationary over a tree. (Curiously, UFOs love to hang out in and around trees). The two travelers sat under the tree and took a rest, and something magical happened. The tree lowered its branches so Mohammed and his uncle were covered by the shade. The monk asked Mohammed to show him his back between the shoulders to look for the mark that the manuscripts mentioned as proof that he was the last prophet, and he found the mark.

The visions of Mohammed created the Islam religion. Mohammed went to meditate in a cave on Mount Hira about nine miles north of Mecca. He spent days and nights engaged in prayer and meditation, going without food or drink. One day he saw on the horizon a tremendous figure like a man, but so much bigger and more beautiful than any man ever seen. The figure started moving toward him and he saw that it was an entity holding in his hand a silken cloth on which there appeared to be writing.

The entity said, "Read."

Mohammed answered, "But I can't."

Again the entity said, "Read."

Mohammed answered again, "What I shall read?"

The angel said, "Recite the name of the Lord, who has created man out of the cloth of blood, recite in the most high, who taught man the use of the pen, who teaches man what, he doesn't know."

After this experience, Mohammed became a little depressed, and he was thinking of committing suicide. He went to throw himself over a precipice, but invisible hands held him back. Mohammed ran away in fear. When he heard a voice calling him back, it seemed to come from heaven and it was a soothing voice that said, "Oh, Mohammed, I am Gabriel, the angel of Allah, and you are indeed the prophet of Allah." Mohammed said of it, "That night there was peace, until the break of dawn." Years after this event, it was referred to as "the night of power" toward the end of the month of Ramadan.

The following event is very important because it happened before in the Christian religion. The writings of the *Apocrypha*, which were rejected by the Catholic Church, mention that the angel Gabriel appeared to Mary announcing that she would give birth to the new messiah. Mary was confused and asked, "How can I bear a child without the addition of a man's seed?" To this the angel Gabriel answered, "Think not, Mary, that you will conceive in the ordinary way. For without sleeping with a man, while a virgin, you will conceive and while a virgin you will give milk from your breast. For the Holy Ghost will come upon you and the power of the most high will overshadow you, without any of the heats of lust. So that to which you will give birth will be only holy because it only is conceived without sin, and being born, shall be called 'The Son of God.'" Then Mary, stretching forth her hands, and lifting her eyes to heaven said, "Take notice of the handmaid of the Lord! Let it be done to me what you have said." (*Mary 11:16-21*)

Since the times of Moses, angels and clouds had been seen all through history. For example, in the 1,400 years since Mohammed's vision, the same phenomenon happened in 1916 and 1917 in Portugal to three children. In 1916, Lucia and two of her cousins Jacinta and Francisco were tending the family flocks in a field east of Mount Cabeco. Around noon a very fine mist began to fall, and Lucia and her two cousins decided to find refuge among the boulders hidden behind the olive grove. The children saw a light, whiter than snow. On another occasion an extraordinary light shone upon them and an entity or angel appeared holding a chalice in its left hand, while suspended in the air. Some drops of blood fell into the chalice, leaving the chalice suspended in the air. The entity or angel prepared Lucia for a meeting with the Virgin, saying that she was the "Angel of Peace."

The miracle at Fatima has all the elements that we have seen in the UFO phenomenon. The year 1915 was the beginning of the supernatural phenomenon or Miracle of Fatima. Lucia and three other friends were tending sheep in Mount Cabeco. After lunch they went to pray, and suddenly saw a strange *cloud*, whiter than snow, hovering above the trees with a seemingly human form inside the *cloud*. Lucia saw the strange *cloud* three times before she saw the visions of the Virgin.

In UFO literature there are thousands of cases in which witnesses have seen camouflaged UFOs inside a *cloud-like* object. On May 15, 1829, Joseph Smith and his friend went into the woods to pray when suddenly a *cloud of light* descended. In Garabandal, Spain, from 1961 to 1965 four pre-teenage girls were visited by invisible entities or angels and the Virgin. Many times the girls fell on their knees in ecstasy and prayed. The archangel Michael appeared with a cup that looked like gold. On another occasion the angel came in a strange light and showed the girls a chalice, in which were falling drops of blood.

So we see the claims given in the *Bible* or *Koran* about angels are true because the same phenomenon materialized in the 19th, 20th and 21st centuries. However, the most important events are the apparition of the angel Gabriel to Mary announcing the coming of "The Son of God" and to Mohammed with the teachings of the *Koran* and the message that he was the last prophet and the last revelations were given to him.

How could God tell Mary that the Son of God was coming and tell Mohammed that he was the last prophet? Let's examine this situation from a human perspective. If a man tells his wife that he loves her but then tells his mistress the same thing, who is being deceived? Obviously both! The same example applies to Gabriel, because he is saying one thing to Mary and saying another to Mohammed. In this case the Jews were deceived because they thought that the new messiah was a Jew. The Christians were deceived because Jesus is not the last prophet. The Moslems were deceived because Gabriel announced the coming of the "Son of God" in Jesus.

So how can God create this mess that is going to bring the human race to the final battle of Armageddon? Obviously, a God of Love would not create this terrible destiny for human kind. The Intelligence behind the UFO phenomenon is responsible for what we call the Jewish, Christian and Moslem religions and there is evidence of it in every religion. The Intelligence behind the UFO phenomenon has been responsible for our spiritual and mental evolution, but at the same time it is responsible of our Day of Doom.

People often think of many of the events that are related in the *Bible* or *Koran* as legends without any historical value. However, I have shown that many are true. For example, in the legend of the battle of Hunayn in which Mohammed was fighting something described as fantasy actually happened. The clans of Hawazin were getting ready to battle Mohammed when coming from Mecca. The commander sent out three scouts to check the area and bring information about the approaching army. The scouts returned speechless in a frightful state. Some of them had their joints dislocated. The scouts told their commander, "We saw white men on pie bald horses and at once we were smitten with thou seest." Another scout said, "We are not fighting people of Earth, but people of heaven, take our advice and withdraw." The commander got angry and said, "Show me a man of courage." Another man volunteered, but he came back in the same state as the others, having seen the same terrifying figures on horses, the very sight of which were unbearable.

Anyone that reads this story will think that it is a product of fantasy. However, a similar event happened in Vienna, Austria, in 1568. A rainbow and fiery beam hovering over the church of St. Stephanie was reported along with sightings of frightening human-like figures dressed in black. The legend said that when those figures were seen on the outskirts of a town or village, their presence would precede the outbreak of an epidemic.

In the year 1559 in Brandenburg, Germany, 15 terrifying men appeared with little heads and fearful faces and carrying long scythes used to cut oats. The swish could be heard at a great distance, but when large groups of people came running to see them, they found the oats remained standing.

Strange men dressed in black were seen in other European communities. Anyone not familiar with this subject will dismiss anything that can't be explained with our everyday common sense.

The well-known legend of the well called Zem-Zem is in *Genesis*. The story says that Ishmael and his mother and Hagar were in the desert and thirsty, and with the help of an angel, a spring suddenly appear to relieve their thirst. Truth or fantasy? True, because a similar event happened in 1858 in France. In a place called Lourdes, a young girl named Bernardette Soubirous reported a series of apparitions, apparently of the Virgin. She was told by the Virgin to dig a hole in the ground and that she would find a spring of sacred water which would cure diseases. So she dug and found a miraculous spring. Many thousands of people have visited the site. The event is similar to the passage in the *Bible* about the well of Zem-Zem, but in the *Bible* an angel helped Hagar. In the case of Lourdes, the Virgin told Bernardette to dig the ground. This supernatural phenomenon in the 19th century makes it possible that the legend of the well of Zem-Zem is true.

Other prophets have been deceived, like Joseph Smith when he was told that the Mormon religion was "The only true and living church upon the face of the whole earth with which, I the Lord am well pleased." (*Doctrines and Covenants 1:30.*) The Jews, Christians, Moslems and every other religion have been told the same—that their religion are the only truth. However, if the word of God is in every religion, then what we have is an illusion. A God of love and truth would never create a false belief; only the Intelligence behind the UFO phenomenon can create this illusion.

The Moslem religion has the same supernatural UFO-like phenomena as the Jewish and Christian religions and their so-called miracles. The phenomenon of the "cloud" is present in the most important event in Jewish history, which is the covenant between the Jewish people through Moses and whatever entity was inside the *cloud*. The ancient Jewish people called the entity Yahweh, but do they really know who was inside the *cloud*?

Further, in most of the miracles—both ancient and modern—the *cloud* is present with the supernatural or angels like those that appear to Mohammed and in the miracles at Fatima, Garabandal, Lourdes and other places. So what we thought was a legend or just a crackpot idea, as in the case of Mohammed, is true. Why? Because the apparitions of entities that some people called angels in the 19th, 20th and 21st centuries give reality to the legend of Mohammed. Someone named Gabriel gave Mohammed knowledge about the *Koran*, just as at Fatima and Garabandal. We humans can't understand the supernatural because it is beyond human reality. We can't ask an extraterrestrial or supernatural entity for an

I.D. to prove who they are. We can call them angel, extra-terrestrial, devil, divine or supernatural, how can we tell the difference? As I show in the miracle at Fatima, it is very clear that a silver object—what we call UFOs—was seen. Other entities, including the so-called angels, make it obvious that the UFO phenomenon is responsible for the so-called supernatural religious miracles.

Further, if we are seeing the same *cloud-like* UFO seen by Moses, then the UFO phenomenon is outside of what we understand as space and time reality. Mankind hours, days, months and years have no meaning for the Intelligence behind the UFO phenomenon. If that Intelligence is behind the Jewish, Christian and Moslem religions and these religions preach an apocalyptic end for mankind, then the Intelligence behind the UFO phenomenon is responsible for our doom. The reason is that any biological species able to travel through space and produce nuclear weapons will be a threat to other existent species already in control of some parts of the universe. In the universe the law of the "survival of the fittest" is alive and well, but more sophisticated than the teeth and jaws going on on planet Earth.

The Intelligence behind the UFO phenomenon is responsible for every religion here on Earth. The question is, if it is responsible for our religious and supernatural thoughts, then are we really free? What are we to them? An experiment? A supply of spare parts? Not long ago every newspaper published an article about a lioness that raised a baby deer. It was wonderful to see the lioness raising the baby deer, but after the baby deer was big enough, the lioness ate it. The story has a similarity with the end of times in the Judeo-Christian and Moslem

religions and the UFO phenomenon. I'll end this chapter
with a thought by Malcolm X, before he was murdered
in 1965. "I did many things as a Moslem that I'm sorry
for now. I was a zombie then, like all Moslems. I was
hypnotized, pointed in a certain direction and told to
march. Well, I guess a man's entitled to make a fool
of himself if he's ready to pay the cost. It cost me 12
years."

CHAPTER 19

WHAT ARE UFOS AND WHERE DO THEY COME FROM?

"What power urges them at such terrible speeds through the sky? Who, or what, is aboard? Where do they come from? Why are they here? What are the intentions of the beings that control them? Before these awesome questions, science—and mankind— can only halt in wonder. Answers may come in a generation—or tomorrow. Somewhere in the dark skies there may be those who know."

— ***Life*** **Magazine, April 7, 1952**

The only evidence that can help answer the first question posed in the title of this chapter are the thousands of eyewitness accounts that we have accumulated since the UFO phenomenon have appeared. Since the beginning of history, there have been reports of UFOs, but because of differences in cultures, times and technological development, these reports have been made within the limited and familiar language of their milieu.

For example, there is the evidence in the prehistoric caves in Altamira, La Pasiega, Ussat, Niaux and Les Tres Freres where designs of what men of the 20th and 21st century call UFOs can be seen next to those of bison and deer. The designs are as old as 15 to 30 thousand years. Since the beginning of recorded history we have eyewitness accounts of the UFO phenomenon.

In the first chapter of this book, I recounted the history of UFOs. In ancient Greece and Rome, UFOs were seen as familiar objects of everyday life, including altars, flaming spears shields, dancing moons and suns, and dragons. As time passed and society developed UFOs were seen in different forms. In the Middle Ages, they were called flying shields, flying spears, dancing moons, dancing suns, dragons and miracles. The descriptions were only slightly different than those from classical times. However, it was in the 19th century that real changes were reported.

Interestingly, it has been in the United States that sightings have reached notoriety. In the 19th century, as the U.S. became an advanced industrial society, UFOs looked like zeppelins or an oblong and cigar form. The belief of UFO scholars that UFOs have always been a little bit ahead of their time is probably correct, but not always.

However, in the 20th century more exactly in 1945, the world became aware of our first nuclear test. In 1946, people in Sweden were seeing rocket-type objects flying their skies. Although UFOs have been around for long time, the really first modem wave in the United States began in 1947. Interested readers can see headlines in the *New York Times* in 1947 about Air Force jets chasing UFOs. With the help of eyewitnesses, we have an unbelievable picture of this phenomenon. The best eyewitness accounts are from the 20th and 21st centuries.

What we know about UFOs is beyond anything we know about space-temporal and ontological reality. For example, we have accounts from witnesses that report astounding capabilities and maneuverability of UFOs.

They travel at fantastic speeds close to the earth's surface, and they have enormous acceleration abilities, from hovering or stationary to supersonic speeds, including straight up flight. Eyewitnesses have seen UFOs descend in an impossible fashion like a "falling leaf." I think that for a spaceship to descend like that is very cool.

Investigators taking measurements of the indentations caused on the ground by UFOs that have landed have calculated their weight at 20 to 50 tons. UFOs make right-angle turns without slowing down, and they hover with a rocking or pendulum motion. They also fly in zigzag or weaving undulations and circle in high turns. They fly on collision course with planes and they suddenly stop in midair just before crashing. They get in dogfights with Air Force planes and do impossible maneuvers that would kill a human. They perform erratic sky dances with one or two other UFOs. They can make themselves invisible and a fleet of UFOs can travel in perfect formation at supersonic speeds.

I think the most amazing feat by these objects is that they can split in two or more vehicles like a cell. Two UFOs can also join in mid-air and vanish. UFOs disguise themselves as a "clouds," creating a mist or fog around themselves. UFOs can not be shot down. They can be lit in different colors, like red, orange, yellow, green, blue and purple. When UFOs land, they leave burned vegetation and at night they suddenly fade away.

Witnesses have seen UFOs dive into the ground and leave no wreckage. When they land, they have turned trees black and the branches dried and carbonized, as though turned into stone. The radioactivity is higher in the vegetation of the landing sites. UFOs don't produce a sonic boon even though they have been tracked at speeds of 18,000 mph. Sometimes UFOs cause cars to stop, televisions and radar to malfunction, and blackouts to occur in cities.

For example, in 1947, ten people in St. Maries, Idaho, reported that eight UFOs had landed near the mountainside. The witnesses said that they came into view at an extreme speed, suddenly slowed, and then fluttered like leaves to the ground. The amazing thing was that when the witnesses went to look at the landing site, they didn't find any wreckage and the trees were without damage. The witnesses said the UFOs "were saucer-shaped and resembled wash-tubes and they were the size of a five-room house." We see in this example that UFOs can make themselves invisible and as I show in the chapter about the Bermuda Triangle, they can abduct a plane and both become invisible or disappear. UFOs can appear or disappear at will, which makes us think they came from another dimension.

The idea that other dimensions exist in the universe would have sounded crazy 50 years ago, but not in 2005. Scientists now believe that for the universe to have come into existence, other dimensions were necessary. New theories, like the superstring theory, postulate the existence of up to 10 dimensions. I think if UFOs come to our dimension from another dimension, they are at the level of "elementary particles" that appear and disappear in the void of the universe. In quantum theory, electrons can materialize in places where Newtonian physics forbids.

According to the greatest minds in physics, like Albert Einstein, Paul Debroglie and Irwin Schrodinger, the wave function only specifies the probability that an atom will have a determined energy level. Quantum theory doesn't say if an atom will be found in a particular measurement. As Born said, "It is only the probability of distribution of events that is causally determined by quantum theory, not the outcome of a specific event."

Witnesses have reported that UFOs have different shapes, including Saturn discs, domed discs, flattened spheres, and flat discs—triangular, cylindrical, elliptical and spherical. On August 18, 1947, in California, a couple observed a vapor trail moving from North to South. A closer observation revealed a piece of "shiny metal" at 600 to 1,000 feet altitude moving at a high rate of speed. It appeared to be rocket-shaped, five feet in length and tilted in a semi-circle. In July 1947, flying balls of fire circled a wide area around Texas, and some people, believing the end of the world was near, began praying. One man grabbed a rifle and shot at the mysterious objects. Sheriff Paul Anderson described them as twelve "orange basketballs of fire" flying over the community, moving in a circle.

These are the same kinds of UFOs still seen in many parts of the world. In the chapter on miracles, I show that this type of UFO is common with such supernatural events. Since the UFO phenomenon and miracles look the same, I have no choice but to say that the UFO phenomenon is responsible for the supernatural, miracles, and religious phenomenon. In Wales in 1908 and 1909, there was a religious revival and a series of supernatural events, such as large lights surrounded by smaller lights, suggesting the idea of UFOs and a mother ship. The lights in the miracle at Fatima and those in Wales gave off smoke—like UFOs do. The Welsh lights blinked on and off—like UFOs. The lights in Fatima, Wales and Garabandal moved in zigzag fashion—like UFOs. At Fatima the appearance of a figure was accompanied by a humming sound and the common sounds in miracles are humming, whizzing, buzzing, whirling and, most common, a buzzing like bees—like UFOs.

The Fatima disc was flat and glowed—like UFOs. It revolved at a high speed and radiated flares of multicolored lights—like UFOs. The Fatima lights zigzagged and dove to the ground then quickly ascended into the sky—like UFOs. The clothing of the multitude that were witnessing the phenomenon were completely wet, and after the phenomenon they were dry—the same as has happened with UFOs.

As recently as November 2004, NASA developed a test plane that flew at 7,000 mph, and was twelve feet long and five feet wide, called the X-43A. It is mounted on a modified Pegasus rocket and carried by a B-52 airplane to 40,000 feet, where it is released and carried by the rocket to 110,000 feet, where it separates and flies at 7,000 mph, but only for ten seconds. UFOs have been tracked as far back as 1947 at 18,000 mph. Someday we probably will be able to achieve that speed, but there are now things that only entities from another dimension can do.

In his masterpiece *The Day after Roswell,* Col. Philip J. Corso (Ret.) reported that he saw alien corpses with an alien craft. He said that the craft was retrieved by the Army and had no navigational controls, no control sticks, wheels, throttle pedals, cables, flaps or rudders, no jet engines, no propellers, no engine, no rocket propulsion or cables, gears or wires. Col. Corso was a man with much experience. He was a former pentagon official and a member of President Eisenhower's National Security Council. A machine like that is beyond anything human reality can imagine.

As long as 5,000 years ago, the Indian epic *Mahabharata* mentions "vimanas" or flying machines that came in a variety of designs and sizes. According to the ancient text, they were quicksilver and could perform complex aerial acrobatics and travel at astonishing speeds. The "vimanas" were used to transport the gods of that era—what we now call aliens.

Aristotle wrote of "heavenly disks" as far back as 4 BC. He said that "a meteor fell out of the sky at Aegospatami and rose up in the wind and descended elsewhere." Pliny, the historian, said that "a spark fell from a star and descended to the earth until it was the size of the moon; at this point the spark stopped dead and hovered in the air for a while." As we see, Pliny and Aristotle are describing UFOs, but they have to explain the phenomenon with familiar vocabulary, like moon and star.

The "Lolladoff Plate," a shocking discovery which appears to show a disk-shaped object in the center, was found in Nepal. The Roman writer Julius Obsequens, reported in his work *The Prodigia* that "things like ships" were seen in the sky of Italy in 216 BC.

A U.S. Air Force report of March 9, 1950, said, "The frequency of reports of this nature has recently increased; instructions have therefore been directed to all radar installations within this command to report scope sightings of unusual objects." General Sanford called UFOs "incredible tales told by credible persons."

There are reports that the beams of light the UFO projects behave in weird ways, including penetration of doors, walls, and any concrete object. In March 1981, two hunters in the Amazon said that a UFO shined a beam of light at them, and one man was immobilized inside the beam.

In September 1976, a witness in California was watching television late at night when the reception started going bad so he went outside and saw a silent UFO that shot a beam of light. Half way off the ground, the beam of light stopped in mid air.

These are amazing feats of technology. U.S. Navy Rear Admiral Delmar Fahrney, a former U.S. Navy Missile Chief, said, "Reliable reports indicate there are objects coming into our atmosphere at very high speeds, and controlled by thinking intelligences." Vice-Admiral and former C.l.A. Director R. H. Hillenkoetter said, "It is imperative that we learn where UFOs come from and what their purpose is."

The question remains, what are UFOs? The best answer is that they are space ships from another dimension. I say from another dimension because of the way they appear and disappear, but it wouldn't surprise me if they manipulate time-space to make us believe. They can come from another universe because an advanced civilization—let's say 400,000 to a million years old—would seem like gods to us. UFOs are here and it seems that had been here from probably before the human race appeared on Earth and they have a plan that I will discuss at the final chapter.

Let's try to figure out where they come from. Since the time of Darwin the concept of life has become less static and more dialectical. We have discovered that bacteria have evolved in the most inhospitable places like in radioactive facilities. There is a bacterium known as methanogens that breathes out methane as a waste product. Scientists have found bacteria at 237 degrees Fahrenheit, in volcanoes and in the coldest places in Antarctic. It was thought in the early part of the 20th century that for life to evolve, there had to be ideal conditions not too far from, or close to, the sun. An atmosphere was also believed necessary for the organisms to develop. This idea is no longer acceptable because life is everywhere. The four most vital elements for life— carbon, hydrogen, nitrogen, and amino acids—are found in asteroids and in interstellar space.

In the year 1849 Andrew Crosse synthesized an organism by the action of electricity on a porous stone soaked with hydrochloric acid and potassium silicate. The organism created was named Arcarus Electricus and was shown in H. M. Noad's lectures on electricity in 1849. A University of Arizona researcher recently found that schreibersite, a phosphorus mineral in meteorites yields a component of nucleic acids when mixed with water.

On March 15, 1806, a meteorite known as Carbonaceous Chondrites showed that life probably has been deposited on planets. The theory known as Panspermia postulates that microscopic life has been carried in the universe by the interstellar wind. The process of life on planet Earth took millions of years. In the beginning, the Earth was inhospitable. The atmosphere was composed of ammonia, carbon dioxide and water vapor. It had no free oxygen until the plants began processing the carbon dioxide. Probably Venus looks like Earth in the beginning of our geophysical history. Since the beginning of life it has been trial and error when it come to life forms.

The great scientist and human being Stephen J. Gould wrote in his masterpiece *Wonderful Life* about a study of a form of life found in a quarry formed 530 million years ago. A greater variety of life forms were found in these ancient remains than in all our oceans. Dr. Charles D. Walcott discovered this ancient sea in the early 20th century. The great variety of life found there didn't have the chance to evolve.

Another important consideration in the evolution of life is periodical mass extinction. The first mass extinction destroyed 90 percent of life on Earth. The most recent and most famous was the extinction of the dinosaurs 68 million years ago. This event allowed a vacuum for the mammals to evolve. It was chance and luck that made our human evolution possible. As recently as 12,000 years ago, in the last mass extinction, all the big mammals, such as the mammoth and saber-toothed tiger perished. Many scientists believe that we are now in the sixth mass extinction because we are destroying our planet.

Life in general has been a product of chance. Mass extinction has been the major trigger of new species. If we look at life in the time scale of the universe, we see the large amount of time that life takes to evolve. Scientist Stephen J. Gould said, "In two or three billion years, the impossible became the inevitable." Scientists believe there are five steps necessary for the transformation of inanimate matter into organic matter: The first step is the formation of the simplest organic compounds. The second step is the transformation of these materials into more complex organic compounds. The third step is the production of key life chemicals, such as proteins and nuclei acids. The fourth step is the transformation to structures, metabolism and energy-producing chemistry. The fifth step is the evolution of metabolism.

The basic ways that simpler organic compounds might have been synthesized is by radiation, lightning, electrical discharge or heat. The result of these processes is that life is one of many possible outcomes. In the 19th century, an experiment verified that life is a natural and regular process in the universe. It is not an exception, it is a rule. So the possibility of life in the universe is infinite. So far we have discovered 110 planets and our solar system is 4.5 billion years old, but the universe is 15 to 20 billion years old. So, life in the universe has had plenty of time to evolve.

Recently, however, physicists have come up with new theories of the Universe, like the superstring theory that postulates the existence of ten additional dimensions. There are other physicists who postulate the existence of parallel universes. The great scientist Michio Kaku in his masterpiece *Hyperspace* states that dimensions exist beyond our space-time reality. Many Nobel Laureate scientists believe that the universe exists in a "higher-dimensional" space. Scientists call the "Hyperspace" theory by the names of Kaluza-Klein Theory and Supergravity. Many scientists believe that the four-dimensional theory is too small to describe the Universe.

In *Hyperspace*, Dr. Kaku describes a being from the fourth dimension as being like what we have called God. Such a being will be able to walk through walls, doors, mountains, and refrigerators and also be able to disappear or reappear at will. The being will have x-ray eyes, and will know the present and future. It will perform miracles.

Physicists know that the concept of a perfect and all-knowing God has no support in nature because quantum theory only makes statistical predictions. Also, even an all-knowing mind needs the support of experience, and the immensity of space and time makes human life and everything absolutely contingent. Our solar system is about one fourth as old as the universe. To put it another way, the universe has existed four times longer than our sun and earth.

To compare the length of human life to the universe: a low-mass star cools off in about one hundred thousand billion years, planets detach from stars by collisions with other stars in about a million billion years, and some stars are high velocity and fly off in about ten billion years.

Scientists believe that in our galaxy alone there are eight billion possible planets and in the known universe there are 100 billion galaxies. Shockingly, even though the universe seems so immense, matter as we know it only counts for 5 percent of reality; 25 percent is made of dark matter. Science doesn't know what the components of dark matter are, but 70 percent is made of dark energy.

Just as our planet is not in the center of our solar system, our galaxy is not the center of the universe. Our species is not the finality of evolution. We are here by chance and luck, thanks to the asteroid that destroyed the dinosaur.

Blaise Pascal in his philosophical masterpiece, *Pensees,* said: "When I consider the brief span of my life absorbed into the Eternity which comes before and after, as the remembrance of a guest that tarrieth, but a day, the small space I occupy and which I see swallowed up in the infinity, immensity of space of which I know nothing and which knows nothing of me, I take fright and am amazed to see myself here rather than there. Now rather than then. Who put me here? By whose command and act were this time and place allotted to me?"

In this marvelous philosophical thought, Pascal shows the absolute contingency of every god, alien, mountain, planet and universe.

CHAPTER 20

THE UFO PHENOMENON AND THE FUTURE OF THE JEWISH, CHRISTIAN AND MOSLEM RELIGIONS

"Nothing in fact—neither wild beasts nor microbes—can be more terrible for man than a species that is intelligent, flesh-eating, cruel; a species which would be able to understand and to thwart the human intelligence; a species whose goal would be precisely the destruction of man. That species is obviously ours."

— Jean-Paul Sartre, French philosopher

We can't talk about the future of the Jewish, Christian and Moslem religions without mentioning their past histories. We can look at the past as enlightenment or as a tragedy. We can learn from it or be sorry about it. However, if we study the past, there are many errors that had been committed in the name of these three religions. Although not God, nor religion, nor ideology justifies the suffering of the poor or the slaughter of the innocent, the history of these three religions is bathed in blood and the suffering of mankind.

The problem of these three religions is that for too long they have been fixated on human sexuality and elaborating a false morality while human suffering has been neglected. This pattern has also been a normal psychological and cultural path of primitive societies. The classic religions believe in sexual taboos. The word "taboo" means a prohibition, saying or doing something for fear of immediate harm from a supernatural force. It also means a prohibition imposed by social custom or as a protective measure. However, this fixation with human sexuality and not with human suffering had been the tragedy of the Jewish, Christian and Moslem religions. It is time to change this false morality and make this planet a better place to live and die.

Since the beginning of history religion has been allied with the ruling classes, increasing the suffering of mankind. For example, in primitive cultures the shaman or magician was allied with the chief running the affairs of the tribe. In Egypt during the reign of Rameses III, the priesthood was the most powerful institution, as it has been in modern times with the Catholic Church and the Moslem mullahs. The priesthood possessed 107,000 slaves, the equivalent of one-thirtieth of the population of Egypt. They owned 500,000 head of cattle and 750,000 acres of arable land. The priesthood received revenues from 169 towns in Egypt and Syria and their property was exempt from taxation.

Rameses III gave gifts to the priesthood, including 32,000 kilograms of gold and a million kilograms of silver. Each year the Pharaoh gave the priesthood 185,000 sacks of corn while the rest of the population starved to death. Slavery was a means for ancient civilizations to dispose of the surplus of prisoners of war, in addition to using them as servants and for religious sacrifices. The code of Hammurabi of 1350 BC mentions slavery.

The tragedy of the Jewish, Christian and Moslem religions is that they didn't stop slavery. On the contrary, they considered it divine and the will of God. Since the time of Moses, for 3,000 thousand years, slavery was an institution respected and accepted. The Mosaic Law made slavery the will of God. For example, *Leviticus 25:44-6* says, "As for your male and female slaves whom you may have; you may buy male and female slaves among the strangers, who sojourn among you, and their families that are with you who have been born in your land and they may be your property. You may bequeath them to your sons after you, to inherit as a possession forever; you may make slaves of them, but over your brethren, people of Israel, you shall not rule one over another with harshness."

And *Exodus 21:1:4-5* says, "If his master gives him a wife and bears him sons and daughters, the wife and her children shall go out alone, but if the slave plainly says, 'l love my master, my wife and my children. I will not go out free,' then his master shall bring him to God and he shall bring him to the door or the doorpost, and his master shall bore his ear through with an awl; and he shall serve him for life."

The Greek and Roman societies became the greatest civilizations man had ever known and also became the largest slaveholders in the ancient world. Slaves constituted a third of the population in Athens. Phillip II of Macedonian finally destroyed the Athenian slave society at the battle of Chaeronea in the year 338 BC. On the orders of the great law-giver Lycurgus, many slaves were freed.

The next major slave society was the Roman-Italian. Between the second century BC and the fourth century AD, 30 percent of the population were slaves. The greatest philosophers and statesmen were pro-slavery; not even the genius of Aristotle saved him from that barbaric custom. He said in his major philosophical-political treatise *Politics*, "The intention of nature therefore is to make the bodies of freemen and of slaves different, the latter strong for necessary service. One who is a human being belonging by nature not to himself but to another is by nature a slave."

Aristotle proves that even the greatest minds sometimes can't surpass the milieu or alienation in which their societies exist. Plato spoke in favor of slavery, saying in his famous philosophical-political treatise, *The Laws*, "Now that each of the citizens is provided, as far as possible, with a sufficient number of suitable slaves who can help him in what he has to do." The great Roman orator Cicero was in favor of slavery and gladiator fights. However, in 71-73 BC, a great slave revolt in Rome led by a famous slave-gladiator named Spartacus made the Roman Empire tremble. He led 100,000 slaves against Rome, but the senator and general, Pompey, defeated him. Spartacus was crucified and exhibited in the "Vie Appia." If he had lived in the 20th or 21st century, he would have been called a communist.

Curiously, no God or angel was present to help those poor slaves. The Roman and Greek gods and philosophers died out, and a new religion appeared as an offspring of Judaism called Christianity. However, the luck of millions of slaves didn't change. On the contrary, it got worse, because like Judaism, Christianity made slavery the will of God.

Christianity didn't want change in the socioeconomic conditions of the slave. Its only advice to the poor and oppressed was servitude and humility. Jesus advised the Pharisee's to "render unto Caesar the things that are Caesar's, and unto God the things that are God's… Blessed is the slave whom, his master returning finds performing his charge…To him who has, more will be given, and from him who has nothing, even that which he has will be taken away." In *Matthew 39*, he says, "But I tell you not to resist an evil person, but whoever slaps you on your right cheek, turn the other to him also." and in *Matthew 40,* "If anyone wants to sue you and take away your tunic, let him have your cloak also."

The Catholic Church became the largest slaveholder. Christianity defended the slave institution of slavery because it believed that slaves had all the spiritual conditions to exercise Christian moral values like humility, patience and forgiveness to enemies. Also, the church believed that man was cursed with Original Sin and was not fit to govern himself. The greatest saints in the Catholic Church spoke in favor of slavery.

Even the great saint and philosopher Saint Augustine claimed that Christianity improved master/slave relations. He said, "You teach slaves to be faithful to their masters from a love of duty rather than from the necessity imposed on them by their status. You make masters more benign toward their slaves out of regard for the one God, who is master of both, and you dispose them to look after their interest rather than keep them down by force."

Saint Augustine believed that the origins of slavery were caused by the sin of Adam. He said, "And what deeds the apostle says when he teaches that slaves are set under their masters? Slaves, be obedient to those who are your earthly masters, with fear and trembling, in singleness of heart, as to Christ rendering service with a good will as to the Lord. Look, he did not make freemen out of slaves, but good slaves out of bad slaves. How much do the rich owe to Christ for creating stability in their homes? If there were an unfaithful slave, there is Christ, who would correct him and would not say to him, get rid of your master. For you have recognized him, who is your true master. He may be impious and hostile, but you are faithful and just. It is unworthy that a just and faithful man serves one who is unjust and unfaithful. He did not say that to the slave, but rather *be a slave!"*

To me it is mind boggling to accept that a God full of love can give this kind of inspiration to a saint. Only a cold alien intelligence can show so little compassion for human suffering. In the *Bible* for example, *Corinthians 7:20* says, "Servants are even commanded in scripture to be faithful and obedient to unkind masters." St. Peter said, "Servants, be subject to your masters with all fear; not only to the good and gentle, but to the forward, for what glory is it if when ye shall be buffeted for your faults, ye take it patiently, this is acceptable with God."

So, while millions of people were living and dying in slavery, where was Christian morality? Fixated in human sexuality, especially women's sexuality. For example, when the congregation went to worship, women had to wear a veil because hair was so seductive that even angels might be sexually attracted during the service. The great Christian St. Geronome said that the women's hair should be completely cut.

St. Paul said to the congregation, "Women should keep quiet in church, they must take a subordinate place. If they want to find out anything, they should ask their husbands at home. For it is disgraceful for a woman to speak in church. A man ought not to wear anything on his head in church. For he is the image of God and reflects God 's glory, while woman is a reflection of man's glory. For man was not made from woman, but woman from man; that is why she ought to wear upon her head something to symbolize her subjection."

Ancient Christians celebrated a feast called "Agape." It was a mate feast and usually it was celebrated on a Sabbath evening. The dinner began and ended with prayer. They believed that the bread and wine represented the body and blood of Christ. However, the worshipers of Dionysus, Attis and Mithras had the same beliefs; at their banquets, people ate the magic embodiment of their gods. The final ritual of the Agape was called the "Kiss of Cove." In some congregations, this was given only by men to men and by women to women. In some congregations, there was no such restriction, and Catholic officials denounced them for having created sexual indulgence and recommended that the lips should not be opened when kissing.

In the third century, the Agape gradually disappeared and the remarriage of widows and widowers was not advised. In 322, in the Council of Nicae, the church declared that women had no souls.

Historians mention that early Christians saw the hand of the devil in every pleasure of the senses and they looked with suspicion on music, white bread, foreign wines, warm baths or shaving the beard.

Ironically, in the 21st century we see in the extreme form of Islam the same extreme third century Christian theocratic customs.

The civilized world in ancient times looked upon the Christians as "harmless fanatics," but Tacitus called them "the vilest of people." Under Roman law, men and women caught in adultery shared the same punishment, which was banishment and confiscation of part of their property. The man gave half of his property and the woman gave a third of hers and always there was a chance of pardon and reconciliation. However, when the Christians were in control, a husband was justified in killing his wife caught in adultery. He could also kill the man she was having the affair with, if he were a slave. Constantine the Great neatly set the example when he killed his wife, boiling her alive, for a supposed sexual affair. The great Christian St. Thomas Aquinas said, "Woman is in subjection because of the laws of nature, but a slave only by the laws of circumstance."

The ancient Christians closed Greek academies and burned the books of poets, philosophers, and scholars, setting back knowledge 1,500 years. The "Dark Ages" was the product of Christian superstition.

In the fifth century, Christians burned the ancient library of Alexandria and the great school of philosophy. The head of the school was a woman named Hypatia. She was a logician, philosopher, astronomer and mathematician. Following a sermon about the evilness of women, a group of Christians went into the school and found Hypatia with a pupil named Synesius of Cyrene. They tore off her clothes and cut her to pieces with oyster shells. Her pupil escaped by saying he was a Christian. Later he became the Bishop of Ptolemais.

Slavery never died out completely and is still around in the 21st century. However, the relationships of the means of production changed and Constantine the Great's social reforms paved the way for feudalism. The difference between the feudal peasant and the slave was very thin. It was the relations of production or the economic basis of society that made the difference. However, in the feudal society the Master became the Lord and the slave became the peasant. The Catholic Church became the largest land and peasant owner before the French Revolution, when the Catholic Church owned one-fifth of the land in France.

The darkest chapter in human history was the Inquisition, which was created by the clergy, and the origin of heresy began with the church. The Council of Enreus (1195) mentions indulgences being sold by the clergy, and bishops selling holy oil and relics. The Council of Avignon (1209) mentions priests gambling with dice for penance and others opening taverns with the clerical collar as an inn sign. The Council of Paris (1209) mentions nuns organizing parties and wandering in the streets at night. Shockingly, while all these activities were going on, the church claimed that the troubadour, poetry and the tradition of courtly love was decadent and a form of paganism.

Heretical movements were an answer to these excesses of the church, and the inquisition an answer to any opposition. St. Thomas Aquinas described heresy as "a sin which merits not only excommunication, but also death." His writings are the basis of Catholic Church theology today.

Scholars believe that the persecutions began between 1163 and 1184, more exactly during the first six years of the pontification of Gregory IX between 1227 and 1233. They estimate that during the witch paranoia in the 16th and 17th centuries, from 200,000 to 1,000,000 million people, mostly women, were burned at the stake. The 13th century inquisitor Moneta said, "How can the fire that burns the houses of the poor and holy men be created by God? How can the God who sends suffering to good men be good himself?"

In Salem, Massachusetts, women were accused of witchcraft and were burned at the stake because they had the symptoms of a possessed person. However, research in the 21st century has discovered that those women had food poisoning, which caused their strange behavior.

The famous philosopher John Hicks questioned, "If God is perfectly loving, He must wish to avoid evil; and if He is all powerful, He must be able to abolish evil, but evil exists; therefore God cannot be both omnipotent and perfectly loving."

Napoleon abolished the Inquisition in Spain in December 1808, but it continued to function sporadically. In 1813, the Spanish court voted that the Inquisition was incompatible with the new constitution. The last execution for heresy took place in 1862, when a schoolmaster named Cayetano Rippoll was hanged as an unrepentant deist. The real end of the inquisition came on June 6, 1869.

The Italian inquisition ended in 1638 after killing 15,000 people. Giordano Bruno was first tried in 1576 and was executed in 1600. Feudalism was faced by new social-economic contradictions between the monarchy and the new raising class, the bourgeoisie. One of the most important events in human history, the French Revolution, was precede by the "Enlightenment" or a revolt of the mind. The great philosophers like Diderot, Rousseau, Voltaire and their philosophies preceded and anticipated the revolution. In 1789 the peasants, workers and merchants stormed the Bastille. The new ruling class declared that their values of freedom, democracy, equality, justice, religious freedom were universal in the famous "Declaration of the Rights of Man." Slowly the peasants advanced in the ranks to become wage workers.

The birth of modern capitalism really happened in England during the Industrial Revolution in the 1830s in which children were forced to work in factories and coal mines 16 to 18 hours per day in the worst possible conditions. The Victorian society lived in the worst hypocrisy, comparable only to modern 21st century society. Oscar Wilde's homosexual affair got more attention in the press than children working 16 hours a day in inhumane conditions.

Slavery and feudalism lived side by side until modern times. In the second half of the 15th century Europeans began to trade along the west coast of Africa, and by the year 1867 between seven and ten million Africans were shipped as slaves to the New World. African traders demanded adult males, and in some areas of Africa, slave trading depleted the population. In Europe, slavery lasted until the 1720s. A quarter to a third of the population of some areas of Thailand and Burma were slaves in the 1st through the 19th centuries. In 1841, India had eight to nine million slaves, and Malabar had 15 percent of the population in slavery. In South America, Chile freed its slaves in 1823. Mexico abolished slavery in 1829; Peru abolished slavery in 1854. England abolished the slave trade in 1807. However, the world coffee market needed slaves and it came back in the 1820s. Lithuania abolished slavery in 1858. Russia abolished it in 1679, but automatically converted its slaves to serfs in chains to the land. Puerto Rico abolished slavery in 1873; Cuba was independent in the 1880s. On May 13, 1888 all slaves in Brazil, where half the population had been slaves around 1800 and a third in 1850, were freed. China abolished slavery in 1906.

Haiti is the only country in the world where a slave rebellion in 1827 succeeded in winning independence. The United States occupied Haiti from 1915 to 1934. In the United States, the cotton industry increased the demand for slaves, especially in the south in Alabama, Mississippi, Louisiana and Texas. In the year 1850 two-thirds of all slaves were engaged in the production of cotton.

Slaves were first brought to the United States in 1619 to Virginia. In the 1660s and 1670s, the laws of slave ownership were written. However, during the reign of "King Cotton," 40 percent of the southerner population were African slaves. In 1720, in South Carolina 64 percent of the population were slaves. In Mississippi from 1810 to 1860, 55 percent of the population were slaves. In 1825, more than 36 percent of the New World slaves were in the south of the United States.

Since the time of Moses the institution of slavery was respected, justified and endorsed by religious leaders and politicians. In the United States in 1820, Thomas Roderick defended slavery saying, "When we turn to the *Testament*, we find not one single passage at all calculated to disturb the conscience of an honest slave holder."

In France, Jean Bodin (1530-1569) was the founder of the antislavery movement, but for most Christians, it was not a sin. Any concern for the slaves was not for their freedom, but for whether they were able to work.

The Pennsylvania Quakers voiced opposition to slavery in 1688. The Vermont Constitution of 1777 was the first document in the United States to abolish slavery. Chief Justice Grannlie Sharpe ruled in 1772 that his master could not forcibly return James Somerset, a fugitive slave from Virginia, to the colonies. Most Northern states abolished slavery, but it continued in the South because of the cotton industry.

Abraham Lincoln's Emancipation Proclamation was on January 1, 1863. The 13th amendment to the U.S. Constitution put an end to slavery. However, a bloody legacy lingered with American society for a long time and there was lynching of African-Americans because of their skin color. The word "lynching" means the killing of a person by a mob in defiance of the law. The term probably originated with Charles Lynch, a hunter who lived in Virginia during the 1700s. The story goes that Lynch and his neighbors took the law into their own hands to punished Tories (British sympathizers).

The term came to be applied to physical punishment. James E. Cuttler one of the first historians of lynching said, "Lynching was an undeniable part of daily life, as distinctly American as baseball games and church suppers." Scholars believe that lynching in the early 19th century was part of frontier life, and there was not much that anybody could do about it. Lynching was legal in the United States until 1893.

The first anti-lynching law was passed in Georgia, but it only made the violation punishable by four years in prison. In 1712, New York punished a slave insurrection by hanging 13 slaves and burning three at the stake, breaking one at the wheel, and starving one to death in manacles. The six remaining slaves committed suicide.

Lynching started in the U.S. as early as 1712. Many times the government sent troops to the plantations where white owners kept black slaves by force. In early 1866, six confederate veterans living in Pulaski, Tennessee, formed the original chapter of the Ku Klux Klan. Curiously, Christianity is the only religion with the idea that Africans were the children of Ham who, as a consequence of his adultery, was banished by God.

In June 1965, a Ku-Klux-Klan leader said in a famous trial. "Integration breaks every moral law God ever wrote. Noah's son was Ham and he committed adultery and was banished and his sons were Hamites and God banished them and they went to Africa and the only thing they ever built was grass huts. No white woman can ever marry a descendant of Ham. That's God's law. I don't care what Lyndon Johnson or anybody else says."

Scholar Richard Maxwell's study of vigilante violence in the United States estimated that between 1868 and 1871, there were more than 400 killings by the Ku-Klux-Klan in the South.

Union General Phil Sheridan calculated that 3,500 whites and blacks were killed between 1865 and 1875. In the 1890s, journalist Ida Wells-Barnett put the number of blacks killed by whites since 1865 at 10,000, with only three white men executed for crimes against Africans-Americans. Author Dorothy Sterling calculated at 20,000 the number of African-Americans killed between 1868-1872.

On February 3, 1893, a major spectacle took place at Paris, Texas, when a young black man was burned before a crowd of 10,000 cheering people. This was the largest reported event in the history of lynching. The only incidents comparable to this monstrosity were the gladiator fights in ancient Rome.

Many scholars believe that in the beginning lynching was a Southern spectacle, and that in the 1880s and 1890s it became widespread in the United States. Other scholars believe that lynching spread from the 1890s to the "Red Summer" of 1919, even close to the 1930s. However, for every known lynching, there were many others unreported. In 1903, a reporter named Henry Waring Ball said, "A miserable negro, this morning, the jail was stormed and the wretched creature carried down Washington Avenue to the telephone exchange, where he was hung up in front of it. While the girls looked on and applauded, everything was very orderly. There was not a shot, but much laughing and hilarious excitement. It was quite a gala occasion, and as soon as the corpse was cut down, all the crowd went to see a game of baseball."

Many victims were roasted and butchered, very often members of the crowd offering cooking solutions. On some occasions, burned remains were chopped and put outside stores to deter blacks who might want to steal.

The act of castration was part of the ritual, and some people took home cooked human remains. Many scholars have tried to explain this tragedy. One said that the South's fundamentalist Christianity, with its lost-cause ideology wanted to create a belief system. Another scholar said that "lynching was a form of tribal sacrifice." Many spectators said that "lynching cleared the air," and others said it was "the kind of painful spasm a community needed."

The scholar Trupier Harris wrote, "Lynchings were sexual events of the extreme sadism of white men. It was caused by jealousy of his mythical sexual potency and larger genitalia." Other scholars claimed that the religious aspect took on an important meaning. For example the taking of human remains would stop the soul of criminals from rising on the Day of Judgement. In the post-slavery South, white men developed a fear of being overwhelmed by the supposed supersexuality of black men.

As recently as 1981 a Klan organization in Alabama randomly selected a black teenager. In the same year a group of whites in Skidmore, Missouri, lynched the town's white bully.

In June 1998 in Jasper, Texas, three white men lynched a part-time musician named James Byrd. They tied him by his feet to the rear of a pickup truck and dragged him to his death. The question is, what was the reason for so much suffering? Why does God allow so much unnecessary suffering?

As the offspring of the Judeo-Christian religion, the Moslem religion has been no different when it comes to human suffering. Slaves were owned in all Islamic societies, both sedentary and nomadic, from Arabia to North Africa, Pakistan and Indonesia. The Islamic states were the Ottoman Empire, the Crimean Khanate and Sokoto Caliphate.

Slavery was practiced before the birth of Mohammed and the rise of Islam. Approximately 18 million Africans were delivered into the Islamic Trans-Saharan and Indian Ocean slave trades between 650 and 1905. The *Qur'an* was the fundamental starting point for Islamic Law, Sharia

and the law of slavery. (*The Scholarly Legal Consensus and
the Qiyas Juristic Reasoning by Analogy.*)

Islamic law regulates the institution of slavery in every
detail from the jihad or holy war to the distribution of
booty to the treatment of slaves. The last Islamic slave
law was promulgated in 1936 by King Ibn Sand of Saudi
Arabia. It restated the teachings of the Qur'an, and
required owners to register slaves with the government
and issue slave trade licenses.

Slavery persisted in Saudi Arabia into the 1960s and
was made illegal in 1962. Some parts of Africa and the
Islamic world retained slavery until the end of World War
I. By the 1930s, Liberia abolished it. Among the Islamic
Berber, Tuareg and peoples of the Sahara, slavery stayed
until 1975. In the Sudan and other parts of Africa, slavery
is still practiced, mostly among the Moslem population.

In many ways, the Moslem religion seems frozen in
the beginning of third century Christianity. For example,
the reason behind women wearing a veil was to prevent sin
or temptation. Clothing was made in a fashion to prevent
sexual arousal. The various schools of Sharia are derived
from the *Koran* and Hadith and some harsh punishments
came from these laws.

For example, women caught having a sexual affair are
stoned to death. In the 1990s, a woman was sentenced to be
stoned to death in Nigeria for having an affair. One of the
consequences of this barbaric custom is something called
"honor killing." Many young women are killed if they
are raped or are in love with a man without the family's
approval. The Moslem religion makes women less than an
object. Women can't shake hands with men. Under strict

271

Sharia law, women can't work or go to school. Fanaticism is a very important ingredient of these religions.

The legend says that in 628 Mohammed sent letters to the great kings, demanding that they should abandon their fate and adopt the religion of Islam. The King of Abyssinia, the King of Persia, Chosrees II, and the Emperor of the East Roman Empire, Heraclius, received letters from Mohammed. The Persian king destroyed the letter in a rage. The Roman Emperor received his courteously, probably thinking it came from a harmless fanatic. The Roman Governor of Egypt was more considerate, as were the Arabian sheiks. The Moslem armies were set in motion for a holy war against idolaters and unbelievers. Mohammed gave a choice: the acceptance of Islam, death, or a payment of a special tax.

Fanaticism is a very important feature of the Moslem religion. As recently as November 2004, a Dutch filmmaker, Theo van Gogh, a relative of the great master Vincent van Gogh, was murdered in Holland because of a film that shows the injustices committed against women in the name of Allah.

In the 21st century, in the Sudan and some parts of Nigeria and Marruecos, slavery is still practiced among Moslems. Another strange custom is the stoning of the devil. Since the time of Moses 3,000 years ago, slavery has been a respected institution endorsed by priests, philosophers and politicians.

In 6,000 years of history, what has mankind accomplished? Absolutely nothing. The only thing that he is doing very well is to refine the methods of exploitation of his fellow human beings. The tragedy of humanity's poor hasn't changed in 6,000 years. Human societies,

with the help of organized religion, have created a
permanent and civilized exploitation, oppression, poverty
and inequality.

In the United States, for example, what does democracy
mean? Freedom, family values, and morality for whom?
For the estimated 500,000 kids working on farms in
subhuman conditions? For the 50 to 70 million people
without health insurance who have to choose between
paying rent, eating or their health? For the many people
making a sub-human minimum wage who have to live in
homeless shelters because they can't afford to pay rent?

In the United States there are 38 million people living
in poverty. In the United States, 12.1 to 12.9 percent of
children are poor. In New York City, 50 to 60 percent
of children are poor. A single mother earning twice the
minimum wage ($10.30) and paying $800 a month for
rent will have $165 a week after taxes for food, clothing,
transportation, school supplies and health care for herself
and her children. Many parents often skip a meal or two
a week, so that their children can eat; sometimes both
parents and children have to skip meals one or two times
a week.

In the United States, by age 15 a child has seen 12,000
simulated murders on television. About 31,000 people are
killed each year by firearms and 75,000 wounded. Eighty
people are shot to death every day. The prison population
is two million people and there are four million parolees.
Some 18,000 people die each year for lack of adequate
health insurance. Upper and middle-upper class families
constitute the top 10 percent of the income distribution,
while 90 percent of the population hardly makes ends
meat.

In the 2004 presidential and congressional elections, the candidates expended four billion dollars. Meanwhile, a doctor used his own money to buy and transform a truck into a medical dispensary to go to his poor neighbors of Paterson, New Jersey, to treat poor children for free. He is a real hero, but the media didn't cover that news at all. How big a difference would four billion dollars make? How many hospitals, schools, day care centers could be opened with that amount of money?

In the presence of so much despair, where are the moral values? What the Western world calls morality is only a circus-media frenzy, fueled by homophobia and sexual paranoia. The poor are still poor, the homeless are still homeless, the uninsured are still uninsured.

Furthermore, what do "democracy, freedom, and moral values" mean for the world? Close to four billion people in the world live on $2 per day. A mother of six children in Mexico said, "We seldom have money to buy milk and other nutritious food. Sometimes I have very little to give to my children." For decades it has been known that in Brazil there are millions of children in the streets, some of whom are killed or raped every day, but no Catholic or governmental institution stops it. In Malawi, Africa children stand on the roadside selling skewers of roasted mice. In Haiti, people are so poor and hungry that they make round swirls of dough with butter, salt and dirt, then they sell it and eat it. In Mozambique, people eat grasshoppers and call them "flying shrimp." In Ghana, people eat anthills. In Angola, people eat a dark dirt called "black salt" mixed with water. In Zambia, balls of edible clay are sold in street markets, as are plants like cactus, seaweed, tree bark, grass and cornstalks.

Relief workers in many Third World countries know that mothers boil water with stones and then tell their hungry children that the food is almost ready in hopes that the children will fall asleep. In Somalia, people eat camel skin. They also eat the skin and bones of dead animals that even vultures don't want, boiling it for soup. In Africa, millions live without food or clean water and every 45 seconds a child in Africa dies of malaria, a largely preventable disease. In the Third World, families are so poor that they use the kitchen table to wake the dead. In India, people die in the streets of hunger. In Third World countries people have to bring their own sheets, toilet paper, and medicines to the hospital because their governments are corrupt and they steal or waste the revenues of the country.

Poverty is so great that in the 21st century there are 27 million slaves in Third World countries because people sell themselves for food or shelter. The slave society is inhumane, but if the master were a good master, he would provide shelter and medical care for his slaves.

In the 21st century if a worker can't pay rent, he will end up in the street. If a worker can't pay health insurance, he may end up dead. The number of hungry people in the world is rising at five million people per year. As I write, more than 170 million children go hungry every day and 10 million die every month of preventable diseases.

In 1963, President Kennedy told delegates to the first World Food Congress that "We have the means. We have the capacity to eliminate hunger from the face of the earth in our lifetime. We need only the will." The world has money and technology to end poverty and hunger. It is just the politics of rich and poor and religious fanaticism that keep the world in these conditions.

In 2005, the great economist Jeffrey Sacks said that we need only $150 billion to contain poverty, yet one trillion dollars per year is wasted in the arms trade. Only three of the world's 180 nations—Canada, France and the United States—produce more food every year than they consume. As we see, poverty and hunger is the most important moral issue in the 21st century. While the world debates the meaning of the word "genocide" in Sudan's Darfur, two million people have been dispatched from their homes. A thousand people die every month, victims of Moslem Janjaweed militiamen attacks. In Africa, one to three million people die every year of preventable diseases. In Third World countries 8,000 children die of Malaria and 5,000 die of tuberculosis every day. In the Congo, since 1998, three to eight million lives had been lost in the civil war. In Rwanda, close to one million people were butchered, the largest holocaust in modern history, while the world watched. Unfortunately there is no oil, like in Iraq, otherwise maybe lives could have been saved.

So after such a long list of calamities like poverty, hunger, scarcity, war for oil, slaughter and disease, what is morality? If to send 100,000 people to their deaths is morality, then what is immorality? To show too much skin or plain homophobia? Then if that is morality, Genghis Khan is a saint. If to pay $37 million a year to a CEO and $6.50 an hour to a poor worker with a family is morality, then what is immorality? To watch the Teletubbies? Who in the world would take the smile of a child, saying that the comic characters of Teletubbies, SpongeBob, the Simpsons (and earlier, Bugs Bunny) are immoral.

I remember when I was a kid, my favorite program was "Felix the Cat." I never saw more than a simple cartoon, not a female or male character, just a cartoon. Not long ago I was shocked to read in the newspapers that a six-year-old boy was accused of "sexual harassment." I couldn't believe it! Jesus says in the *New Testament in Mark 10:14-15* and *Luke 18:16-17,* "Suffer the little children to come unto me, and forbid them not; for of such is the kingdom of God."

Nobody remembers the beautiful things that Jesus said. A famous minister in a Sunday Mass said, "I have never seen a man in my lifeI wanted to marry, and I am going to be blunt and plain: if one ever looks at me like that, I am going to kill him and tell God he died." Laughter and applause followed. In the story of Mary Magdalene, when she knelt before Jesus, anointed his feet with precious myrrh, let her tears fall upon them, and dried them with her hair, Jesus said of her that "Her sins were forgiven, because she loved so much."

The state of the world after three thousand years of the Jewish, Christian and Moslem religions is a nightmare, and it is not over yet. The final goal of these three religions is to establish the Kingdom of God on Earth, after the final battle called "Armageddon." It will be the last battle of mankind because the prophecies say that one-third of mankind is going to perish after Jesus comes in a cloud. The Jews, Moslems, and everyone must convert to Christianity. Then the New Kingdom of God will appear in the New Jerusalem coming down from the heavens.

So after so much suffering in this life, it is not over yet, because Armageddon is coming, and after that, if you are a sinner (whatever that means), Hell will be waiting for you.

So if human destiny is written in the Jewish-Christian-apocalyptic, end-of-time religions, then we should be worried because it means the end of mankind.

I think it was unfortunate that mankind adopted these three religions as a hope for salvation. If mankind had embraced Jainism, Confucianism or Buddhism, the Inquisition, the Crusades, the Dark Ages, the First and Second World War never would have happened. Nor would the Armageddon that is around the corner happen.

The religion of Jainism is a good example of a non-violent religion. Basically there are no absolutes. The moral basis of the Jain religion is Ahimsa or non-violence. All life is sacred and inviolable, even that of the poor animals that we eat. Buddhism is another alternative. Its doctrine is that a good moral life is the basis from which an understanding of the true nature of things must begin. Confucianism and Taoism are indigenous to China and are mostly philosophical systems lacking any cult element. Confucius taught ethics and morality. He had no concern with the spiritual or supernatural world. He was concerned with the ethical and moral relationship between human beings. If we had adapted these sets of values as the basis of our moral values, then we wouldn't have so many crooked politicians.

Before any Jew, Christian or Moslem wants to start Armageddon, he unfortunately has to put the UFO phenomenon into the equation, which means that probably it won't be Jesus coming in a cloud, but an alien invasion. I don't feel sad or disappointed to know that the UFO phenomenon is the source of every religion and supernatural event in the life of mankind. Erik Von

Daniken shows in his work that an extra-terrestrial or extra-temporal Intelligence is behind the greatest works of ancient civilizations. The Hindu religion is the clearest example of UFOs in ancient times. The *Ramayana* and *Mahabarata* were written 5,000 years ago—2,000 years before Abraham and Moses, 3,000 years before Jesus, and 3,600 years before Mohammed. The scriptures mention the "vimanas," what men in modern times have called UFOs.

For example, *Rama* describes a vimana: "The radiant vimana gave forth a fierce glow. The fully equipped vimana shone brilliantly, when it set out, its roar filled all four points. The beautiful celestial car possessed the radiance of fire. Bhima, riding in his vimana of solar effulgence, whose noise was like the roaring of thunder clouds. It seemed there were two suns in the firmament. The whole sky was ablaze when he ascended into it, blazing with a mighty radiance, like a flame on summer night, like a comet in the sky. When drawn into battle, by those white horses, that chariot looked exceedingly resplendent, like a celestial car that is borne along the sky and like Cukra's celestial car."

The chariot could move in a circular course or move forward and do diving movements. The vimanas are described as round, sometimes boat-shaped, they glow in the dark, and they have twin rows of nozzles along the sides. The similarity with the sightings of UFOs in the 19th, 20th and 21st century is overwhelming. For example, in Bismark, North Dakota, in 1953 at 8:05 p.m., 45 people saw a UFO as a red glowing light making long sweeping movements. A witness said, "It would remain stationary, then hop up several degrees, very quickly, almost instantaneously. It would stop, move to the left and then swerve down in a sort of slanting motion, repeating these maneuvers several times." Another witness said, "It's brighter than the brightest star I've ever seen. It changed colors from white to green."

In Georgia and Alabama, eleven policemen saw UFOs. They were "fast moving, noisy, basketball-size, brightly lit with red, green, orange, or all white, blinking and revolving," said Georgia State Trooper Sam Taylor. "It was oblong, but not quite thin enough to make it cigar-shaped. It seemed solid and when I saw it, it gave off a gentle white glow." The witness, a Vietnam flying veteran, added, "I was absolutely mystified. What I saw was certainly no airplane or natural phenomenon."

In another case, two military policemen at Hunter Air Force Base near Savannah, Georgia, were on routine patrol when one of the policemen, a former helicopter crew chief, said that he spotted a cluster of lights in the sky at about 2,000 feet. The lights were tracked across the sky, flashing red, orange, blue and white. The UFO then disappeared behind the trees, only to return 15 minutes later and hover at one end of the deserted runway, its lights flashing brilliantly. It began moving toward the patrol car. "When it got closer, we could see the lights were clustered underneath a metallic-looking saucer-shaped body. I thought it was going to hit us, at least smash the blue light on top of our car."

He said that he kept his foot on the gas pushing near 100 mph, with the UFO in close pursuit. The policeman said he had difficulty keeping the car on the road at that speed and could hardly see through the windshield because of the red and white flashes of the UFO's lights, which he described as "just a few feet above us." One of the policemen said, "l was terrified when the saucer chased us. I was crouched under the dashboard just waiting for it to hit our roof lights."

So what is in store for mankind? It presently appears that religious fanaticism is going to be in every human affair. Politicians are going to use religion for their advantage, fueled by greed. So, Armageddon is going to be closer and closer to fulfillment. If there is no Armageddon, probably the world will be divided into religious groups. We will go back to the Dark Ages in a society where watching the Teletubbies will be a sin, reading a crime, and Sharia law applied to anyone breaking religious precepts.

I believe the only way to end the problems of mankind is to end poverty. That is the major moral issue in the 21st century. If we take care of that problem, everything else will fall into place. People will stop emigrating to the United States or Europe. The only reason people emigrate from Mexico and other countries is because in their countries all the wealth is in the hands of few families who own the banks, factories, farms and so forth. The rest of the population is poor and hungry.

The superpowers do not enforce social justice in the Third World countries because they are predators themselves. You don't need to be a rocket scientist to know that ending poverty is the end of the major problems for mankind. Everyone knows that the wealth of the world is in the hands of probably 500 families and corporations. So if Armageddon came to be, followed by an alien invasion, than it would be the end of mankind as we know it. I don't think they will come to listen to Frank Sinatra or play a game of chess with me or have a cup of coffee in the mall. It will be the end.

CHAPTER 21

PROPHECIES AND FINAL WARNINGS TO MANKIND

"I've often wondered, what if all of us in the world discovered that we were threatened by an outer power from outer space, from another planet, would we all of a sudden find that we didn't have any differences between us all?"

— Former U.S. President Ronald Reagan

Since the beginning of recorded history there have been prophets and prophecies. The Jewish, Christian and Moslem religions are not the only eschatological-apocalyptic religions. In the United States the prophecies of the Hopi Indians talk about coming apocalyptic events in the U.S. and the world. They are so sure of the coming events that in the 1940s they even went to the United Nations to warn the world.

The ancient Maya mythology gives 2012 as the year that cataclysmic events are to destroy the planet. The prophecies of Nostradamus said that after an economic collapse, a war will follow that will take the lives of one third of human kind. *Revelation,* the last book of the *New Testiment* predicts that the angel Gabriel will herald the slaying of one third of humanity during or after Armageddon.

Interestingly, most of the end times prophecies fit neatly into our times: the 20th and 21st centuries. The

Hindu mythology mentions that we live in the times of the Khaly-Yuga where there is turmoil, despair and war.

The Jews were tormented with the idea of doomsday. The *Old Testament* has many prophecies concerning the destruction of the world and the Day of Judgement. In the middle of the 10th century, fanatics appeared in France, Germany and Italy prophesying that the end of the world was around the corner and telling people to stop any earthly affairs. The site of the Last Judgement was expected to be Jerusalem. In the year 999, thousands of pilgrims moved to the Holy City to await the coming of the end of the world. People in Europe sold their houses, farms, and castles because they believed that the Lord was coming. Many churches, castles and buildings fell into ruin because it was not worthwhile to fix them.

The end was coming and all classes left their homes. Nobles, knights, serfs, women and children traveled to the Holy City. On the trip to Jerusalem the large mass of serfs and nobles sang psalms and looked to the sky for signs. They expected the heavens to open and to see the Son of God descend in clouds to purify the world. In the year 1000, the number of pilgrims increased. Every time thunder or a meteor appeared, the entire city of Jerusalem rushed into the streets weeping and gibbering with terror. Fanatic preachers kept provoking the peregrins during any natural disaster.

In the year 1213, mass hysteria instigated by religious fanatics made 30,000 children go on a crusade to liberate Jerusalem, following five previous attempts by older people. Many of the children perished on the way; others were turned back from Italian seaports. The children that reached the Middle East were captured and sold by the Saracens into slavery.

In the following centuries, especially during the times of calamity like "the Great Plague" in 1345 and 1350, there was an appearance of comets, a shower of shooting stars, earthquakes, and floods. The prophets of doom would appear and announce that the last judgement and end of the world were near.

In the 19th century, especially in the United States, many influential prophets of doom appeared. Harriet Livermore preached that the coming of the Lord would take place in Jerusalem and it would begin His thousand-year reign. She believed that the American Indians were descendants of the tribes of Israel and urged congress to save them and transport them to Jerusalem to watch for the coming of the Lord. She kept two huge Arabian stallions to provided transportation for herself and the Savior on his glorious re-entry into Jerusalem.

Perhaps the most famous prophet of doom in the 19th century was William Miller. He initially prophesied the end of the world from 1831 and until 1834. People were alarmed from Canada to Pennsylvania and from Boston to Ohio. At the height of his preaching, he had 50,000 followers. He again set the date of the end of the world and judgement for April 1843. However, nothing happened and his followers were disappointed. He then changed the date to between 1843 and 1844, and again nothing happened.

Not disappointed with his failure, he set the day for March 21, 1844. The prophet sat in his house reading the *Bible* and waiting for the blast of the angel Gabriel. Followers went to graveyards to be with departed loved ones and wait to rise up to heaven. Some climbed into trees or on barn and house roofs. Some of them built wings and to try to fly into the arms of the Lord and some of them broke their legs. Others gathered in large houses dressed in their ascension garments waiting to be transfigured.

However, the idea of the end of the world and Day of Judgement is still fresh with Jewish, Christian and Moslem fundamentalism. For example, Christian fundamentalists believe that the purpose of the Apocalypse is to create a paradise here in earth, and the victory of Christ over Satan and the Antichrist. The doctrine of the "The Rapture" is the moment when Christ takes every believer into a glorious resurrection. All Christians who died in the faith in the last 2,000 years and those who are alive when Jesus comes in the air will be supernaturally "translated" without warning.

Fundamentalists believe that Christ will bring all the departed saints with him. In the *New Testament* it says that Christ will come without warning to take his church to heaven. The Antichrist confederacy will sign a seven-year treaty with Israel and the Jews have to be converted to Christianity. Fundamentalism says that the Antichrist will rise in Europe and will take over the ten-nation confederacy of the newly revived Roman Empire. The treaty will mark the beginning of the last seven-year period, known as Daniel's Seventh Week leading to the battle of Armageddon.

The war known as Gog and Magog is possibly a war between Russian-Arab armies against Israel. God will also release a Chinese army of 200 million men that will destroy the world. When the sixth trumpet sounds, it will kill a third of human kind, and the angel Gabriel will be responsible for that event. The Battle of Armageddon will be fought in or around Jerusalem and the focus of the battle is Planet Earth and the souls of mankind.

In every religion there is the expectation of a savior. The Buddhists and Hindus are waiting and searching for the next avatar. The Moslems are expecting the appearance of the Mahadi, a messiah-like figure mentioned in the Koran.

Before Jesus, there were people who were believed to be messiahs. For example, Gamaliel speaks of one self-proclaimed prophet who is mention in the Jewish *Antiquities of Josephus, Book XX, Chapter 11.* His name was Theudas and he claimed to have crossed the Jordan. He attracted many followers, but the Romans arrested him, and cut off his head and displayed him in Jerusalem.

Gamaliel also speaks of Judas the Galilean who is the same prophet Josephus refers to in the twelfth chapter of the second book of the Jewish wars. He attracted many people and on one occasion, nearly 30,000 men.

In apostolic times, there was a self-proclaimed prophet named Simon the Magician who people in Samaria regarded as the power of God. In the years 178 and 179 of the Christian era, in the reign of Hadrian, a false messiah name Barcochebas appeared at the head of an army. The emperor sent Julius Severus to capture him and put him to death.

Socrates, the ecclesiastical historian, mentions that in the year 434 a false messiah whose name was Moses appeared on the Island of Candia. He said that he was the ancient liberator of the Hebrews resuscitated to free them again.

A century later in 530, a false messiah appeared in Palestine named Julian. He proclaimed himself a great conqueror who, at the head of his nation, would destroy the whole of the Christian people. The emperor Justinian sent troops against him and killed him.

In the eighth century, a Spanish Jew name Serenus claimed to be the Messiah. He preached, had disciples and died.

In the 12th century several messiahs appeared. The 13th century was very rich in false messiahs, probably seven or eight. They appeared in Arabia, Persia, Spain and Moravia. One in particular, whose name was David El Re, was a very famous magician. He converted hundreds of people, but he was murdered. In the year 1666 Sabbatai Zebi, born in Aleppo, claimed to be the messiah.

You can laugh at the ingenuity of the prophets of doom and their followers, but it is only in the 20th and 21st century that all those prophecies have become self-fulfilling. The reason is that some countries have the nuclear power to kill 32 times every man, woman, child and dog on this planet. Also, they have bacteriological, chemical, and germ warfare—and more that we don't know about it.

As I write in the beginning of this chapter, since the beginning of history there have been prophets and prophecies about the possible end of the world. Some scholars believe that the Pyramids of Egypt contain prophecies about the end of the world. Some claim that the prophecies ended abruptly in the year 2000. However, since the time of Jesus there have been outstanding prophecies. I will start with the one that Joseph Smith received on Christmas Day of 1832.

The most important revelation after the *Book of Mormon* was "The Civil War Prophecy," which said,

"Verily thus saith the lord concerning the wars that will shortly come to pass, beginning at the rebellion of South Carolina, which will eventually terminate in the death and misery of many souls; and the time will come that war will be poured out upon all nations, beginning at this place. For behold, the southern states will call on other nations, even the nation of Great Britain as it is called, and they shall also call upon other nations and then war shall be poured out upon all nations."

In my opinion, this part of the prophecy predicted the alliance between the United States and Great Britain in the war against Iraq in the 21st century. Obviously this prophecy goes beyond the Civil War prediction into the 21st century. It continues, "And it shall come to pass after many days, slaves shall rise up against their masters and thus with the sword and by bloodshed, the inhabitants of the earth shall mourn, and with famine and plague and earthquake and the thunder of heaven and the fierce vivid lightning. Also the inhabitants of the earth shall be made to feel the wrath and indignation and chastening hand of an almighty God, until the consummation decreed hath made a full end of all nations."

I can see that this part of the prophecy as relating to the final apocalypse.

Sister Maria Faustina, a Polish nun who died during the invasion of Poland in 1938, had written the following prophesy on February 22, 1931: "The Lord manifested himself to me today, and he said to me, 'Before coming as the just judge,I shall come as the king of mercy. Before judgement day arrives, there will appear a sign in the heavens and over the earth; that sign will be the sign of the *cross*, and from each of the wounds in my hands and in my feet there will issue *a bright light* that will *illumine the whole earth* for a few minutes. This will be the end of time.'"

This prophecy was very significant because the signs of the cross and the flash of light had been seen for hundreds of years.

The vision seen by Constantine was seen before and around his time. In the years from 1961 to 1965 in Garabandal, Spain, four pre-teen girls were visited by invisible beings and the Virgin. The girls were often seen falling on their knees in ecstasy, praying and taking up the customary attitude for receiving Communion. The girls opened their mouths and swallowed something. St. Michael the archangel appeared on one occasion with a cup of gold.

Another time, the angel gave Communion to Conchita, one of the seers. Suddenly the host appeared on the tongue of Conchita with many people as witnesses. It did not seem to have been put there, but just materialized. On another occasion, the angel came in a strange light and showed the girls a large chalice into which were falling drops of blood.

The apparitions happened between 1961 and 1965. Conchita reported the following prophesy: "The Virgin told me about this on January first, 1965, up in the pine grove. I can not say what it will consist of, because she did not command me to do so. And when it is going to be, she did not tell me so I do not know. What I do know is that it will be visible to everybody. I do not know whether people will die because of it. They could only die from the shock of seeing it. The punishment is considered on whether or not mankind heeds the blessed Virgin's message, and the miracle, if it does take place, then I know what it will consist of because the Virgin told me, but I am not allowed to say. What is more, I have seen the punishment. What I can assure you is if it comes it is far worse than if we were enveloped in fire, worse than if we had fire above us and fire beneath. I do not know how long a time will elapsed after the miracle, before God sends it."

During the so-called miracle at Fatima, in one of the prophecies, the Virgin said, "When you see a night *illuminated* by an *unknown light*, know that this is the great sign given by God, that he is about to punish the world for its crimes, by means of war, famine and persecution of the Church and the Holy Father." Interestingly, the only unknown lights that we know are the UFO phenomenon lights. Shockingly, five Popes refused to give the third secret and one Pope passed out after reading about it. The third secret seems to mentions a great natural or man-made disaster.

On May 12, 1973, Sister Agnes Katsuko entered the Institute of the Handmaids of the Holy Eucharist. She was incurable deaf. The first extraordinary event took place one month later when a brilliant light emanated from the Tabernacle. The phenomenon occurred a number of times and was often accompanied by something like a *fog* or *smoke*, which gathered around the altar. On one occasion Sister Agnes saw a multitude of beings similar to angels surround the altar in adoration before the host. She also was visited by an angel that she described as having "a round face, an expression of sweetness, covered with a shining whiteness like snow." The angel guide prayed and gave her messages.

During the evening of June 28, 1973, Sister Agnes discovered on the palm of her left hand a cross-shaped wound three centimeters long by two centimeters wide, which caused her terrible pain. The following week during the late evening hours of July 5, a small opening appeared in the center from which blood began to flow. On Thursday and Friday nights, the pain became unbearable. In the early morning of July 6, the angel appeared and said, to Sister Agnes, "The wounds of Mary are much deeper and more sorrowful than yours. Let us go to pray together in the chapel."

After entering the chapel, the angel disappeared, so Sister Agnes turned to the statue. She said, "I suddenly felt that the wooden statue came to life and was about to speak to me. She was bathed in a brilliant *light,* and at the same moment a voice of indescribable beauty struck my totally deaf ears." The vision told her that she was going to be healed of her deafness.

Another message was given on August 3, a First Friday. A heavenly voice came from the statue and warned. "Many men afflict the world. In order that the world might know His anger, the heavenly Father is preparing to inflict a chastisement on all mankind." On October 13, the statue of the Virgin gave another warning to mankind: "As I told you, if men do not repent and better themselves, the father will inflict a terrible punishment on all humanity. It will be a punishment greater than the *deluge,* such as one will never have seen before. *Fire* will fall from the *sky* and will *wipe out* a great part of humanity, the good as well as the bad, sparing neither priest nor faithful. The survivors will find themselves so desolate that they will envy the dead."

Following the message the dazzling light that covered the statue slowly disappeared.

Mankind has never been so close to a nuclear disaster as now, because we have the perfect combination—greed and religious fanaticism. It is the perfect combination for the last battle of mankind, the "Battle of Armageddon" or the battle for Jerusalem. A battle of such proportions that as the prophecies in the *Bible* said, one-third of mankind will perish.

One interpretation of *Revelation* is that the battle of Armageddon will be a frightful carnage of such proportions that the human mind can't conceive of it. In the middle of this battle, there will be an enormous earthquake. The shock from the earthquake and battle will produce a complete destruction of the world. A nuclear blast could make the earth's axis shift and create more earthquakes and destruction.

Interestingly, the Virgin Mary at Fatima, Portugal, in 1917 gave a somber prophecy. She said that "nations will be annihilated." The prophecy fits neatly with the modern world. During, the so-called Cold War, the world knew who had nuclear weapons. However, since the fall of socialist Russia, the dangers of nuclear proliferation has increased more than ever. There is a black market of weapons of mass destruction, and it is only a matter of time before an Osama or a Hitler gets his hands on it.

Since the 1990s there has been a rumor that Russia lost more than 100 nuclear suitcases. The fact is that all over Russia, there are all kind of nuclear, bacteriological, and chemical weapons that are easy to steal, buy or exchange. A recent study said that half of Russia's nuclear arsenal is unaccounted for, perhaps four thousand weapons. Where are they? Nobody knows. The world has more than 30,000 nuclear weapons and enough highly enriched uranium and plutonium for 240,000 nuclear weapons. The United States has approximately 10,640 nuclear weapons, Russia has approximately 8,600, China has approximately 400, France has approximately 350, England has approximately 200, Israel has more than 200, India and Pakistan have more than 200, North Korea has probably close to 10 nuclear devices, Iran is getting ready to build something, Brazil has nuclear reactors but is keeping the press out of its facilities. South Africa and Japan have the technology to build nuclear reactors.

Right now the U.S. has more than 2,000 intercontinental land-based hydrogen bombs and 3,456 nuclear weapons, submarines roaming the seas 15 minutes from their target, and 1,750 nuclear weapons in intercontinental planes ready for delivery. As I write, 2,500 nuclear weapons remain on hair-trigger alert, ready to be launched at the press of the button. Russia has a similar number of strategic nuclear weapons, with approximately 2,000 nuclear weapons on hair-trigger alert. The world has enough nuclear power to kill every child, woman, man and dog 32 times.

In November 2004, Russia President Vladimir Putin said, "We are not only conducting research and successful testing of the newest nuclear missile systems, I am certain that in the immediate years to come, we will be armed with them. These are such systems that other nuclear states do not have and will not have in the immediate years to come."

So welcome to a new democratic, nuclear apocalypse and end-of-time arms race.

There are also chemical and bacteriological weapons. For example, not long ago, the Russians perfected a form of anthrax and Ebola disease for which the West has no vaccine. Who knows what other kinds of nuclear, bacteriological, chemical and germ weapons the U.S. and Russia have. As I write, there are more than 2,000 labs in the world with the money and the know-how. It is a matter of time before someone like Osama Bin Laden or Hitler takes control of weapons of mass destruction.

In passing I would like to ask, who in the world is going to believe that the combination of the U.S., France, England, Europe, and the world can't find Osama Bin Laden? Who in the world is going to believe it? Since the 1950s the U.S. has had technology that can hear the drop of a pin on the moon. Obviously if Osama dies, it will mean the end of the War on Terror, which means millions of dollars will be diverted to military enterprises. It has to be diverted to civilian enterprises, like hunger, homelessness, health insurance, education, day-care centers, and training for a new work force.

There are more prophecies, such as in the *Koran*, which mention that we will know that the end is coming by the length or tallness of the buildings. Interestingly, there are skyscrapers everywhere in the modern world. The *Koran* says, "Watch for the day when the sky will bring forth a visible smoke that will envelope the people, this will be terrible, then the people will cry, 'Lord remove from us this torment, truly we are believers.'…We shall remove the torment for a little while, but you will certainly revert to your evil courses…On the day when we shall seize you, with a great seizure, then certainly we shall exact retribution." *(Koran 44:11-13, 16, 17)*

One of the most important problems in modem society is "global warming." Many well-paid scientists don't believed in global warming, but big changes are going on in the planet. For example, the Arctic Ocean ice has shrunk from 5 to 10 percent at an accelerating rate. In Alaska, a village named Shishmaref is melting into the ocean. Over the past 30 years, the Inupiaq Eskimo village has lost 100 to 300 feet of coastline, half of it since 1997. The temperature in Alaska has risen four to five degrees Fahrenheit in the past 30 years, and world wide, it has risen just under one degree. The oceans will rise 20 feet if the western shelf in Antarctic melts. That means that New York, Florida and other coastal cities will be partially submerged.

Interestingly, there are prophecies that mention such disasters and indicate the rising of the levels in the ocean. American's "Sleeping Prophet," Edgar Cayce said, "Los Angeles and San Francisco will be destroyed before New York City. The southern Atlantic coast, Georgia, South Carolina, and North Carolina will disappear beneath the ocean. The Great Lakes will empty into the Gulf of Mexico. The western coast of North America will be inundated, for several hundred miles inland. Similar cataclysmic disturbances will occur around the world. Northern Europe will be transformed 'in the twinkling of an eye' as land submerges and the ocean rolls inland."

The great prophet Nostradamus, who predicted great apocalyptic natural disasters, wrote in the *Epistle to Henry II*: "There will be a solar eclipse, more dark and gloomy than any since the creation of the world, and it shall be in the month of October that a great movement of the globe will happen; and it will be such that one will think the gravity of the earth has lost its natural balance and that it will be plunged into the abyss and perpetual blackness of space. There will be portents and signs in the spring, extreme climate changes, nations overthrown and mighty earthquakes."

Scientists believe that a change or shift in the polar axis would create apocalyptic natural disasters, including huge tidal waves that would smash the coastlines, hurricanes with winds of hundreds of miles per hour, and earthquakes of great magnitude. Volcanoes would pour out huge lava flows with poisonous gases and ash. Climates would change instantly and the summers and winters would be more intense. If the polar cap melts, it would instantly raise sea levels to 50 feet.

The *Bible* has many prophecies about major natural disasters like earthquakes and polar shifts. For example, in *Revelation 16:18-20*, John's vision of the end of life is very similar to what scientists think will happen with a polar shift: "And there were voices, and thunder and lightning, and there was a great earthquake, such as was not since men were upon the earth. So mighty an earthquake and so great that the great city was divided into three parts, and the cities of the nations fell, and every island fled away and the mountains were not found."

Scientists have predicted a great earthquake in California that can propagate the whole seismic fall of the world. *Isaiah's 24:1-24:18-20* says, "Behold the Lord will lay waste the earth and make it desolate, and he will twist its surface and scatter its inhabitants. For the windows of heavens are opened and the foundations of the earth tremble. The earth is utterly broken, the earth is rent asunder, the earth is violently shaken. The earth staggers like a drunken man; it sways like a hut; its transgressions lie heavy upon it, and it falls, and will not rise again."

In the chapter on UFOs and natural disasters, I show that many times UFOs have been seen near earthquake faults and during storms. So it is not impossible that they are manipulating the human natural environment. A super-advanced civilization could manipulate reality. *Matthew 24:29* says, "Immediately after the tribulation of those days, shall the sun be darkened and the moon shall not give her light and the stars shall fall from heaven, and the powers of heaven shall be shaken."

There is some evidence that points to a sudden change of the earth axis. For example, the mystery of the frozen mammoths is still unsolved and the sudden death near the end of the last Ice Age of more than 50 millions animals in the United States alone and millions more world wide. The mystery is that frozen mammoths have been found with fresh food in their stomachs. These great animals gave the name to the Pleistocene period. The extinction was of colossal proportions, in a violent cataclysm like men never have seen.

The scholar Frank C. Hibben in his masterpiece *The Lost Americans* said, "The Pleistocene period ended in death. This was not ordinary extinction of a vague geological period, which fizzled to an uncertain end. This death was catastrophic and all-inclusive...In the great bone deposits of Nebraska, we find literally thousands of these remains together. The young lay with the old, whole herds of animals were apparently killed together, overcome by some common power."

Scientists have found 39 frozen mammoths, some with soft parts. A few had their eyeballs intact. The most amazing thing is that they had fresh food in their stomachs. One of the mammoths, named Dima, estimated at 44,000 years, was found with its flesh in good condition. Another has been estimated at 9,000 years.

Just at the end of the last Ice Age, two mammoths came from Alaska and the rest from Siberia. In Mexico, a mammoth bone was found that was dated at 690 BC. A tusk from Bavaria, Germany, was dated at 1900 BC. The late scientist Ivan Sanderson said that for a mammoth to freeze and not be able to digest the food, the temperature of the air had to drop to minus 150 degrees Fahrenheit.

Evidence of both a sudden freeze and a sudden warmer climate is overwhelming, as evidence of an axis shift, for that matter. For mammoths to be found with fresh food in their stomachs, after 40,000 years with no time for to the organisms to assimilate the food, the freeze had to be *sudden*. Some mammoths were even found standing.

In the *Bible* there are prophecies that mention natural catastrophes like a polar shift. *Peter 3:10* says, "But the day of the Lord will come, as a *thief* in the night, in which the heavens shall pass with great noise, and the elements shall melt with fervent heat. The earth, also, and the works that are therein shall be *burned* up." This prophecy fits neatly with a magnetic pole shift.

Moreover, the *Bible* mentions that there will be many signs in the sky, like lights. Since the beginning of history signs in the sky have preceded a war, natural disasters and even important historical events. For example, in 1917 the Virgin appeared in Portugal and said that there would be signs before the Second World War. Amazingly, on January 25, 1938, extraordinary lights were seen in all of Europe and parts of North America. The *New York*

Times had an article on January 26, 1938, that said, "Aurora Borealis Startles Europe, People Flee in Fear, Call Firemen."

In England, newspapers said it was, "the most violent display of an aurora borealis in 50 years. From 6:30 to 8:30 p.m., the people of London watched two magnificent arcs raising in the east and west, from which radiated pulsating beams like search lights in dark red, greenish and purple." I would point out that only UFOs present these characteristics.

Another newspaper said, "Police stations, fire brigades, newspaper offices all over the country called asking 'Where is the fire?'" People were in fear in Austria and Portugal. It was something rarely seen in Western Europe. The lights were also seen in Spain. During this period all transatlantic and radio communications were interrupted. The phenomenon was a vivid "red glow" that fits with the description of a UFO.

In Bermuda, many people thought that the light was caused by a ship afire at sea. In Canada, electrical disturbances disrupted wire services. In France, thousands asked whether it was a fire, a war, or the end of the world. A common aurora borealis does not cause so much disturbance, but it is known that UFOs cause electrical disturbances. (See chapter on UFOs and electric disturbances.)

There have been other displays of extraordinary lights, for example in 1972 in Mount Zion, Israel, and on June 12, 1974, in northern Spain. Professor of Physics Dr. Mueller Markus from Switzerland, who happened to be in Spain, said of the event seen by millions: "It is difficult for me to speak of what I saw with my own eyes. Never

have I seen anything like it in my entire life." He reported
that there were no clouds in the sky and that it was about
an hour after sunset when the light appeared in the north,
like a huge *bolt* of *lightening* suspended between heaven
and earth, but not moving. He said, "It was a somewhat
frightening color of red, something like blood and I had
the impression that the other world was breaking into this
world to tell us something...It could not possibly have
been a purely natural phenomenon."

The jagged red bolt of light, remained about 20 miles
high for an hour. Then it began to change and to form a
kind of writing in the sky, something like the lines of an
electrocardiogram or the lines drawn on a Richter scale
measuring an earthquake. Over this writing appeared a
great *cloud* of *light* of amazing brilliance in the shape of
an "M' from which spread horizontal blue wings.

The next day newspapers reported it to have been seen
all over Northern Spain as far as Majorca. In Barcelona,
traffic jams occurred because people stopped their cars
to stare into the sky. On radios, television and even at
football stadiums, announcements were made. It was
indeed widely viewed. Some people made the suggestion
that a satellite had been shot down from Nabonne in
southern France, resulting in a cloud of gas in the sky.
However, aviators said the cloud was too high for this
kind of phenomenon to happen. The *Diario* of Barcelona
said, "This was a brilliant light of vast dimensions. Some
think it was over 300 feet wide." The world press failed to
report the lights over Spain.

Life on earth has been wiped out many times by
various catastrophes, such as asteroids and shifts of the
axis. Man himself is creating the next mass extinction.

The jungles in the Amazon are being destroyed at a rate of the size of England. Scientists believe there are 2,000 bodies that cross earth's orbit that are big enough to destroy human civilization. Scientists have located only 10 percent or 200 of 2,000. Moreover, statistics tell us that every million years, four objects can strike earth and kill millions. Scientists also believe that every 1,000 years, a 250 yards diameter asteroid could hit earth, creating within 40 seconds huge tidal waves that would destroy the coastlines.

Scientists believe that there are 20 million objects in earth's crossing. One of these objects collides with earth every 100 years. On August 10, 1972, from Utah to Alberta, Canada, many witnesses saw a huge meteor streaking across the atmosphere. The speed was measured at 31,000 miles per hour and it burned for 100 seconds and came within 31,000 miles from the ground. We were lucky that that it escaped to the upper atmosphere.

In the late 1980s, American surveillance spy satellites detected something big hitting the Atlantic Ocean off South Africa. The blast was big enough to register on seismographs. From 1991 to 1994, a new space watch camera using the latest technology discovered four asteroids that came close to earth, within half of the distance of the moon. In February 1994, six U.S. spy satellites detected a fireball coming into our atmosphere at 45,000 miles per hour. We were lucky this time because it exploded in the ocean about 12 miles off the Fuji Islands.

In mid-July of 1994 a comet named "Shoemaker-Levy 9" collided with Jupiter. We don't know how much damage Jupiter sustained from the impact, but we know that if earth had been impacted, there would be nobody to tell the story. On March 23, 1989, the asteroid named "1989 F.C.," and later called "Asceleus," passed within 400,000 miles. It was half a mile wide and had the energy of 5,000 nuclear bombs. In 2005, scientists predicted that an asteroid will get closer to earth in 2023, maybe before.

So there are many reasons for mankind to unite in a society and world based in justice and peace. The future of mankind is very uncertain, and only a united the human species can survive. Life on Planet Earth is in a very thin balance, with no guaranties from nature or gods. Many prophecies mention something coming from the sky and causing great destruction on planet earth, maybe ending life as we know it.

I was surprised to learn that another great president, George Washington, had a "supernatural" vision. Wesley Bradshaw originally published it in the *National Tribune* (Vol. 4, No. 12) in December 1880. Washington recounted:

> "I do not know whether it was owing to the anxiety of my mind or what, but this afternoon, as I was sitting at this table engaged in preparing a dispatch, something seemed to disturb me. Looking up, I beheld standing opposite a singularly beautiful female. So astonished was I, for I had given strict orders not to be disturbed, that it was some moments before I found language to inquire the purpose of her presence. A second, a third, and even a fourth time did I repeat my question, but received no answer from my mysterious visitor, except a slight raising of her eyes.

By this time I felt strange sensations spreading through me. I would have risen, but the riveted gaze of the being before me rendered volition impossible. I assayed once more to address her, but my tongue had become useless. I even thought it had become paralyzed. A new influence, mysterious, potent, irresistible, took possession of me. All I could do was to gaze steadily, vacantly at my unknown visitant. Gradually the surrounding atmosphere seemed filled with sensations, and grew *luminous*. Everything about me seemed to rarify; the mysterious visitor herself becoming more airy and yet more distinct to my sight than before. I now began to feel as one dying, or rather to experience the sensation which I have sometimes imagined accompanies dissolution. I did not think, I did not reason, I did not move. All, alike, were impossible. I was conscious only of gazing fixedly, vacantly, at my companion.

Presently I heard a voice saying 'Son of the Republic, look and learn;' while at the same time my visitor extended her arm eastwardly. I now beheld a heavy white vapor at some distance rising fold upon fold. This gradually dissipated, and I looked upon a strange scene. Before me lay spread out in one vast plain all the countries of the world—Europe, Asia, Africa and America. I saw rolling and tossing between Europe and America, the billows of the Atlantic; and between Asia and America lay the Pacific.

'Son of the Republic,' said the mysterious voice as before, 'look and learn'. At that moment

I beheld a dark, shadowy being, like an angel, standing, or rather floating, in mid-air between Europe and America.

Dipping water out of the ocean in the hollow of each hand, he sprinkled some upon America with his right hand, while with his left hand he cast some on Europe. Immediately a cloud arose from these countries, and joined in mid-ocean. For a while it remained stationary, and then it moved slowly westward, until it enveloped America in its murky folds. Sharp flashes of lightning gleamed through it at intervals; and I heard the smothered groans and cries of the American people.

A second time the angel dipped water from the ocean and sprinkled it out as before. The dark cloud was then drawn back to the ocean, in whose heaving billows it sank from view.

A third time I heard the mysterious voice saying, 'Son of the Republic, look and learn.' I cast my eyes upon America and beheld villages and towns and cities springing up one after another until the whole land, from the Atlantic to the Pacific, was dotted with them.

Again I heard the mysterious voice say, 'Son of the Republic, the end of the century cometh. Look and learn.' And with this, the dark, shadowy figure turned its face southward, and from Africa I saw an ill-omened specter approach our land. It flitted slowly over every town and city of the latter. The inhabitants presently set themselves in battle array against each other. As I continued looking, I saw a bright angel on whose brow rested a crown of light on which was traced the word 'Union' place an American flag between the divided nation, and say, 'Remember, ye are brethren.' Instantly, the inhabitants, casting from them their weapons, became friends once more, and united around the National Standard.

And again I heard the mysterious voice saying, 'Son of the Republic, look and learn.' At this, the dark, shadowy angel placed a trumpet to his mouth and blew three distinct blasts; and taking water from the ocean, he sprinkled it upon Europe, Asia and Africa. Then my eyes beheld a fearful scene: from each of these countries arose thick, black clouds that were soon joined into one. And throughout this mass there gleamed a dark-red *light*, by which I saw hordes of armed men, who, moving with the cloud, marched by land and sailed by sea to America; which country was enveloped in the volume of cloud. And I dimly saw these vast armies devastate the whole country and bum the villages, towns, and cities that I beheld springing up.

As my ears listened to the thundering of the cannon, the clashing of swords, and the shouts and cries of millions in mortal combat, I again heard the mysterious voice saying 'Son of the Republic, look and learn.'

As the voice ceased, the shadowy angel, for the last time dipped water from the ocean and sprinkled it upon America. Instantly the dark cloud rolled back, together with the armies it had brought, leaving the inhabitants of the land victorious. Then once more I beheld the villages, towns, and cities springing up where I had seen them before; while the bright angel, planting the azure standard he had brought in the midst of them, cried in a loud voice: 'While the stars remain and the heavens send down dew upon the earth, so long shall the Union last.' And taking from his brow the crown on which was blazoned the word 'Union,' he placed it upon the Standard, while people, kneeling down, said, 'Amen!' The scene instantly began to fade and dissolve and I at last saw nothing but the rising, curling vapor I at first beheld.

This also disappearing, I found myself once more gazing upon the mysterious visitor who, in the same voice I had heard before, said, 'Son of the Republic, what you have seen is thus interpreted. Three great perils will come upon the Republic. Learn to live for his God, his land, and his Union.'

With those words the vision vanished, and I started from my seat and felt that I had seen a vision; wherein had been shown me the birth, progress, and destiny of the United States."

I would like to end this chapter with a prophecy by Abraham Lincoln that fits perfectly with 21st century United States of America. Lincoln was probably the greatest president of the United States and great men sometimes have visions of the future. On November 21, 1864, he said, "I see in the near future, a crisis approaching that unnerves me and causes me to tremble for the sake of my country. Corporations have been enthroned and an era of corruption in high places will follow, and the money power of the country will endeavor to prolong its reign by working upon the prejudices of the people until all wealth is aggregated in a few hands and the Republic is destroyed."

Lincoln's prophecy fits neatly with all the corruption we see in the country. For example, the fraud in the elections of 2000, the lie about Iraq and the war for oil, Enron, the future privatization of Social Security to be followed shortly by Medicare. Trillions of dollars go into arms manufacturing; Lockheed got $200 billion right after September 11.

The great writer George Orwell said, "We live in an age of the deceived, where to tell the truth is a revolutionary thing." We live in an age where ignorance is wisdom, patriotism is imperialism, and honesty is mockery. The poor citizens, in addition to living in desperate conditions without health insurance and with a subhuman minimum wage, have their patriotism and honesty challenged every day, while politicians wrap themselves in the American flag and get away with lies and more.

The last patriotic war was fought against Hitler. Since then, wars had been fought only to keep an ideology alive: the ideology of "greed" for the benefit of only a few.

Chapter 22

Conclusion

"If we banish man...the Universe becomes quiet; silence and night take over. All is transformed into a vast solitude, where unobserved phenomena take place in darkness and deafness. It is the presence of man that renders natural existence interesting. Why should we not make of man an eager center? Man is the unique end from which we must begin and to which everything must return. If I omit my existence and the happiness of my fellows, what can the rest of nature mean to me?"

— Diderot, *Encyclopedie*

Man's inhumanity to man has lasted for 6,000 thousand years, 3,000 of those years with the help of organized religion. Man's heart is like stone—insensible to the suffering of his fellow man. To accept the fact that his gods are not divine would be a shock.

Unfortunately, humanity's gods are not divine; they are not even from heaven. They are of extra-terrestrial or extra-temporal origin. I don't know where they come from, but the human race is in terrible danger of becoming extinct because of religious fanaticism and greed. The major moral issue in the 21st century is to end poverty, which will solve other problems, such as the spread of disease and terrorism. The only way for the human race to survive is to unite in a more just and peaceful society because there are many challenges ahead, like earth changes and wars.

The visions of Abraham and Moses were real, the visions of Jesus were real, and Mohammed's visions were real. So were those of the Greeks gods, the Mayas gods, the Aztecs gods, the Incas gods, and the Hindus gods. Why? Because the Intelligence behind the UFO phenomenon is behind every aspect of our religious and supernatural life. We know this because UFOs have been seen all through history, especially in the 19th, 20th and 21st centuries in ways that strongly suggest a relationship between UFOs and religion. The biggest similarity is in the lights and physical effects of both phenomena.

There are some clues in the *Bible* about the UFO phenomenon. For example, *Ephesians 6:12* says, "For our wrestling is not against flesh and blood, but against principalities and powers, against the rulers of the world of this darkness, against the spirits of wickedness in the high places."

I think that we probably are part of a cosmic game in which we are not even important players, just accidental ones. The more one reads about UFOs, mythology and religion, the more one sees the similarity of the phenomena. For example, African mythology mentions the "Abahambi, Abanutayo" or the "fiery visitors" that came from the sky. In the 21st century, people will think that is fiction without a material basis. However, when you see the same phenomenon in the 20th or 21st centuries, then it is no longer a myth or legend, but the truth.

In South Africa on a summer afternoon in 1969, two people were walking in the country when suddenly they saw an "eerie reddish glow" that looked like a bubble and was clearly luminous. The two men stared at the phenomenon, and after a few minutes noticed a flock of sheep acting curiously. Cows gathered around the mist as if attracted to its "glow." As the two witnesses stared at the glowing fog, there was no sound and the sheep were lifted upwards as if pulled by force. The sheep remained standing vertically, and when the mist went away, the sheep went back to the ground. One had strangely vanished and was never found.

The tribes had a legend about a "red glow" that ate cattle and had been seen in the area, but this incident confirms the reality of the myths and legends about "fiery visitors" from space. Why? Because the myths and the actual appearances of the UFOs are similar. In other words, the UFO phenomenon is the origin of the myths and legends that many people think are fictions.

My point in this book has been to show that what we thought were myths, legends, and folklore are true and that the Intelligence behind the UFO phenomenon is responsible. All the visions of saints, prophets, shamans, etc., are real. The god Quetzalcoatl is as real as Yahweh and Allah and Zeus. The Intelligence behind the UFO phenomenon is responsible for creating this reality. So, Abraham, Moses, Jesus and Mohammed were right, but unfortunately their visions didn't came from God, but from the Intelligence behind the UFO phenomenon.

Grim as this may sound, I don't see a reason for mankind to be unhappy because the gods of our childhood are gone. This is the time to start working to unite to end poverty. I don't see any other way for mankind to survive the terrible future ahead.

There will never be democracy, freedom, moral values or family values as long there are close to four billion people living on $2 dollars a day and there is no social justice.

We must stop the slaughter in the name of Jesus, Yahweh, and Allah because human life is sacred.

Bibliography

A
Bill Adler, *Letters to the Air Force*

B
Jim Baggott, *The Ghost in the Atom*
David Barclay and Therese Marie Barclay, *UFOs: The Final Answer?*
George Berkeley, *Philosophical Writings*
Otto Binder, *What We Really Know about Flying Saucers*
Willian J. Birnes, *Unsolved UFO Mysteries*
Ralph Blum, *Beyond Earth Man Contact UFOs*
Josef F. Blumrich, *The Spaceships of Ezekiel*
The Holy Bible
John Bowker, *The Meaning of Quantum Theory*
Fawn M. Brodie, *The Life of Joseph Smith*
Courtney Brown, Ph.D., *Cosmic Explorers*
A.C. Bhaktivedanta Swami Prabhupada, *Bhagavad Gita As It Is*
David Bender, *Islam: Opposing Viewpoints*

C
Joel Carmichael, *The Birth of Christianity*
Cicero, *The Nature of the Gods*
Dr. Edward J. Condon, *The Complete Report Commissioned by the U.S. Air Force Scientific Study on Unidentified Flying Objects*
Janice T. Connell, *Meetings with Mary*
Col. Philip J. Corso (Ret.), *The Day after Roswell*
Maurice M. Cotterell, *The Mayan Prophecies*

D

Charles Darwin, *On the Origin of Species*, *The Voyage of the Beagle*

Paul Davies, *About Time*

R.L. Dione, *God Drives a Flying Saucer*

Barry Downing, *The Bible and Flying Saucers*

E

Frank Edwards, *Flying Saucers: Serious Business*

Albert Einstein, *The Theory of Relativity*

Robert Emenegger, *UFOs: Past, Present and Future*

Eusebius, *The History of the Church*

F

Lawrence Fawcet, *Clear Intent*

Bruce Feiler, *Walking the Bible*

Paris Flammonde, *UFOs* Exist

Charles Fort, *The Book of the Damned*

Raymond Fowler, *UFOs:* Interplanetary Visitors

Sigmund Freud, *Moses and Monotheism*

John G. Fuller, *Incident at Exeter*

G

H.A.R. Gibb, *Mohammedanism: An Historical Survey*

Gavin Gibbons, *On Board the Flying Saucers*

William R. Goetz, *UFOs: Friend, Foe or Fantasy?*

Michael Grant, *Constantine the Great*

Brian Greene, *The Elegant Universe*, *The Fabric of the Cosmos*

H

Charles Haggood, *Path of the Pole*

Richard H. Hall, *The National Committee on Aerial Phenomenon (NICAP)*

J.E. Hanaver, *The Holy Land*

Graham Hancock, *Fingerprints of the Gods*

Stephen Hawking, *Brief History of Time*, *Black Holes and Baby Universes*

Gerald S. Hawkins, *Stonehenge Decoded*

Werner Heisenberg, *Physics and Philosophy*

Donna Hill, *The UFO Evidence*

Hans Holzer, *The UFOnauts: In Quest of Ghosts*

David Hume, *On Human Nature and the Understanding*

Colin J. Humphreys, *The Miracles of Exodus*

Dr. J. Allen Hynek, *The Hynek UFO Report*

I

John and Katherine Imbrie, *Ice Ages:Solving the Mystery*

J

William James, *Varieties of Religious Experience*

C.G. Jung, *Flying Saucers: A Modern Myth of Things Seen in the Skies*

K

Michio Kaku, *Hyperspace*

Immanuel Kant, *Critique of Pure Reason*

Werner Keller, *The Bible as History*

Major Donald E. Keyhoe, *The Flying Saucers Are Real*, *Flying Saucers From Outer Space*

Lawrence David Kusche, *The Bermuda Triangle Mystery Solved*

L

Michael Lindemann, *UFOs and the Alien Presence: Six Viewpoints*

Martin Lings, *Muhammad, His Life Based on the Earliest Sources*

David H. Lund, *Death and Consciousness*

Alan Landsburg, *In Search of Myths and Monsters*

M

Hyam Maccolay, *The Book of Mormon*

John E. Mack, MD, *Abduction: Human Encounters with Aliens*

Ann Madden, *The Yahweh Encounters*

Eugene H. Maly, *Prophets of Salvation*

Theophile James Meek, *Hebrew Origins*

Howard Menger, *From Outer Space*

Susan Michaels, *Sightings:UFOs*

N

Michael Normar, *Historic Haunted America*

O

Everett C. Olson, *Concepts of Evolution*

P

Heinz R. Pagels, *Perfect Symmetry*

Blaise Pascal, *Pensees*

F. David Peat, *Superstrings and the Search for the Theory of Everything*

Regine Pernoud, *Joan of Arc: By Herself and Her Witnesses*

E. Royston Pike, *Mohammed: Founder of the Religion of Islam*

Bob Pratt, *UFO Danger Zone*

R

John Revard, *The Laws of Physics*

Milton J.S. Rudwick, *Georges Cuvier, Fossil Bones and Geological Catastrophes*

Les Roddy and Charles E. Sellier, Jr., *In Search of Historical Jesus*

Edward J. Ruppelt, *The Report on Unidentified Flying Objects*

S

Carl Sagan and Thorton Page, *UFOS: A Scientific Debate*

Beth Scott, *The Christian Faith*

Kelly L. Segraves, *Sons of God Return*

John Spencer, *The UFO Encyclopedia*

L. Jerome Stanton, *Flying Saucers: Hoax or Reality?*

Brad Steiger, *Project Blue Book*

Lee Strobel, *The Case for Christ*

T

Robert Temple, *The Sirius Mystery*

Barbara Thiering, *Jesus and the Riddle of the Dead Sea Scrolls*

Keith Thompson, *Angels and Aliens*

Richard L.Thompson, *Alien Identities*

ABOUT THE AUTHOR

I have been researching UFOs since 1987, traveling extensively in Europe and South America. I have also studied Hindu mysticism for 26 years. My hobbies include playing chess and listening to music, especially classical and jazz. I have participated in 17 marathons, 11 triathlons and hundreds of races. I work in sales.

Made in the USA
Monee, IL
07 June 2021

70439992R00194